The Menu

and the

Cycle of Cost Control

Third Edition

Paul J. McVety
Susan Desmond Marshall
Bradley J. Ware

KENDALL/HUNT PUBLISHING COMPANY
4050 Westmark Drive   Dubuque, Iowa   52002

Contents

Preface

To be successful in today's modern foodservice industry regardless if the foodservice establishment is a classical fine dining or family style or limited serve the operation has to be profitable to stay in business. In order to be profitable management needs to develop and implement a strategic fiscal plan that contains financial goals, policies, procedures and controls. These goals, policies, procedures and controls must be properly executed by all employees for a profit to be realized. This book was written primarily to provide the necessary knowledge to hospitality and culinary students who aspire to be a member of a management team operating a profitable foodservice operation.

Organization of the Textbook

Unit 1: The Menu
In Chapter 1: The Foodservice Industry Today and Chapter 2: Concept Development we explore seventeen different segments of the foodservice industry, how to develop a foodservice concept, and the key elements to analyzing a market survey. In Chapter 3: Developing the Sales Menu, Chapter 4: Layout and Design of the Menu and Chapter 5: Exploring Menus we discuss the foundation to all foodservice establishments the menu. How to develop, layout, and design a professional sales menu is explained. Eleven sales menus from excellent foodservice establishments throughout the United States are reviewed and analyzed.

Unit 2: The Cycle of Cost Control
Once the concept and sales menu are developed Chapter 6: The Big Picture: Income Statement and Chapter 7: Determining Portion Costs and Selling Prices clearly explains how fiscal goals from the profit and loss statement correlate to establishing selling price for items listed on the menu. Costing out recipes, providing effect yields and executing portion controls are critical components discussed within this chapter. Chapter 8: Purchasing Controls, Chapter 9: Receiving Controls, and Chapter 10: Storage and Inventory Controls discuss cost saving controls to properly procure ingredients, receive, store and manage inventories. After establishing standardized food and beverage cost controls we discuss how to manage through proper planning, monitoring, analyzing, forecasting sales and expenses in Chapter 11: Daily Production Control and Analysis and Chapter 12: Sales Controls and Analysis.

Unit 3: Essential Operating Expenses
The final two chapters review two major expenses: labor and equipment costs. Chapter 13: Labor Cost Control explains how labor controls contribute to the bottom line in all foodservice establishments. Labor Cost Control includes topics such as wages, salary, benefits, federal taxes, hiring the right employee, tip declaration, preparing payroll and determining payroll deductions and net pay. Chapter 14: Menu Equipment Analysis reviews guidelines to purchasing equipment and identifying the necessary equipment needed to produce the menu.

New Features for the Third Edition

The Menu and the Cycle of Cost Control third edition will feature the first edition of WebCOM™ a website that offers round the clock access for students to participate in online interactive activities which includes: nine cost control spreadsheets; click, drag and drop menu design exercises and a number of forms which include recipe costing, purchasing, receiving, inventory, yield test, etc. Additional chapter review questions as well as additional practice exercises have been incorporated.

WebCOM™ website offers a number of benefits to teachers such as power point presentations, test bank questions, and numerous classroom activities.

WebCOM™ allows the authors to provide teachers with information on new menu designing techniques, new menu regulations, updated labor laws and new information on nutrition. We have placed more emphasis on nutrition particularly addressing how to design healthy menus.

Look for the WebCOM logo

This indicates the spread sheet can be found online on the WebCOM site.

The Authors

The Menu

The Foodservice Industry Today

objectives

Upon completion of this chapter, the student should be able to:

1. define the two main divisions of the foodservice industry.
2. discuss the various segments within each of the two main foodservice divisions.
3. list the segments within the foodservice industry in order of importance regarding their market share percentages.
4. introduce new foodservice trends and sales figures within each segment.

key terms

Branding
Chain Restaurant
Commercial Industry
Commissary
Cook-Chill System
Cycle Menu
Dinner Houses
Family Dining Restaurants
Fine Dining Restaurants
The Food Guide Pyramid

Franchise
Franchiser
Franchisee
Health Maintenance Organizations
Non-Commercial Industry
Outside Foodservice Contractors
Preferred Provider Organizations
"Sous Vide"
Traditional Board Plan

Introduction

The foodservice industry can be broken down into two main divisions: the commercial industry (for-profit), and the non-commercial industry. The *commercial industry* operates to create earnings in excess of expenses (food, labor, and overhead), in order to pay investors and owners; while the *non-commercial industry* runs to keep facilities operational, by bringing in enough money to cover day to day expenses. Profit is not the major objective of the non-commercial division. The commercial industry, in terms of market share, dwarfs the non-commercial division by almost a 3 to 1 ratio.

In this chapter, commercial and non-commercial segments appear in order of importance based on their market share percentage. A summary of the most significant segments of each foodservice division is presented and broken down into 2003 retail sales, industry share, and nominal growth with an inflation assumption rate of

2.1% for 2003 and 2.2% for 2004 for food purchased away from home. (Figure 1.1) The chapter examines the trends that each segment is currently employing to win over potential customers. By briefly describing each segment, the chapter sheds light on the diversity and the enormous potential the food industry holds for current employees, as well as future employees.

Limited Service

The limited service or fast food industry is the largest of all the commercial or non-commercial segments. This segment includes burgers (McDonald's®), pizza (Pizza Hut®), chicken (KFC®), sandwiches (Subway®), Sweets (Smoothie King®), Mexican (Taco Bell®), and seafood (Long John Silver's®).

SEGMENT	2003 Retail Sales equivalent *A (billions)	Industry Share	Nominal Growth *B	
			2003	2004
Limited-service restaurants	$141.130	32.8%	2.6%	3.0%
Full-service restaurants	127.733	29.7	3.3	3.5
Vending/office coffee	27.123	6.3	−5.5	−2.0
Business & Industry	20.300	4.7	−5.5	−2.0
Supermarket Foodservice	18.716	4.4	3.0	3.0
Convenience Stores	15.488	3.6	3.5	3.0
Primary/Secondary schools	13.952	3.2	2.5	1.5
Recreation	12.395	2.9	1.0	2.0
Lodging	11.292	2.6	−3.0	1.5
Colleges/Universities	9.721	2.3	2.5	2.5
Other *C	7.359	1.7	3.5	3.0
Hospitals	6.656	1.5	−1.0	0.0
Nursing Homes	5.816	1.4	2.0	2.0
Other retail	4.945	1.2	3.5	4.0
Military	3.490	0.8	3.0	2.5
Airlines	2.158	0.5	−10.0	0.0
Bars/Taverns	1.998	0.5	2.5	2.5
TOTAL INDUSTRY	**$429.912**	**100.**	**1.6**	**2.4**

*A excludes alcoholic beverages and sales tax; *B nominal growth includes an inflation assumption of 2.1% and 2.2% for 2003 and 2004, respectively, food away from home; *C includes penal institutions, child centers, continuous-care retirement centers and other noncommercial operations.

FIGURE 1.1 The Foodservice Industry 2003–2004

Source: Technomic Inc., 2004

While limited service continues to target the children's market by including give-aways such as popular toy characters with certain meals; this service segment is also making a concerted effort to reach the adult population. Subway® offers a variety of wraps such as Asiago Caesar Chicken and turkey breast and bacon. McDonald's has successfully attracted a more health-conscious segment of the population by offering (chef, garden, grilled chicken Caesar) McSalad Shaker Salads as well as the Fruit' n Yogurt Parfait (with or without granola) for dessert. Newly designed offerings such as the Big N' Tasty and the grilled chicken breast filet have enticed an adult market and resulted proportionately in increased sales.

In recent years legislators, consumers, and nutritionalists have expressed concern over the obesity rate in this country and limited service establishments have responded in kind to those concerns. McDonald's® now offers all white meat chicken McNuggets that have 40 percent fewer calories and fat than the dark-meat McNuggets. Pizza Hut® has introduced Fit N' Delicious pizza that has less cheese, and comes with toppings such as chicken or vegetables that are leaner and healthier than sausage or pepperoni. Smoothie King® now has low-carb, high protein smoothies available in banana, chocolate, and strawberry. Trimming fat and calories has become a reality and the foodservice industry is meeting this challenge head-on.

Another trend that has proven to be successful is the creation of store fronts within retail locations: Dunkin' Donuts® and Taco Bell® are seen in gas stations and convenience marts, while McDonald's® is now in Wal-Mart®. With a large variety of food offerings and the seemingly endless arenas where these franchises (a legal arrangement made between two consenting parties: the franchiser or parent company, and the franchisee or individual unit owner) are opening, quick service should continue to dominate the foodservice industry.

The characteristics of limited-service outlets are similar in nature, regardless of the type of food item involved. In limited-service outlets (1) the menu is often à la carte, and each item is individually priced (or patrons select combination meals so that they are perceived by patrons as having special value); (2) the menu tends to be simple and requires limited food preparation; and (3) the average check is usually low, resulting in the need for high volume in terms of patronage. The ability to take out at the counter or to pass by a drive-thru enables a facility to keep down labor costs. (Figure 1.1)

Full Service

The full service segment of the commercial industry encompasses dinner houses (Applebee's®), family dining (Denny's®), and fine dining establishments (Restaurant Daniel). Each one of these sub-segments also has unique characteristics.

Dinner houses generally attract customers who favor fresh salads, spicy foods (Mexican), fresh chicken, fish, and desserts. Dinner house menus are usually moderately priced and easy to prepare. The turnover rate in most dinner houses is higher than that in fine dining restaurants. Some dinner houses such as Houlihan's®, have added global cuisine dishes that include Caribbean, Mexican, and Italian entrées to their menus in order to capture the ever increasing multi-cultural market. Applebee's® in partnership with Weight Watchers International Inc. ® has introduced a menu section that includes the Weight Watchers logo along with selected food items, while T.G.I. Friday's has created a number of Atkins low-carbohydrate menu items such as Tuscan Spinach Dip served with vegetables or Garlic Chicken with mixed vegetables. The creation of these various products reflects positive changes in the foodservice industry in an effort to combat the obesity issue. Most dinner houses serve alcohol on the premises and are frequently either part of a national chain or a franchise, although they can be independently operated.

A *chain restaurant* is an operation where the menu, atmosphere, policies, and procedures are established by a parent company. Each operation is an integral part of a larger assemblage and is a replica of the other. A *franchise*, on the other hand, is a legal unit consisting of two consenting parties: the *franchiser*, or parent company, and the *franchisee*, or individual unit owner. The franchise grants the franchisee the exclusive rights to market products and services while using the franchiser company name, logo, and marketing and promotional strategies. The franchisee is legally bound to follow policies and procedures established by the franchiser. A franchise, in contrast to a chain restaurant, is individually owned.

Family dining restaurants feature home-style cooking and moderately priced menus that are easy to prepare. These dining facilities appeal to all age groups, including children, teenagers, young adults, "middle agers," and seniors. Many have rather extensive children's menus, and some offer alcohol such as beer, wine, and a limited number of mixed drink selections. Generally, the turnover rate is high, as is that of the dinner house.

Family dining restaurants are sometimes associated with signature items such as the home style biscuits, beef stew, and noodles served at Bob Evans®. Denny's® has "lighter fare," in the form of fresh salads and a chicken sandwich in addition to its usual offerings. Oriental, Mexican, and Italian specialties have also been added to other family dining menus to better accommodate all tastes.

Fine dining restaurants are often independently owned. The menu is more complex in terms of preparation, so the average check is high. In many fine dining establishments, a wine list is available for guests to select from, also contributing to a higher check average. The turnover rate is low because lunch and dinner are often served in multiple courses (appetizer, soup, salad, entrée, accompaniments, and dessert). The customer expects excellent service from a professional waitstaff that is knowledgeable in wine and food pairings. Service is generally slower-paced and relaxed. Guests expect the dining experience to last two hours or more. (Figure 1.1)

Vending

Foodservice vending is also a current success in the industry. Vending machines are found in retail, business and industry operations, recreation facilities, lodging, schools, colleges/universities, hospitals, military installations, and in airline terminals. Vending has developed as one of the fastest growing foodservice segments. The old unattractive vending machines have been phased out and new machines with glass fronts attractively market and display products to customers. New food items include pizza, fresh salads, deli sandwiches, and vegetarian items. Many of the items for sale have brand names that customers can identify: White Castle®, Blimpies®, Veryfine®, Otis Spunkmeyer®, and Haagen-dazs®.

Similar to other foodservice segments, vending is also facing challenges regarding nutrition and obesity. School administrators are now urging the U.S. Department of Agriculture (USDA) to set up nutritional guidelines. Donna Wittrock, Executive Director of Food and Nutrition for the Denver Public School system wants the USDA to create regulations on chips, soda, and candy purchased in vending machines. Many school districts have already replaced common vending snacks with more nutritious items such as fruits and vegetables.

Vending technology now also allows customers to use debit cards or smart cards, or to go online for coupons and other promotions (give-aways such as sports tickets, bicycles, hats, etc.). Customers perceive this as an added convenience and also as getting something extra for their money. Thus, vending sales have increased and customer satisfaction is on the rise. Large food companies have also paired up with major food suppliers (ARAMARK® with NABISCO®). This arrangement has created a win-win situation with increased product sales and brand recognition for suppliers. This trend will obviously continue throughout the decade. (Figure 1.1)

Business and Industry

Business and industry have been part of the non-commercial foodservice industry for over 100 years. However, dramatic changes in this segment have only recently occurred with the turning over of business and industry operations to *outside foodservice contractors*, such as ARAMARK®, Host International®, Marriott®, and ARA®. Generally when a business or industry wishes to obtain an outside contractor, bids are taken. After a company or client finally selects the outside contractor, a number of scenarios may occur regarding payment. The outside contractor may elect to run the foodservice establishment for a fee, take a portion of the profit, or collect a percentage of sales. In some cases, the outside contractor may ask for both a fee and a share of the profits, or a combination of a fee and a percentage of sales.

No matter what negotiations take place, the advantages of selecting an outside contractor outweigh the disadvantages. The advantages of allowing an outside contractor to run a foodservice operation are numerous. First and foremost, the business can focus on its major vision instead of concerning itself with running the foodservice operation. Secondly, the outside contractor brings in a professional staff of managers and chefs who are specially trained, so time and dollars are saved on training. Thirdly, outside contractors already have their own policy and procedures in place, so that an easy transition can occur when they begin running the foodservice operation. At times management is forced to answer to two figureheads, the company or client, and the central office, and this can prove to be a disadvantage since having to appease more than one boss can be difficult and can also diminish management's effectiveness. (Figure 1.1)

Supermarket Foodservice

Supermarkets, in order to survive, must depend upon high volume. To increase volume, supermarkets must not only intensify product sales, but they must also expand services. Today, supermarket delis offering soups, salads, pastas, sandwiches, and entrées with all the accoutrements, and desserts are seen in east coast chains, such as Publix®, Shaw's®, and Stop & Shop®. Supermarkets that have had their own in store retail outlets for years are now leasing space to well known franchises. Kroeger's®, for example, has joined forces with Chick-Fil-A®. The theory behind this venture is to keep customers on property for as long as possible so that they will spend money. Markets are also selling healthier foods. BREAD & CIRCUS® provides natural foods grown without pesticides or herbicides, as well as organically fed poultry, game, and fish. Vegetarian and ethnic foods are also featured. The convenient locations of most supermarkets, coupled with their growing one stop credo, make them attractive to customers with time constraints. (Figure 1.1)

Convenience Stores

Convenience stores have expanded their product line as well as the services they offer. The hot dogs, hamburgers, ready-made sandwiches, bread, milk, soda, and coffee that were once commonplace offerings are now but a part of an extended menu that includes fresh-squeezed juices, sandwich wraps, soups, salads, pastas, gourmet pizzas, sandwiches to order, and bakery items. Convenience stores have also joined forces with limited-service giants in order to establish a larger market share. For example, Taco Bell® and Blimpies® have teamed up with Circle K®. Petroleum companies are also entering the convenience store segment and are establishing lucrative partnerships with quick-service companies as well: Amoco®, for instance, has united with McDonald's®. Other associations will undoubtedly follow this course in order to provide customers with extra service and the convenience of one stop shopping.

Some convenience stores, such as 7-Eleven® and Circle K®, are expanding their product line without increasing manpower. These stores provide microwaves for patrons to heat up the meals they purchase in the store. Customers then stand in line to pay in the traditional convenience store manner. (Figure 1.1)

Primary and Secondary Schools

Most elementary and secondary school lunch programs in the United States are run by the federal government through the National School Lunch Program that was established in 1946. The U. S. Department of Agriculture (USDA) conducts the program, and is responsible for seeing that each school system receives its rightful disbursement of surplus food and an endowment that is based on family need and population. Today, with the ever-growing expenses associated with employee benefits and labor cost, more school systems are hiring outside food contractors to run their school lunch programs to reduce costs.

School systems, regardless of how they operate, follow certain nutritional guidelines, most notably, *The Food Guide Pyramid* established by the U.S. Department of Agriculture/U.S. Department of Health and Human Services. The Food Guide Pyramid is a daily guide to food choices that is divided into five major food groups. It is recommended that individuals eat breads, cereals, pasta and rice, vegetables and fruits, milk, yogurt and cheese, meat, fish and poultry, and eggs and nuts. A modified fat, oil, and sweet intake is also encouraged. Some school systems are now asking for student input concerning menu offerings. Students are asked to rate current food items on menus and the results of these polls are then evaluated and considered in developing menus for the upcoming year. Although student input is important, daily menu offerings must still meet Federal Dietary Guidelines.

Another trend in many school systems is the use of the *branding* technique, which incorporates well-known brands that children have come to know through media advertising. Branding offers students a larger variety of menu choices, as well as student satisfaction at no additional cost to the school. School systems are also remodeling their cafeteria into food courts and snack bars offering a variety of food selections. In Florida's Broward County and North Carolina's Charlotte County schools, students may choose from a variety of foods such as pizza, fresh salads, and deli bars. School administrators, in an effort to keep students on campus, are offering attractive alternatives to traditional fare. The immediate appeal of healthy and more comprehensive food programs to special interest groups, parents, and educators is growing due to data that supports the fact that proper nutrition improves student concentration and performance. In Savannah, Georgia, Carole Rowe, LD, MS, RD, was successful in introducing healthier options to children at several elementary, middle, and high schools. Students were able to select fresh fruit or juice, salads, and two to three vegetable selections daily. (Figure 1.1)

Recreation

Whether the venue is an amusement park, art museum, concert hall, convention center, cruise line, exposition, national park, stadium, or zoo, the recreational foodservice industry recognizes that patrons are a captive audience. Although entertainment was at one time thought to be the primary draw, and food considered but an additional offering, the recreational foodservice industry has had to change its way of thinking to compete in today's competitive market. Food is now an integral part of the overall recreational experience. In recreational facilities across the country, more sophisticated items such as shrimp, sushi, salads, burritos, bratwurst, and gourmet pizza are being added to the stand-by offerings of hot dogs, hamburgers, sandwiches, peanuts, popcorn, pretzels, ice cream, and beverages. Today, in upscale stadiums across the country, food selections are creative and pricey. The use of open kitchens to attract patrons and to keep them on premises is a clear example of how food has become an important part of the entertainment equation. Delivering a complete entertainment package to the customer is imperative, as commercial operations in close proximity continue to compete with other recreational foodservice facilities in terms of market share.

Outside foodservice contractors have also made advances in the recreational foodservice industry. ARAMARK®, for example, now manages Walt Disney World's® foodservice operations. Sportservice® runs more than fifty professional sports arenas in the United States and Canada, and Sodexho Marriott Services® manages several college stadium concessions throughout the United States. (Figure 1.1)

Lodging

Today, hotels and resorts are offering a wide range of services to guests and local residents. Bistros, fine dining restaurants, specialty restaurants, cafés, bars, night clubs, delis, snack bars, markets, coffee houses, room service, catering and banquet facilities are commonplace in a number of lodging establishments. Many hotels and resorts are currently franchising or leasing to popular chain restaurants to run their foodservice operations in order to decrease the number of services that they themselves must provide. Food courts featuring brand names such as Pizzeria Uno®, Nathan's Hot Dogs®, and Cheesecake Factory® are also appearing in hotels.

Hotel companies are also bringing in big name chefs to make menu changes and to create new concepts. Hilton Hotels Corporation®, located in Time Square, partnered with Larry Forgione to create Restaurant Above, which highlights Forgione's New American cuisine. Mark Miller, founder of Coyote Café in Santa Fe, New Mexico, served as a consulting chef for Westin Hotels and Resorts®. Hotels are coming up with innovative ideas to meet customer needs and to keep investment costs down. (Figure 1.1)

For years the lodging industry has known that the more time guests spend on property, the greater the possibility that these patrons will spend money there. By keeping guests on premises and drawing customers from surrounding communities, an establishment can greatly increase its revenue and profit. Guests are more likely to stay at a facility and local customers are more apt to visit the property when there are a variety of dining options. Catering and banquet facilities that specialize in business meetings, conventions, wedding receptions, brunches, special occasions, and community events also attract patrons who stay in the hotel or resort while attending these events, as well as customers from the local community.

Colleges and Universities

For years, college foodservice has primarily revolved around the traditional board plan: a fixed plan that includes a predetermined number of meals (19–20 per week). The traditional board plan essentially controls where and when a student can eat.

College students today do not want to be tied down to such restrictive plans. They want the flexibility to eat on campus when the need arises, but also want the option to be able to go out for a meal or to eat alone in their dormitories. Many students do not eat breakfast and are grabbing food and beverage items to go, such as sandwiches and coffee. Students also like the option of having a pizza and a beverage delivered to their room at any time of the day or night.

Many colleges are listening to students and are offering several alternatives to the traditional meal plan, while also insuring food sale revenue. Some colleges are providing the option of a reduced number of meals per week. Debit cards are commonly accepted on college campuses to buy snacks, soda, sandwiches, and pizza. Cash credits are also popular for purchasing pizza, sandwiches, beverages, and other convenience items, in place of complete meals. Students may enjoy pasta, pizza, hamburgers, sandwiches, beverages, and desserts at retail shops found in student unions as well. Chains and franchises such as Burger King®, Subway®, and Pizza Hut® are now common on many college campuses and offer students a sense of freedom and flexibility that had not previously existed.

More sophisticated choices are now being offered to students who elect to dine in a residential hall. In addition to meat and potatoes, Oriental and Mexican dishes are finding their way on to foodservice menus. College campuses are also paying closer attention to student nutritional concerns and are offering low-cholesterol, low-fat, low-calorie and vegetarian entrées, in place of beef and fried foods. At Southern Oregon University Jeff LaMagra, Director of Foodservices, offers a number of low-cal items such as fruit smoothies, sushi, rice bowls, vegetarian stir-fry, and low-fat, low-calorie sauces to accompany pastas. Colleges and universities such as Harvard University, University of Massachusetts, and Boston College, are offering display cooking to their students.

If traditional board plans seem unpopular with many college students, the opposite is true among administrators, faculty, foodservice directors, and parents. Administrators and faculty like the idea of students eating together, because they believe that such an experience provides students with a sense of belonging. Foodservice directors today must plan menus and control production and food costs. Food is often purchased in high volume to allow colleges the option of providing inexpensive meal plans. With a traditional meal plan, parents have some assurance that their son or daughter is receiving three meals daily. (Figure 1.1)

Other Segments (Penal Institutions, Child Centers and Continuous-Care Retirement Centers, Etc.)

Penal Institutions

Today, inmates are being incarcerated for a longer period of time, due to new and stricter laws such as the "three strikes and you're out" decree. As a result, correctional facilities continue to experience an increase in population. At a time when communities are facing budget cuts, tax payers and politicians agree that correctional facilities must also be held responsible for reducing their budgets.

Government allocations of vegetables, fruits, eggs, cheese, and milk to prisons are being reduced, eliminated, or reshuffled to other government agencies; yet, foodservice departments are held responsible to develop budgetary alternatives in order to break-even. Foodservice directors are now reevaluating their menus by examining costs and making food adjustments in an effort to diminish overall food costs. Many correctional facilities that once relied on cook-serve systems, are now incorporating cook-chill systems into their foodservice departments in order to curtail expenditures.

The *cook-chill system* is a process in which large quantities of food are cooked, chilled, and then reheated for service. The food is prepared in large computerized kettles that accurately record and regulate product temperature. Then, the food is cooked rapidly and mixed to prevent deterioration. The cook-chill system has improved the overall quality and consistency of many food products, is easier to maintain, and requires less supervision than traditional systems. The cook-chill system usually produces food items in a centralized location called a commissary. A *commissary* is a food operation that produces food items at one site and transports them to another location (in this case, another correctional facility within the same district). The cook-chill system frequently allows foodservice departments to decrease the number of civilian cooks on staff, which in turn lowers labor cost. Other correctional facilities are selecting private contractors such as ARAMARK®, Compass Group North America®, and Sodexho® in an effort to cut expenditures. (Figure 1.1)

Child Centers

The child care industry has grown tremendously in the last decade due to an increase in the number of single-parent households and homes in which both spouses work. The child care industry falls under the auspices of the United States Department of Agriculture (USDA) which administers the Child and Adult Care Food Program (CACFP) that was established in 1978. The CACFP provides the USDA with meal pattern guidelines, funding, and appropriate literature on nutrition and the foodservice industry. Other responsibilities of the program include monitoring, training, and providing technical support to administrators and staff in child care centers.

Many child care centers follow the USDA meal pattern requirements that guarantee that all meals are well-balanced and focus on "the individual needs of infants and children over one year old." (McAteer 1981, 4) Menus should be carefully planned, so that the right food combinations are represented in order to provide the necessary nutrients needed for growth. Reaching this goal becomes difficult when food is not prepared on premises. In some cases, food is received from outside sources such as vendors, schools, and foodservice operations. Nutrition must be an integral component in all child care facilities. Children need to learn on a daily basis how nutrition and food relate to long term health. The child care industry, similar to schools and nursing homes, is now turning to outside foodservice contractors such as ARAMARK®, in an effort to deliver nutritious and well-balanced meals. (Figure 1.1)

Continuous-Care Retirement Centers

Continuous-care retirement facilities cater to clients who are financially secure. These individuals are accustomed to eating at country clubs and dining restaurants. In order to meet the needs of this sophisticated market, life care/elder care facilities are employing experienced chefs to create elaborate menus. Registered dietitians are also being hired as consultants to work in conjunction with chefs to produce low-fat, low-cholesterol, and low-sodium menus, for a health conscious market. The number of continuous-care retirement centers (that provide a comfortable and convenient life style), will continue to expand well into the next century as baby boomers gracefully enter retirement. Retirement Corporation®, Manor Care®, Hyatt®, and Marriott® are currently serving this market. (Figure 1.1)

Hospitals

The dramatic increase in HMOs *(Health Maintenance Organizations)*, and PPOs *(Preferred Provider Organizations)*, has contributed considerably to the financial difficulties facing hospitals today. Over the last few years, a dramatic reduction in Medicaid and Medicare benefits has forced individuals to turn to these providers who offer financial savings (in some cases up to 30% annually). Although HMOs and PPOs offer monetary savings to plan participants, member freedom concerning choice of physician and length of hospital stay has been sacrificed. Both HMOs and PPOs emphasize and promote ambulatory care, whereby patients are treated outside the hospital whenever possible. Savings from both plans come from scrutinizing physician costs and reduced hospitalization.

Reduced patient stays at hospitals have meant a demand for fewer meals and therefore decreased revenue. As a result, foodservice departments are now attempting to cut costs whenever possible. Some foodservice departments are joining forces geographically to expand their purchasing power. Others are revaluating their menus and reducing the number of food items they offer. Computers are being used to reduce labor and to increase productivity.

In most hospitals, the foodservice department provides food for the staff, physicians, nurses, patients, and in some cases, catered events. Meals can range from breakfast, lunch, dinner, and snacks to elaborate catered functions. Hospitals have registered dietitians on staff who work in conjunction with the foodservice director and chef to ensure that all menu items meet dietary guidelines. This working relationship is imperative because many patients in hospitals are on strict diets (e.g., low-sodium and low-fat etc.), which must be carefully followed. Hospitals are generally more concerned about health and nutrition than in the marketing of goods and services, however, in some hospitals patients can call up their orders on the phone, similar to room service in a hotel, and select items from a menu. Hospitals, in addition, are offering their employees options such as grab-and-go items to take home, and convenience stores and cafés on premises. Food items include homemade soups, Caesar salad, couscous, specialty sandwiches, and bottled flavored waters. Global cuisine is also gaining popularity in some hospitals. (Figure 1.1)

Nursing Homes

American are now living longer, which means occupancy levels in health care facilities are also steadily increasing. Nursing homes generally cater to patients who are elderly and suffer from gastrointestinal difficulties or digestive problems. Since many patients are on bland or soft diets, nursing homes must provide high protein and nutritious food items. A registered dietitian or consultant is usually hired on a part-time basis to provide this expertise. The cost of providing nutritious and attractive meals to patients in these facilities is currently a major challenge. As food costs and labor costs continue to climb, both state run and independently owned nursing facilities are looking for solutions to curb costs while continuing to deliver quality food.

Two systems that allow for a reduction in labor costs are the cook-chill system and *"sous vide."* The cook-chill system is a process in which large quantities of food are cooked, chilled, and then reheated for service. The food is prepared in large computerized kettles that accurately record and regulate product temperature. Rapid cooking follows. The cook-chill system allows nursing homes to decrease the number of cooks on staff, which in turn lowers labor costs. "Sous vide" is a procedure of packaging raw or undercooked food items, which are subsequently placed in an airtight sealed pouch. The pouch is then cooked, refrigerated, and frozen. When needed, the pouch is reheated and served immediately. Both methods have proven to decrease labor costs in many nursing homes by reducing the number of full-time cooks on staff.

Nursing homes also use outside foodservice contractors to run their foodservice operations. Compass Group North America® and Sodexho® are leaders in this area. Consolidation is also taking place, whereby for-profit chains such as Manor Care®, and Beverly Enterprises®, are buying large numbers of nursing homes in an effort to reduce overall costs. (Figure 1.1)

Other Retail (Department Stores, Discount Stores, and Cafeterias/Buffets)

Department Stores and Discount Stores

In this segment, the goal of keeping the patron on property for as long as possible to increase the probability that additional money will be disbursed on site is key. For years, department stores have accommodated customers by serving meals in upscale dining rooms. Today, department stores such as Macy's®, NeimanMarcus®, Nordstrom's®, SaksFifth Avenue®, and Marshall Field's® provide complete dining facilities, cafés, and upscale coffee bars to captivate their clientele. Some upscale retail stores even offer wine tastings, and have gourmet gift and wine shops. Discount stores are now joining forces with well-known fast-food chains by leasing them lucrative space, for example K-Mart® houses Little Caesars®. The market share of this segment is due to increase, as department/discount stores, such as Lord & Taylor®, Dayton-Hudson®, Wal-Mart®, and Home Depot® continue to explore new ideas to capture a larger share of this market. (Figure 1.1)

Cafeterias and Buffets

One of the fastest growing foodservice segments in the commercial sector is cafeteria/buffets. A very successful company in this segment includes Buffets, Inc.®, which operates Old Country Buffet®, HomeTown Buffet®, Country Buffet®, and Country Roadhouse Buffet & Grill®. These buffet restaurants use a scatter system instead of a traditional straight-line cafeteria system, which allows customers to more easily choose from a large selection of foods. Menus can include soups, salads, breads, entrées, vegetables, and desserts, which are made from scratch using the freshest ingredients. Other cafeteria/buffet chains include Buffet Partners, LP®, and K&W Cafeterias®. These cafeterias/buffets offer homestyle foods at affordable prices that appeal to many families, in which both spouses work and do not wish to cook when they come home. Cafeterias/buffets offer convenience for busy families today. (Figure 1.1)

Military

Military troops, bases, and departmental budgets have all been curtailed in the last decade. Military foodservice is attempting to cope with these changes by reducing manpower whenever possible, and incorporating automated systems such as vending machine courts. When vending machines are not feasible, dining halls are taking cues from institutions and restaurants, and are using branding. Branding has the potential to increase revenue on many military bases by introducing food items that are familiar and popular with enlistees. Limited-service, via convenience foods such as sandwiches, pizza, and beverages, is also commonplace on numerous military bases. Food and drink establishments have opened on bases and cater both to commissioned officers and enlistees to eliminate the additional overall costs of maintaining two separate facilities. Restaurants are also focusing their energies on married enlistees with children to provide them with more nutritious and freshly prepared foods on base. (Figure 1.1)

Airlines

The transportation industry is affected by time constraints placed on the traveler. Whether it is a short domestic flight or an overseas airplane flight, this segment attempts to satisfy the food and beverage needs of its customers in order to heighten the satisfaction of the overall travel experience. Airlines offer a variety of food items such as sandwiches, snacks, and beverages on commuter flights and complete meals featuring an appetizer or soup, salad, entrée with accompaniments, and dessert on longer flights. Airline commissaries provide food for one or several airlines and in some cases use a cycle menu. A *cycle menu* repeats all the food items after a set number of days. Most airlines run a six-day cycle menu to decrease the possibility that a customer might receive the same entrée during a round-trip flight.

Airline feeding has gone through many changes over the last decade. Current trends of reducing snacks and beverages on commuter flights are being rethought, and are being replaced by branded items that appeal to travelers. For example, Starbucks® coffee is now served on United Airlines®. Other airlines have begun to hand out bag lunches at boarding gates (something Luftansa® has done for years), in order to reduce costs. Airline commissaries are also serving ethnic dishes in-flight due to the influx of multi-cultural travelers. Health-conscious travelers are accommodated with fresh fruit and vegetables, low-fat, low-cholesterol, and vegetarian items.

In addition to catering to travel clients, many terminals now have vending machines, employee cafeterias, and small sandwich and beverage outlets for their workers. Although this segment of the foodservice operation has traditionally been a non-commercial endeavor, outside foodservice contractors such as Host International®, are now being used as well. As in other foodservice segments, brand identity is increasing at airport terminals across the country. CA One Services® (a subsidiary of Delaware North Cos.®) manages operations with brand-name recognition such as Amercio's Pizzaria® and Lefty's Bar and Grill®. CA One Services® also runs big-name operations such as McDonald's® and Applebee's®. (Figure 1.1)

Bars and Taverns

The foodservice segment made up of bars and taverns consists of properties that are for the most part independently owned. Chain operations are not as common in this segment as in other foodservice sectors. Today there are many variations of bars and taverns that appeal to a wide range of markets. These include sports bars, brew pubs, wine bars, and teen clubs that serve non-alcoholic beverages. Appetizers, soups, salads, sandwiches, burgers, and desserts are also popular fare at these establishments. More upscale properties offer brick-oven pizza, calzones, and pasta as well as signature drinks. Bars and taverns also provide entertainment and recreation, music, pool tables, big-screen TVs and video games. Operators use promotions such as drink specials, prizes, wine and beer tastings, free appetizers with drinks, v.i.p. parties for businesses, sporting events parties for the Super Bowl and the World Series, and charity functions to increase sales. (Figure 1.1)

Review Questions

1. What is the major difference between the commercial and the non-commercial foodservice industry? Name and discuss two segments of the commercial food-service industry.

2. Explain the advantages and disadvantages of selecting an outside foodservice contractor. Cite examples of foodservice contractors who have entered into the foodservice industry.

3. Define "branding" and discuss the advantages of introducing this marketing technique into a foodservice operation. Give examples of where branding is used in the foodservice industry.

4. What is the key to running a successful lodging establishment?

5. Discuss the influence of Health Maintenance Organizations and Preferred Provider Organizations on the hospital foodservice sector.

6. Discuss three alternatives to traditional university board plans. What are the advantages and disadvantages of these plans?

7. Why is vending proving to be such a lucrative proposition?

8. Identify and discuss two systems that have reduced overall labor costs in nursing homes.

9. Discuss the alternatives to the home cooked meal.

10. Discuss food trends in the airline industry.

Bibliography

Andorka Jr., Frank H. "Counting on Food Courts." *Hotel & Motel Management.* 20 April 1998, 46–47.

Bartlett, Michael. "1996 Annual Forecast." *Restaurant & Institutions.* 1 January 1996, 18–22.

Battaglia, Andy. "As top freestanding sites become harder to find, restaurants aim to synergize." *Restaurant News.* 19 July 1999, 49–52.

Briley, Margaret E., Cynthia Roberts, Gray Simpson, and Deborah Simpson. "Identification of Factors that Influence the Menu at Child Care Centers: an awarded theory approach." *Journal of the American Dietetic Association* 94.3 (March 1994): 276–81.

"Choose to offer choice," *Foodservice Director.* 15 November 2003, 44.

"How Corporate Foodservice Is Performing." *Foodservice Director.* 15 May 1996, 67–74.

Hume, Scott. "Friends & Enemies." *Restaurants & Institutions.* 1 January 2004, 67–73.

Hutchcraft, Chuck, and Deborah Silver. "2001 A Foodservice Odyssey." *Restaurants & Institutions.* 1 January 2001, 44–60.

"Industry Forecast." *Restaurants & Institution.* 1 January 1997, 29–37.

King, Paul. "Contract Foodservice Operators raise the stakes, play for keeps in stadium arena segment." *Nation's Restaurant News.* 28 June 1999, 154–158.

Kotschevar, Lendal, and Marcel Escoffier. *Management by Menu.* 3rd ed. Chicago: The Educational Foundation of the National Restaurant Association, 1994.

Grossbauer, Sue. "Room Service In Patient Feeding." *Foodservice Director.* 15 April 2000, 150.

LaVeachia, Gina. "New Demands of Captive Customers." *Food Management*. August 1996, 38–42.

Matsumoto, Janice. "Health Care." *Restaurants & Institutions*. 15 September 2000, 56–59.

McAteer, Michael, and Michael Healy. "Child Care Food Program Facts for Sponsoring Organizations." *Food & Nutrition*. April 1981, 4–5.

"Menu overhaul in Ga. schools adds culture, healthier options." *Foodservice Director*. 15 November 2003, 28.

Michaelides, Stephen. "Different Strokes for Different Folks." *Food Management*. August 1996, 46–50.

"Navy Exchange to Debut Foodcourts." *Foodservice Director*. 15 January 2001, 5.

"On The Fly." *Restaurant News*, 6 September 1999, 26–28.

Perlik, Allison, and Margaret Sheridan. "A Future in Flux." *Restaurant & Institutions*. 1 January 2004, 52–60.

"Prison forgets inmate weight." *Foodservice Director*. 15 December 2003, 28.

Ruggless, Ron. "Hotels tap mainstream trends, big-name chefs to exploit hot economy." *Nation's Restaurant News*. 28 June 1999, 160–165.

"Segment Trends." *Restaurants & Institutions*. 1 January 1996: 28–38.

Sheridan, Margaret. "Staying Power." *Restaurant & Institutions*. 15 January 2000, 61–67.

"Sportservice Revitalized." *Foodservice Director*. 15 February 2001, 26.

Stockham, Ann. "Schools." *Restaurants & Institutions*. 15 September 2000, 70–72.

"Vending Study: Average Sales Grow 9%." *Foodservice Director*. 15 October 2000, 63–68.

Wallace, Rande L. *Introduction to Professional Foodservice*. New York: John Wiley & Sons, 1996.

Weiss, Robert J. "Health Maintenance Organizations-PPOS-Who Pays for Medical Care: The American Health-Care System and How to Use It" The Columbia University College of Physicians & Surgeons Complete Home Medical Guide, 1989.

Weiss, Robert J. "Preferred Provider Organizations-PPOS-Who Pays for Medical Care: The American Health-Care System and How to Use It" The Columbia University College of Physicians & Surgeons Complete Home Medical Guide, 1989.

Weiss, Shari. "On the line (Piccadilly Express take-out food services)." *Nation's Restaurant News*. 29 March 1999, 16.

Wolson, Shelley "Growth in Branded Entrées." *Food Service Director*. 15 February 2000, 136.

Wolson, Shelley. "Pushing Bigger Buys." *Foodservice Director*. 15 November 2000, 150.

Yee, Laura. "Weighing in." *Restaurant & Institutions*. 1 January 2004, 39–42.

Concept Development

objectives

Upon completion of this chapter, the student should be able to:

1. list and explain the components of a customer survey and feasibility study.
2. write a feasibility study for a foodservice concept.
3. evaluate if a foodservice concept can be successful in a selected community.

key terms

Community Geographics	*Feasibility Study*
Concept	*Foodservice Concepts*

Introduction

A Risky Business

Bank officials state that investing in a foodservice business is a high risk investment. It is also well known that 80% of the individuals who open a foodservice operation today find themselves out of business in a year. How can so many people fail at making a profit, and find themselves out of business?

This chapter explores the reasons why 80% of owners fail, and more importantly, why 20% succeed. The steps in developing a foodservice concept are discussed highlighting topics such as market demographics and community geographics.

Developing a Concept

This is where it all starts! Let's begin to develop a concept for a foodservice operation. The concept is the foundation that contributes to building a profitable foodservice operation. The concept includes more than the type of cuisine to be served and the type of atmosphere. It is defined as a matrix of the owner's business philosophy and operational procedures, the customer survey and community geographics, financial feasibility plans, strategic advertising, and management goals and objectives. The concept becomes the strategic business plan, which acts as a blueprint for what needs to be accomplished.

An Owner's Philosophical Approach

How a person designs a concept depends on his/her philosophical approach about getting into business. There are two fundamental entrepreneur approaches. Both involve owners who invest time and money (see Figure 2.1). The first type will be labeled Investor A, and the second, Investor B.

Investor A is a person who enters the foodservice industry solely for a maximum profit to be returned on his/her financial investment (ROI). The style and type of foodservice operations are important but are truly secondary to reaching a financial goal. Whether it is a quick-service, family, or fine dining food concept, the goal is to invest in the best concept that will bring the greatest profit. The investor does not want to fail and lose money. He/she is usually not an expert on foodservice systems, but is knowledgeable about foodservice operations. Investor A's expertise is in finance and financial systems. Investor A is sometimes known as a silent owner who wants to invest by "filling the gap," as he/she is usually less involved in daily operational activities. "Filling the gap" means to have a customer survey and feasibility study completed on a community. If the analysis indicates there are 50 classical French restaurants, 60 steak and seafood restaurants, 44 Italian restaurants and one Chinese restaurant that is very busy, the cuisine restaurant that indicates "a gap" when comparing numbers is the Chinese cuisine. The type A investor would then "fill the gap" by investing in another Chinese cuisine restaurant even though he/she does not prefer Chinese cuisine.

Investor B is a person who enters the foodservice industry as an active owner. This owner is instrumental in the creation, development, and implementation of the concept. This person also wants to reach a profitable financial goal and invests "sweat equity" in

Type A

1. Primary investment goal is maximum return on investment.
2. Selection of style and type of foodservice concept are secondary.
3. Is not an active owner in daily operations, low sweat equity.
4. Is not an expert in foodservice systems. Is a financial expert.
5. Analyzes a customer survey, feasibility study, and financial strategic plans.

Type B

1. Primary investment goal is maximum return on investment.
2. Selection of style and type of foodservice concept are very important.
3. Is active in the daily operations, high sweat equity.
4. Is an expert in foodservice systems. Is not a financial expert.
5. Does not analyze a customer survey, feasibility study and financial strategic plans.

FIGURE 2.1 Characteristics of Type A and B Investors

operating the business. "Sweat equity" is the amount of time and physical work a person performs on a specific task. Investor B is usually an expert in foodservice operation systems who hires the financial experts. The style and type of foodservice concept, be it quick service, family, or fine dining, is very important to this owner. The type of cuisine and style of atmosphere are the primary elements of a concept, and must be very clear and well defined. If type B investor loves classical French cuisine and wants to open a French restaurant, he/she will, regardless of the number of classical French cuisine restaurants in the same community. Investor B does not select a concept based on customer surveys, feasibility studies, or the "filling the gap" theory.

Why Owners Fail

People who fail within the first year of their business, do so due to a lack of knowledge in one or all of these areas: finance, management, and foods. The ultimate reason for closing a business is not making enough money (sales/revenue), to pay the bills. How does a person get into this situation? An individual might begin a business underestimating the capital needed. An owner might not properly forecast the expenditures (expenses) for the entire concept. A major expense often forgotten is that of paying the purveyors in cash (COD). For the first six months after opening a business, many owners do not receive a line of credit until they can indicate a good cash flow. Once the owner establishes a good working relationship with the purveyor, the purveyor allows the owner to order food on credit. The purveyor then sends a bill (statement) at the end of the month.

At times, owners mismanage people. The inexperienced owner will hire friends or family members, thinking that a great friendship makes for a great working relationship. This rarely works, as it is difficult to take orders from and to fire friends or family members. Many owners have difficulty saying no to their employees or not saying yes often enough. This usually results in employees taking advantage of, or constantly fighting with the owner. In either scenario, a negative attitude emerges in the service sector, resulting in the loss of customers.

A lack of understanding of foods and foodservice systems is a third area that causes foodservice operators to fail. The great taste of food is the number one reason customers patronize a foodservice operation. The owner must have a knowledge of ordering, purchasing, receiving, storing, preparing, producing, and serving foods, as well as a working knowledge of health and sanitation codes (laws). Owners who do not know how to implement controls on food and beverages operate at a high food cost and are more apt to serve an inconsistent quality of food to customers.

Owners must be knowledgeable in all three areas in order to successfully manage a foodservice operation. Does this mean that the owner has to be the chef, the bookkeeper, the bartender, the waitstaff, the front of the house manager, as well as all of the other employees? No, the owner is not, and clearly should not be, all of these employees. But, he/she does need a working knowledge of these positions.

Successful owners are knowledgeable about these positions, and have the following in common:

1. They enjoy eating and learning about the cuisine they have chosen.

2. They enjoy being with, and working with their target market. If you do not like children, why open a family restaurant?

3. They start at the level at which their experience indicates they should start. Most start with a small scale foodservice concept and later expand as their experience, knowledge, and business grow.

4.   Most start with a traditional cuisine. Operating a successful foodservice business while offering an unfamiliar style of cuisine is difficult to do. More customers are familiar with American cuisine than Hungarian cuisine.

5.   They are also willing to learn from everyone. They know the direction in which they want to go, are good leaders, and understand their limitations.

Selecting a Foodservice Concept Category

The foodservice segments discussed in chapter two can be classified into one of two categories, Quick-Service or Full Service (family restaurants, dinner houses, or fine dining establishments).

Quick-service concepts represent foodservice operations that need to generate a high volume of sales due to low check averages. A check average is the amount of money a customer spends for a meal. Fine dining foodservice concepts have the opposite effect; they generate a low sales volume because they generate a high check average. Family concepts generate a moderate volume of sales and a moderate check average.

Once an owner decides which category his/her foodservice operation fits into, everything connected with the concept (especially the design and the planning of operational procedures, such as designing the menu) is implemented based on the principles of that category. (Figure 2.2) Let us begin by examining the quick-service category in Figure 2.2. The quick-service concept needs a high sales volume due to low product cost and a low check average. What types of foodservice operations typically fit into this concept? Hamburger, chicken, pizza, taco, sweet, and sandwich shops are examples of foodservice operations that need to generate a high volume of sales.

Quick-Service concepts must be designed for speed and efficiency. All of the operational procedures, as well as the design and layout of operations, are focused on what can be done to reduce the time it takes a customer to order food, and to leave as a satisfied customer. Customers must not be too comfortable or encouraged to have too leisurely a lunch. National fast food hamburger chains target a 13 to 20 minute staying time for lunch customers. In order to accomplish this goal, four carefully planned design elements must be considered: comfort, lighting, noise level, and menu design.

It is more comfortable to pull out a chair, sit down, and adjust the chair until you are comfortable. In a quick-service concept, the chairs and tables are intentionally designed not to move, forcing the customer to conform to the space provided. After 15 or 20 min-utes the customer is ready to leave. Stationary chairs and tables alone do not get the job done.

The lighting and the noise level also affect a customer's comfort. Bright lighting encourages customers to act quickly. Having an open kitchen where customers can see active employees rushing to fill orders, hear equipment timers, hear employees shouting orders, and witness customers giving orders, also contribute considerably to a quick turnover atmosphere.

The menu design and layout must encourage speed. The menu items are followed by the price. There are no long, colorful descriptions to slow down customer decision-making time. The grouping of food categories: breakfast, lunch sandwiches, desserts, and beverages, contribute to a reduction in selection time.

Once the concept category has been selected, stay focused on that concept throughout the planning and design of the foodservice operation. Do not mix a quick-service, high sales volume concept when trying to plan for a fine dining, high check average concept.

Foodservice Concept Categories	Capacity	Turn-Over Rate/Hour	Check Average	Meal Periods	Eating Time per Minutes	Lights	Noise Level	Seat Comfort	Square Ft. per Person
Quick-Serve	Under 100 Seats	10x Per Hour	Low-Below $7	Breakfast & Lunch	20 or less	Bright	Loud	Less Comfortable	7–12
Full Service Family	Over 100 Seats	1–1.25 Per Hour	Moderate $15–$25	Lunch & Dinner	45 to 60	Casual Bright/Dim	Pleasant	Comfortable	12–15
Dinner House	Over 100 seats	3/4–1.25 Per Hour	Moderate $15–$25	Lunch & Dinner	45 to 90	Casual Bright/Dim	Pleasant	Comfortable	12–15
Fine Dining	Under 100 Seats	1/2–3/4 Per Hour	High $65–$200+	Dinner	60 to 150	Low/Dim	Quiet/relaxing	Very Comfortable	15–24

Foodservice Concept Category	Parking	Menu Design	Type of Service	Rest Rooms	Lobby Design	Uniform Color Scheme	Style of Music
Quick-Serve	Self	Limited Selection No Copy	Counter Self Serve	Basic Design Small	Simple Design Small Sq. Ft. Foyer Only	Unique Design Use of Colors Primary	No Music
Full Service Family	Self	Large Selection Use of Copy	Table Service	Modified Design Large Sq. Ft.	Modified Design Moderate/Large Sq. Ft. Foyer and Lobby	Designed for Theme. Less Use of Primary Colors	Little Use of Music. Style Fits Theme
Dinner House	Self	Moderate/Large Use of Copy	Table Service	Modified Design Large Sq. Ft.	Modified Design Small/Moderate Sq. Ft. Foyer and Lobby	Designed for Theme. Less Use of Primary Colors	Little Use of Music. Style Fits Theme
Fine Dining	Valet	Moderate Selection Elegant Use of Copy	Tableside Service	Elegant Design Use of Fresh Cut Flowers, Perfumes, Large Sq. Ft.	Elaborate Design Moderate/Large Sq. Ft. Foyer and Lobby	Sophisticated To Casual Design More Use of Pastel and Earth Tone Colors	Offers Classical Soft, Background Music

FIGURE 2.2 Foodservice Concept Categories

The philosophy of these two concepts does not blend well, and the designs are not compatible. On the other hand, a quick-service concept might blend with a family concept, or a family concept with a fine dining concept. Blending concepts is difficult to accomplish and is not recommended for inexperienced foodservice operators.

Customer Survey and Feasibility Study

A customer survey is used to study the market a foodservice operation will target. A feasibility study is a customer survey that includes additional information about the community. It is essential to both complete and understand these studies in order to maximize profits. Although both surveys are not required, they are highly recommended. Remember that about 80% of the people who jump right into the foodservice business are unemployed at the end of the year. Before you jump, please think about where you want to land!

Elements of a Customer Survey

Customer surveys study the demographic statistics of potential customers. There are eight key demographic factors:

1. Age
2. Gender
3. Occupation
4. Income

5. Ethnic Background
6. Household Size
7. Education
8. Food Preference
9. Disposable income

The purpose of studying customer demographics is to identify and learn about customers. Who are they and what do they demand? A basic principle of economics is the law of supply and demand: analyze what your customers are demanding and supply them with what they want. Customer demands range from simple to complex. Being able to identify and fulfill customer demands is what will make a foodservice operation profitable. A knowledge of demographic information increases knowledge about the customer.

Age

Age generally indicates the amount of social, work, and life experiences a person has had. A 20 year old customer has different demands than a 60 year old customer. The 20 year old desires foods, beverages, a style of music, dining room decor, menu prices, and portion sizes that are not the same as those of a 60 year old customer. Both customers have different views on education, work experiences, disposable income, dietary needs, and family. Identifying and understanding a targeted age group can assist one in developing a foodservice concept. Hiring 20 year old servers, in a restaurant that targets a 55 to 65 year old market, is likely to cause an uncomfortable atmosphere. The 18 to 20 year old servers and the 55 to 65 year old customers do not usually have much in common. A generation gap (Figure 2.3) causes communication beyond the standard service questions to become more difficult for both age groups. Targeting a 25 to 30 year old customer, and employing an 18 to 20 year old waitstaff, establishes a much more comfortable atmosphere as the two groups have more in common.

Does It Really Exist? Yes!

Topic	20 Year Old Person	60 Year Old Person
Food Preference	Still Exploring	Established
Work Experience	Just Starting Career Four Years Experience Searching for Career	At The Peak of Career 44 Years Experience Been There, Done That!
Families	No Nest Little Interest	Empty Nest Becoming Grandparents
Education	Average 14 Years Completed	Average 18 Years Completed
Diets	Seafood See food and eat! High Calorie Non Restricted	Moderate To Restricted Due To Health Concerns
Number of Wars Lived Through	One: Desert Storm	Four: World War Two Korean War Vietnam War Desert Storm
Type of Car	Not Paid For Not Expensive Over 60,000 Miles Parents Car	Paid For! Expensive Under 60,000 Miles
Music	Great! Loud Important	Okay Not As Loud Not As Important
Disposable Income	Champagne Taste Beer Wallet	Imported Champagne Taste Champagne Wallet
Outlook on Life	Free Spirit Live For Today Don't Worry About Tomorrow	Savoring More Moments

FIGURE 2.3 Generation Gap

Gender

The knowledge of whether your market is predominately male or female will aid you in choosing the types of cuisine, the portion sizes, the balancing of calories, and the nutritional elements on the menu, as well as the decor.

Occupation

The type of work your market does throughout the day will help you to establish guidelines concerning menu selections and portion sizes. If you are feeding people who do a lot of physical work, the food items and portion sizes should be heartier. Customers who are doing less physical work may prefer a food section that has fewer calories and smaller portions. Knowing the types of occupations your customers have may help you in knowing the companies that employ them. It is important to research the financial strength of companies, particularly if 75% of your targeted customers work in two textile factories; what if these factories close three months after you open your restaurant?

Income

Knowing the customer's income bracket assists you in determining the selling price on the menu and in forecasting annual sales. The targeted customer must have enough disposable income to support the proposed check average. Disposable income is money that is left over after all the personal bills, city, state, and federal taxes have been paid. The greater the market income, the greater the amount of disposable income.

Ethnic Background

Having a knowledge of the culture, race, or language of the targeted market can assist you in selecting the cuisine(s) or traditional ethnic dishes to place on the menu. Understanding cultural traditions can help you in designing and decorating the front of the house.

Household Size

A knowledge of household size (defined as the number of people living within a family), and of the number of households in a selected community, can greatly contribute to your feasibility study. There must be enough customers within the targeted geographical region to support the foodservice operation.

Education

The higher the education level of your market, the more open the market is to trying new foodservice operations. People who have a higher level of education usually have more disposable income and tend to dine out more frequently.

Food Preferences

Understanding which foods customers prefer will assist in sales and will contribute to the bottom line profit. To determine customer preference, collect and compare the menu of direct and indirect competition. "Direct competition" refers to those foodservice operations that are similar in their style of cuisine, check average, targeted market, and concept. An example of direct competition is a family steak and seafood restaurant competing with another family steak and seafood restaurant. Indirect competition refers to foodservice operations that do not have the same concepts or style of cuisine, but which compete for the same customers in the same geographical region.

Collect menus from both direct and indirect foodservice operations. Compare the same menu classifications and subclassifications on the menus, for example, soups with soups, beef entrées with beef entrées. If ten out of ten menus offer French onion soup, it is a good indication that the customers in this community enjoy French onion soup. If only one out of ten menus features French onion soup, and the other nine feature chicken soup, it would be obvious that chicken soup is preferred. Other research methods include:

    A.   Asking potential purveyors about which foods are the most popular. Purveyors keep usage charts that indicate how much food a foodservice operation uses. This information is not readily available to the general public.

B.   Visiting the direct competition. Observe on a busy Friday or Saturday night. Talk with the customers, waitstaff, cooks, and the owner. Analyze their menus as well as the entire operation. Determine the signature items on the menu. Put your detective's hat on and investigate.

C.   Visiting supermarkets at which your targeted customers shop. Visit the day after a busy shopping day. Take note of which foods are left on the shelves to determine the foods that customers do not like. Talk with the store owner and counter personnel about which food products are popular.

D.   Analyzing the types of specialty markets in the community. If there are a number of successful gourmet shops and high quality pastry shops within the community, this would indicate that customers are familiar with and appreciate quality specialty foods.

The purpose of studying the demographics of the target market is to gain as much insight and understanding of what these people look for in a dining experience. Knowing as much as you can about your customers greatly increases your chances of operating a financially successful foodservice operation.

Community Geographics

One of the most important decisions an owner makes is where to locate a foodservice operation. A prime location will greatly increase the visibility of the operation. High visibility will increase the customer count and sales due to impulse diners. Impulse diners are people who base their decision to dine at a foodservice operation on the taste of the food and the location of the foodservice operation. High visibility also reduces advertising expenses.

In researching factual data about a community, collect current information on the geographic region and on the neighborhood in which the foodservice establishment will be located. Helpful information includes: population growth, economic growth, financial stability, unemployment rate, type of industries, commercial tax rates, prime interest rate, real estate values, zoning regulations, building codes, state board of health codes, highway and road development, public services offered, potential sales generators, crime rate, school systems, purveyors, and competition.

Population Growth

Population growth determines if the population is growing, declining, or maintaining its current number. If there is a great decline, examine why people are moving away. In a small community the customer base may be too small to support the foodservice operation, while in a large city a small decline may not greatly affect the customer base.

Economic Growth and Financial Stability

Is the city on the brink of bankruptcy? Are the taxes frequently being increased? What is the prime interest rate? Are companies relocating? What are the commercial tax rates? Is the unemployment rate high as compared to the state and national rate? How many businesses have "for sale" signs in their windows? What are the top five industries in the community? What is the commercial real estate value? Are the local banks branches or bank headquarters? Does the community have more jewelry and shoe stores than pharmacies and liquor stores? Have the building permit applications and the number of building permits being issued increased or decreased? Answering these questions will give you a better understanding of the economical and financial stability of the community.

Zoning, and Local and State Codes

There are several types of zones, such as residential, commercial, industrial, school, hospital, no parking, tow, preservation, and environmental zones. All zones have either local, state, or federal codes associated with them. The only zone a commercial business cannot operate in is a residential zone. All zones require permits and licenses in order to open a business.

Highway and Road Development

In surveying the community and the exact neighborhood where the foodservice operation may be located, map out roads that are under construction and those that will soon be under construction. Find out the community's plans for road repairs and sewer development. Also note where one-way streets, stops signs, reduced speed limits and traffic lights are located. People will avoid foodservice operations that they find difficult to get to. Foodservice operations located on two-way streets have higher sales than foodservice operations located on one way streets. Easy access into and from the foodservice operation's parking lot is also important. Stop signs, low speed limits, and traffic lights allow people, both driving and pedestrian, to have more time to look around and notice the foodservice operation.

Public Services Offered

What services does the community offer you as a taxpaying business person? Normally, only fire, police protection, and street snow removal services are offered.

Potential Sales Generators

A sales generator is a location where potential customers gather and where sales might be generated. Some examples of sales generators are: factories, office buildings, churches, movie theaters, civic centers, busy intersections, sport arenas, and shopping malls. All of these places are where large groups of people congregate and become potential sales for foodservice operators. Successful owners identify two or more sales generators as part of their customer base profile. They do not simply say, we will locate the foodservice operation next to a large office building or near a busy intersection and hope that customers will come to dine. Owners will analyze the needs of the people at the sales generators and work hard to fulfill their needs.

Crime Rate

No one is going to dine in a foodservice operation located in a high crime neighborhood. If people have a fear that something bad may happen at a particular site, they will not go there.

School Systems

A large number of schools (elementary, junior high, and high schools) in a community indicate a stable customer base. Communities that have numerous schools have a lot of children, which usually indicates a lot of families. Most of these families will also own their own houses. People who own their houses usually have a more difficult time just picking up and leaving town. Communities with numerous schools are positive indicators in selecting a family style foodservice concept.

Purveyors

Research the types of purveyors, where they are located, and the services they offer. Get to know these people, not just their telephone numbers and prices. Select purveyors who are willing to build a long term business relationship with a foodservice owner.

When analyzing research data, make sure that there are more positive indicators than negatives before locating a foodservice concept in a particular community. There is no scientific method or magical formula that indicates how to become an instant success. There are many financially successful foodservice operators who can teach you how to become successful. All of them have worked hard and have learned by their mistakes. Successful foodservice operators understand the importance of planning and implementing food and beverage cost controls, and financial controls. They also know how to manage people.

Review Questions

1. Explain the differences between quick service, family, and fine dining foodservice concepts.

2. List reasons why foodservice operations fail.

3. What is the importance of conducting a customer survey?

4. List and explain the importance of ten components in a community geographics survey.

5. Describe the two types of investors.

Bibliography

Conducting a Feasibility Study for a New Restaurant.
    National Restaurant Association and Cini-Grissom
    Associate Inc. 1983, Washington D.C.

Developing the Sales Menu

objectives

Upon completion of this chapter, the student should be able to:

1. identify and discuss the major classifications on a menu.
2. select and describe menu listings based on variety, balance, and composition.
3. define and discuss Truth-in-Menu.
4. distinguish between nutrient and health claims on a menu.

key terms

Balance
Classification/Headings
Composition
Descriptive Copy
Health Claim
Menu2™

Menu Listings
Nutrient Claim
Subclassification/Subheadings
Truth-in-Menu
Variety

Introduction

Developing a menu takes time and careful planning. Within this chapter the basic components of menu development are defined and explained: menu classifications, menu listings, variety, balance, composition, and descriptive copy. Truth-in-menu guidelines and the new menu labeling regulations are also examined.

Menu Classifications

The restaurant concept must first be defined in order to plan a proper menu. The number of *classifications or headings* on a menu depends upon the type of restaurant. Most menus have the following classifications: **appetizers, soups, salads, sandwiches, entrées, accompaniments,** and **desserts.** There are, of course, other more nontraditional classifications such as: side orders and beverages which might appear on a luncheon menu, or a pasta section on an ethnic menu. A list of menu classifications with a brief explanation of each follows.

Appetizers

The major purpose of an appetizer is to stimulate the palate before the meal. The portion size is generally small and when accompanied with wine or spirits tends to be spicy. Appetizers can either be hot or cold and include: beef, poultry, fish or seafood, fruits, and vegetables.

Soups

Soups can be either hot or cold and are usually served after the appetizer. Soups are divided into three major categories: clear or unthickened soups, thick soups, "Specialty" soups. Clear soups consist of: bouillons, broths, consommés, and thin vegetable soups. Thick soups encompass: bisques, chowders, creams, potages and purées. "Specialty" soups are representative of certain countries or regions, and include: Minestrone, French Onion, or Gumbo. Cold soups also fall under the "National" or "Specialty" category and are often served in warmer climates: cucumber, gazpacho, fruit, and vichyssoise are a few examples of cold soups.

Salads

Salads are generally served as an accompaniment or as a main course on the menu. Salads should be fresh and served at the proper temperature whether hot or cold. Accompanying salads can be served in lieu of the appetizer or soup and are sometimes referred to as first course salads. The major purpose of the first course salad is to enliven the palate. Grilled vegetables, fish or seafood, specialty meats, or fruits can be utilized. In fine dining restaurants, the accompanying salad is served before the entrée. These salads are designed to cleanse the palate; they should be light in nature, and consist of mixed greens such as Bib and Belgian endive. Main course salads or cold plates are referred to as cold entrées. Lobster salad, chicken salad with apple and walnuts, or grilled vegetable plates with aged balsamic and pecorino are a few examples of cold entrées.

Sandwiches

Sandwiches can be served cold or hot and might contain beef, poultry, fish or seafood, and vegetables. Sandwiches are generally found on the luncheon menu and can be simple to elaborate: ranging from a chicken salad sandwich, to a grilled swordfish sandwich provençale served open faced.

Entrées

Entrées are usually also separated into hot or cold sections on the menu. Hot entrées are the largest classification on the menu and are sometimes further broken down into *subclassifications or subheadings*. These can include: meat, poultry, fish, and seafood. Cold entrées make up a smaller classification; therefore, subclassifications are not warranted. Generally, a listing of main course salads or cold plates follows the cold entrées.

Hot Entrées

Meats

Meats are the largest subclassification on the menu and contain: beef, lamb, pork, and veal. Menu listings should be adequately represented to ensure proper cross-utilization. Cooking techniques must also be well balanced and include: braising, broiling, frying, grilling, roasting, sautéing, and smoking. An adequate representation of cooking techniques facilitates proper rotation of kitchen equipment and takes into consideration customer preferences.

Poultry

The poultry subclassification on the menu includes chicken, duck, pheasant, quail, and turkey. Poultry is relatively inexpensive to procure and can be cooked in a variety of ways: baked, barbecued, braised, fried, grilled, roasted, and smoked. Poultry can be cross-utilized with relative ease throughout the menu in appetizers, soups, salads, and entrées. Chicken and turkey, over the last decade, have risen in popularity, due to health concerns over high-fat and high-cholesterol in the diet. They have become healthier alternatives to red meats.

Fish and Seafood

Fish and seafood are rich in flavor and are an excellent source of protein. Fish and seafood listings can be numerous, and include freshwater fish and saltwater fish such as: flatfish, round fish, mollusks, and crustaceans. Fish and seafood can also be prepared a number of ways: baked, broiled, fried, grilled, poached, roasted, sautéed, and smoked. Unfortunately, fish and seafood are highly perishable, and therefore, should be carefully handled and served immediately.

Cold Entrées

As mentioned earlier, cold entrées generally encompass main course salads or cold plates. Main course salads might consist of: a grilled duck salad with vegetable couscous and fall greens, or Caesar salad with lobster. Cold plate listings might include herb salad with cured scallops and brioche sticks, or a fruit and cheese plate with an assortment of smoked meats. Cold entrées are a welcomed addition to the menu for patrons who prefer lighter fare.

Accompaniments

Accompaniments on the menu consist of vegetables, potatoes, rice, and pastas. Both vegetables and starches are low in calories and are relatively inexpensive to prepare. Accompaniments can be cooked in a variety of ways: baked, grilled, roasted, sautéed and steamed. When accompaniments are prepared correctly and presented with the appropriate entrées on an à la carte menu, they can contribute considerably in increasing the overall check average.

Desserts

Desserts are relatively inexpensive to prepare and when merchandised and served correctly are extremely profitable. A variety of choices should be included in the dessert section of the menu: fresh cakes, cobblers or crisps, fruits, ice creams, pies, puddings, sorbets, specialty items, and tarts.

Menu Listings

Once the menu classifications have been selected, *menu listings* must be chosen. The menu listings in each classification vary depending upon the demographics, the type of restaurant, the geographical location, the accessibility of product, the equipment capacity, and the skill level of employees. All these factors must be considered when preparing menu listings. After the tentative menu listings are assembled, they should be reexamined in terms of variety, balance, and composition.

Variety

Variety refers to the diversity of product, hot and cold offerings, the cooking techniques used, the color, configuration, taste, height, and texture of the menu items. Each component of variety must be fully addressed within each menu classification.

Hot and Cold Items

The number of hot and cold items on a menu has a direct correlation to the geographical location of the restaurant and the season. Hot or cold items can be offered in appetizer, soup, salad, sandwich, entrée, and dessert categories.

Cooking Techniques

Each classification of the menu should incorporate a variety of cooking techniques when possible, in order to facilitate equipment equalization within the kitchen, and to ensure customer satisfaction. (Figure 3.1)

Menu Classification	Cooking Techniques
Appetizers	Baking, barbecuing, frying, grilling, and smoking
Soups	Simmering
Salads	Grilling, poaching, roasting, and smoking
Sandwiches	Baking, barbecuing, broiling, frying, grilling, and roasting
Hot Entrées	
Meats	Braising, broiling, frying, grilling, roasting, sautéing, and smoking
Poultry	Braising, barbecuing, broiling, frying, grilling, roasting, sautéing, and smoking
Fish and Seafood	Baking, broiling, frying, grilling, poaching, roasting, sautéing, and smoking
Cold Entrées	Grilling, poaching, roasting, and smoking
Accompaniments	Baking, roasting, sautéing, and steaming
Desserts	Baking, poaching, and freezing

FIGURE 3.1 Menu Classifications and Cooking Techniques

Color

A variety of vibrant, as well as earth tone colors, certainly adds eye appeal to any presentation. Scrod with bread crumbs, rice, and cauliflower is less attractive than roast ham with raisin sauce, au gratin potatoes and French green beans with almonds. Today, patrons have come to expect an eye-appealing plate which has the proper balance of vibrant and earth tone colors. Remember, 50 percent of sales is based on visual presentation.

Configuration

A variety of configurations of food items on a plate has a direct relationship to eye appeal. Configuration takes into consideration special cuts, slices, molds, and loose or whole food items. The rather flat configuration of a roasted tenderloin of beef entrée, served with zucchini provençale, and lyonnaise potatoes, is far surpassed in attractiveness by the mixed configurations offered in a tuna steak with citrus butter, rice pilaf, and asparagus presentation.

Taste

Be careful not to overload the menu with too many spicy or bland foods. Spicy, as well as bland foods, need to be balanced throughout the menu. When composing any plate, remember this fundamental rule: spicy entrées are desirable with bland accompaniments and bland entrées are advisable with spicy accompaniments.

Height

The aesthetic qualities of each food item on the plate are enhanced through a presentation which incorporates a variety of heights. An entrée of veal schnitzel, potato pancakes, and shredded red cabbage are all fairly level in height, whereas, sirloin steak, garlic mashed potatoes, and broccoli offer diverse heights.

Texture

Menu items can contain a variety of textures. These textures include crispy, liquid, chewy, solid, and soft. A complete meal should have an abundance of textures rather than just one or two. For instance, a Chinese menu might encompass: crispy fried wantons, liquid egg drop soup, slightly chewy and crispy mandarin orange salad, solid, chewy, and soft, Peking duck with pancakes, soft rice, and slightly crispy stir-fried vegetables.

Balance

Within each menu classification, there must be a proper *balance* of food items, hot and cold offerings, cooking techniques, colors, configurations, tastes, heights, and textures. Appetizers should include meats, poultry, fish, seafood, fruit, and vegetable selections. There should also be a somewhat equal number of hot and cold offerings in the appetizer classification. Cooking techniques might include: baking, barbecuing, frying, grilling, and smoking. Color, configuration, taste, height, and texture must also be examined when composing the appetizer classification. Proscuitto with Chanterelles and Tomatoes, Grilled Chicken Tortilla with Fresh Salsa, Fried Rock Shrimp with Organic Greens and Chive Mustard Sauce, and Goat Cheese Bruschetta with Pan Seared Garden Tomatoes demonstrate the fundamental principles of balance.

Composition

Composition refers to the presentation of food on a plate. Both variety and balance are an integral part of composition. When composing a plate, keep in mind traditional food combinations such as: roast ham with sweet potatoes, or au gratin potatoes, and green beans; or lobster with corn on a cob, baked potato, and cole slaw. Looking to traditional combinations can greatly simplify the task of composition development.

Descriptive Copy

Descriptive copy essentially introduces the menu listings to the customers. Depending upon the menu listing, descriptive copy includes some or all of the following elements: size of portion, geographical origin, product, primary and secondary ingredients, method of preparation, and appropriate accouterments. For instance, a menu item listed as BAKED STUFFED LOBSTER might include the following descriptive copy: a two pound Maine lobster stuffed with crab meat, scallops, and seasoned Ritz® cracker crumbs, baked, and served with drawn butter. When writing a descriptive copy, remember the following:

1.   Keep the explanation simple, clear, and concise.

2.   exclude words such as "best," "colossal," "extraordinary," "magnificent," and "superb."

3.   use appropriate food terminology such as: chilled, glazed, flaky, grilled, medallions, sautéed, toasted, and whipped.

Truth-in-Menu

Once the major components of the menu have been developed, an examination of legal regulations should be addressed. Legally, each food item description advertised on the menu must be completely accurate. Several states have passed *truth-in-menu* legislation to deter deceptive advertising on the menu. If a restaurant violates truth-in-menu, legislation fines, court expenses, and negative publicity can result. In an effort to regulate truth-in-menu, the National Restaurant Association published and adopted an Accuracy in Menu position paper, in February 1977. See Appendix A.

Menu Labeling Regulations

In 1990, Congress passed the new menu labeling regulations under the Nutritional Labeling and Education Act (NLEA). The law was initially targeted for the packaged food industry, which was required to have food analyzed by a lab, in order to scientifically substantiate nutrient information. Under the same act, in May 1994, new menu labeling regulations were enacted. Medium sized restaurants, where nutrient and health claims were made on placards, posters, and signs, had to provide customers with documentation. In 1995, smaller restaurants were also made to comply with the new menu labeling regulations.

Beginning on May 2, 1997, the Food and Drug Administration (FDA) determined that all nutrient and health claims on a menu must be scientifically substantiated. These new menu labeling regulations affect the whole restaurant industry, including caterers, delis, take-out establishments, casual and fine dining restaurants, and institutional foodservice.

Restaurants that make nutritional or health claims, or use symbols such as a heart, a fruit, or a vegetable to signify healthy food items or meals have to follow the new menu labeling requirements. Restaurants must be made aware of what constitutes a nutrient or health claim. A *nutrient claim* usually makes a statement about a menu item containing a specific nutrient. Cholesterol free, fresh, healthy, natural, low in fat, light or lite, and reduced are common nutrient claims on restaurant menus. A *health claim*, on the other hand, stresses the relationship between the food item or meal with disease prevention.

For example, fruits and vegetables in relation to cancer. According to the FDA, restaurants cannot alter any health claim statements or fabricate their own health claims.

Once a restaurant makes a nutrient or health claim regarding a menu item or a meal, it must substantiate that claim. The FDA has stated that recipes appearing in a published cookbook that have a nutritional analysis with each recipe, computer generated databases, and menus endorsed by a dietary association or health professional organization suffice in filling this requirement. Nutrient and health claim information must be made available to all patrons either through a brochure, pamphlet, recipe file, notebook, bulletin board, or poster. Claims do not have to be printed directly on the menu. If the menu does not make any nutrient or health claim, or use symbols to denote healthy food items or meals, these new menu labeling regulations are not applicable.

Implementing a Healthy Choice Menu

Professionals in the foodservice industry have been working very hard to keep up with customers' demands to have a menu that offers them a choice to consume a healthy meal. Many foodservice companies have been adapting their menus to offer a variety of healthy menu items such as appetizers, soups, entrée salads, entrées and desserts. Customers who want to maintain a healthy life style are requesting more information on nutrition such as how many calories, how much sodium, how much cholesterol, and how many grams of fat are in the dishes listed on the menu.

The challenge for foodservice managers and chefs is how to serve customers who want to maintain a healthy life style and also serve customers who do not want to maintain a healthy life style while dining out. How do they provide the necessary information on the menu to satisfy both customers without upsetting either party?

In the past customers frowned upon menus that communicated healthy menu items by using a designated logo or symbol such as a heart. Customers who wanted to eat healthy did not want to be singled out by letting other people in their party know they wanted to eat healthy. Customers who did not want to eat healthy but knew they should eat healthier dishes found the heart label to be annoying. Today customers are demanding companies in the foodservice industry—from limited serve to fine dining establishments—provide customers with nutritional information and a greater selection of healthy menu items so they can make an informed choice of what to eat.

Menu2™

Many chefs and managers are meeting their customers demand by providing more nutritional information and a greater selection of healthier menu items. One system that does provide a foodservice establishment an excellent way of disseminating nutritional information and providing the customer with a greater selection of healthier menu items in a comfortable manner is Menu2™.

Menu2™ was developed by internationally renowned, pioneering television gourmet Dr. Graham Kerr (Kerr Corp). Dr. Kerr defines Menu2™ as *a voluntary initiative by hotels and restaurants to provide their customers with a brief, non-intrusive guide to the primary nutritional values of foods offered on their menus. The nutrition numbers are shown on a second menu, hence Menu2, which is offered by the waitstaff and never presented other than in response to a customer's request.*

The waitstaff server would greet customers providing them with the primary sales menu and asking if anyone would like to order from Menu2™. At the customer's request Menu2™ would be provided to the customer. Using this method of communicating allows for customers to receive what they desire without making anyone uncomfortable.

Dr. Kerr indicates: *the nutritional analysis is rounded off and used as a guide only. Every item on the Menu2™ is assessed for comparative purposes. Establishments using Menu2™ are required to include a minimum of two appetizers, two main entrées and two desserts, when added, do not exceed 1,000 calories or contain more than 39 grams of fat and less than 7% calories from saturated fat. The numbers include total calories 350, total fats 12, saturated fats 2 (in parentheses) and carbohydrates 45, i.e. 350-12(2)-45. These reasonable/moderate dishes are not highlighted in any way. They are found to be reasonable/moderate only by their numbers compared to other dishes. As a result, nothing is labeled as "healthy" or "low fat" or in any way as a means to medicate.*

Chefs and managers who are offering Menu2™ in their restaurants are excited about the positive results Menu2™ has provided them and their customers. They stated that Menu2™ is an excellent solution to offer all their customers a great dining experience.

For more information about Menu2™ and Dr. Graham Kerr go to his website at www.grahamkerr.com

Review Questions

1. Name the six menu classifications and create eight menu listings for each.

2. How does variety and balance play an important role in composition on a menu?

3. Write a descriptive copy for the following menu items:

    Crabcakes

    Seafood Corn Chowder

    Caesar Salad

    Grilled Swordfish with Citrus Salsa

    Brown Rice Pilaf

    Peach Crisp

4. List five common misrepresentations on a menu and explain how they might be avoided.

5. What impact do the new labeling regulations have on restaurants?

Bibliography

Broihier, Catherine. "Decoding the New Menu Labeling Regulations." *Restaurants USA*, October, 1996, 9.

Drysdale, John A. *Profitable Menu Planning*. New Jersey: Prentice Hall, 1994.

"National Restaurant Association Accuracy in Menus." Washington, D.C., 1985.

www.grahamkerr.com

Menus

L'Epicureo, Providence, Rhode Island

Layout and Design of the Menu

objectives

Upon completion of this chapter, the student should be able to:

1. identify menu classifications according to the restaurant's concept.
2. highlight menu items.
3. discuss the essential elements of printing type: typeface, typesize, spacing of type, weight of type, and upper and lowercase letters.
4. discuss how to utilize color effectively on the menu.
5. discuss how paper selection relates to menu usage.
6. discuss how menus are printed.

key terms

Bold Print
Grade
Italic Printing
Laminated Cover
Leading
Letterspacing
Light Print
Lowercase
Medium Print
Opacity
Padded Cover
Points

Proof
Ream Weight
Reverse Type
Sans Serif Type
Serif Type
Set Solid
Texture
Typeface
Uppercase
Weight of Type
Wordspacing

Introduction

The layout and design of a menu must be carefully planned in order to produce a menu that is readable and easily understood. The correct placement of headings, subheadings, and menu items, the highlighting of menu items, fundamentals of type, color presentation, paper usage, construction of covers, and printing are examined in detail. All of these elements have a direct relationship to the overall appearance of the menu and can make a favorable and lasting impression on patrons when done correctly.

Layout

Layout is nothing more than the placement of headings, subheadings, and menu items on the menu.

Identifying Menu Classifications or Headings

Generally, the classifications used on a menu reflect the type of restaurant and its offerings. When naming menu classifications, make sure that they are easily identified and not misleading to the customer. A list of menu classifications and names you might find in a casual dining restaurant follows. (Figure 4.1)

Appetizers	=	Beginnings
Soups	=	Hearty Alternatives
Salads	=	Refreshing Complements
Entrées	=	Repast
Desserts	=	Finale

FIGURE 4.1 Menu Classifications

Occasionally, a restaurant, such as a sports bar with a distinct theme, identifies menu classifications with names appropriate to a particular sport. Figure 4.2 uses menu classification names which are appropriate to baseball.

Appetizers	=	Singles
Soups	=	Doubles
Salads	=	Triples
Sandwiches	=	Home Runs
Entrées	=	Grand Slams
Side Orders	=	Extra Innings
Desserts	=	Bases Loaded

FIGURE 4.2 A list of menu classifications and names in a sports bar

Sequence of Menu Classifications or Headings

The sequence of classifications on a menu should be listed in the order that they are consumed: appetizers, soups, salads, entrées, followed by desserts. Sometimes the sequence and type of menu classification varies depending on the foodservice establishment and meal period. For instance, a family restaurant which serves lunch might list appetizers, soups, salads, sandwiches, entrées, side orders, and then desserts. A classical French restaurant most likely would list appetizers, soups, entrées, and finish with salads (to cleanse the palate), before dessert is served.

Organizing Menu Subclassifications or Subheadings

Oftentimes subclassifications are listed under major classifications on the menu. On a typical dinner menu, below the entrée classification, the subclassifications might read: meat, poultry, fish, and seafood. These subclassifications are not subject to any particular sequence; meats for example, need not precede poultry. Once subclassifications have been finalized, the menu items must be carefully selected.

Listing Menu Items

Menu items should be grouped by the type of product. Under the entrée classification, for example, the poultry subclassification should list all chicken dishes together. Menu items should also be listed based on profitability, in lieu of price. Many restaurants list the most expensive menu items first and then proceed in descending order. When restaurants do this, customers tend to focus on the price instead of the item, and this can have a negative impact on sales. Profitable food items should be strategically placed at the top and bottom of a column. Less profitable food items can be located in the middle of a column, as patrons generally focus on the top and bottom first, and then skim the remaining food listings.

Highlighting Menu Items

After the menu items are selected, arranged, and listed, it is imperative that food items be placed in an appropriate position on the page. The type of menu a restaurant utilizes has a direct correlation to where a patron's eye focuses. On a one-page or three-page menu, customers generally look to the center upper third of the menu page. However, on a two-page menu, the eye usually focuses on the middle section of the right-hand side. Regardless of the type of menu the restaurant uses, management can utilize merchandising space to highlight specials, signature items, highly profitable food, or beverage selections.

Design

Once the placement of headings, subheadings, and menu items have been completed, attention must be given to the design process. The most important factors to consider in the design phase are readability and customer acceptance of the menu. The menu should be designed to reflect the restaurant's atmosphere and decor. For example, a classical French menu might have a leather or suede menu cover with the restaurant's name and logo embossed in gold. Inside, a light cream colored paper with Times Roman type in black. This menu would certainly give patrons a favorable first impression and hint at what is to come throughout the meal. A menu is an overall reflection of the restaurant and can set a positive or negative mood for the entire dining experience.

Typefaces

The *typeface* or style of lettering that is selected for a menu has an impact on the patron. Typeface must be legible and compatible with the overall design of the menu. Most importantly, the selection of a particular typeface should disclose the charm and individuality of the restaurant. Commercial script typeface, for example, implies elegance and is often used on classical menus.

There are several different kinds of typeface or styles of lettering employed on a menu. A typeface which is frequently utilized is Serif type. *Serif type* has letters that are slightly curved, such as Palatino, and is easier to read. Serif type is often used for menu items and descriptive copy on the menu. On the other hand, *Sans Serif type*, which is more difficult to read because of its blocky letters, might be utilized for headings and subheadings on the menu. Figure 4.3 offers samples of type found on a menu.

Print generally comes in four forms: normal, bold, script, and italics. *Normal* printing, such as Times Roman, which is the easiest to read, can be employed for headings, subheadings, menu items, and descriptive copy on the menu. *Bold print*, as in the case of Bondi Regular, should only be utilized for headings and subheadings on the menu. *Script*, generally referred to as Commercial Script, due to the difficulty of its readability, should only be used for headings, subheadings, and menu items. However, in some cases, when descriptive copy is limited on the menu, Commercial Script might be employed. In *italics printing*, letters are slanted upward towards the right, which also makes readability difficult. Italics are generally used for headings, subheadings, and key phrases in descriptive copy. Remember, script and italics are problematic to read, and must be used sparingly on the menu. If the patron has difficulty reading a menu, this has a negative effect on sales.

Type Size

Type size on a menu should be large enough so that the patron can read the menu clearly and easily. Printing that is too small makes reading the menu problematic. On the other hand, printing that is too large can take up valuable merchandising space.

Type size on a menu is measured in *points*. On any menu, there should be a variation of point sizes. For instance, headings and subheadings can be 18 point type, menu items 12 point type, and descriptive copy 10 point type. If all of the type sizes are the same on a menu, it can be very monotonous to read and may again jeopardize sales. (Figure 4.4)

Spacing of Type

The amount of spacing between each letter in a word is referred to as *letterspacing*; and the amount of spacing between each word is known as *wordspacing*. Both influence the readability of type on the menu. Letters and words should be typeset so that they are not too condensed or too far apart, to make for easier reading. Attention to the vertical spacing between the lines of type, known as *leading*, is also important. Leading, similar to type, is also measured in points. When there is no leading between lines on a menu, this is referred to as *set solid*. Generally, three point leading should be utilized on a menu to simplify reading. (Figure 4.5)

Serif

Times Roman

Flaky pastry shells filled with freshly chopped tomatoes sautéed in butter with parsley and shallots. Topped with poached eggs and covered with Hollandaise sauce.

Bookman

Flaky pastry shells filled with freshly chopped tomatoes sautéed in butter with parsley and shallots. Topped with poached eggs and covered with Hollandaise sauce.

Garamond

Flaky pastry shells filled with freshly chopped tomatoes sautéed in butter with parsley and shallots. Topped with poached eggs and covered with Hollandaise sauce.

Palatino

Flaky pastry shells filled with freshly chopped tomatoes sautéed in butter with parsley and shallots. Topped with poached eggs and covered with Hollandaise sauce.

Sans Serif

Avant Garde

Flaky pastry shells filled with freshly chopped tomatoes sautéed in butter with parsley and shallots. Topped with poached eggs and covered with Hollandaise sauce.

Futura

Flaky pastry shells filled with freshly chopped tomatoes sautéed in butter with parsley and shallots. Topped with poached eggs and covered with Hollandaise sauce.

Erie

Flaky pastry shells filled with freshly chopped tomatoes sautéed in butter with parsley and shallots. Topped with poached eggs and covered with Hollandaise sauce.

Helvetica

Flaky pastry shells filled with freshly chopped tomatoes sautéed in butter with parsley and shallots. Topped with poached eggs and covered with Hollandaise sauce.

FIGURE 4.3 Samples of Type

4-Point Type

Flaky pastry shells filled with freshly chopped tomatoes sautéed in butter with parsley and shallots. Topped with poached eggs and covered with Hollandaise sauce.

5-Point Type

Flaky pastry shells filled with freshly chopped tomatoes sautéed in butter with parsley and shallots. Topped with poached eggs and covered with Hollandaise sauce.

5 1/2-Point Type

Flaky pastry shells filled with freshly chopped tomatoes sautéed in butter with parsley and shallots. Topped with poached eggs and covered with Hollandaise sauce.

6-Point Type

Flaky pastry shells filled with freshly chopped tomatoes sautéed in butter with parsley and shallots. Topped with poached eggs and covered with Hollandaise sauce.

7-Point Type

Flaky pastry shells filled with freshly chopped tomatoes sautéed in butter with parsley and shallots. Topped with poached eggs and covered with Hollandaise sauce.

8-Point Type

Flaky pastry shells filled with freshly chopped tomatoes sautéed in butter with parsley and shallots. Topped with poached eggs and covered with Hollandaise sauce.

9-Point Type

Flaky pastry shells filled with freshly chopped tomatoes sautéed in butter with parsley and shallots. Topped with poached eggs and covered with Hollandaise sauce.

10-Point Type

Flaky pastry shells filled with freshly chopped tomatoes sautéed in butter with parsley and shallots. Topped with poached eggs and covered with Hollandaise sauce.

11-Point Type

Flaky pastry shells filled with freshly chopped tomatoes sautéed in butter with parsley and shallots. Topped with poached eggs and covered with Hollandaise sauce.

12-Point Type

Flaky pastry shells filled with freshly chopped tomatoes sautéed in butter with parsley and shallots. Topped with poached eggs and covered with Hollandaise sauce.

14-Point Type

Flaky pastry shells filled with freshly chopped tomatoes sautéed in butter with parsley and shallots. Topped with poached eggs and covered with Hollandaise sauce.

FIGURE 4.4 Samples of Type Sizes

16-Point Type

Appetizers Entrées Desserts

18-Point Type

Appetizers Entrées Desserts

20-Point Type

Appetizers Entrées Desserts

22-Point Type

Appetizers Entrées Desserts

24-Point Type

Appetizers Entrées Desserts

FIGURE 4.4 Samples of Type Sizes (continued)

Solid

Bananas Foster . . . A Brennan creation and now World Famous! Bananas sauteéd in butter, brown sugar, cinnamon and banana liqueur, then flamed in rum. Served over vanilla ice cream. Scandalously Delicious!

1-Point Leading

Bananas Foster . . . A Brennan creation and now World Famous! Bananas sauteéd in butter, brown sugar, cinnamon and banana liqueur, then flamed in rum. Served over vanilla ice cream. Scandalously Delicious!

2-Point Leading

Bananas Foster . . . A Brennan creation and now World Famous! Bananas sauteéd in butter, brown sugar, cinnamon and banana liqueur, then flamed in rum. Served over vanilla ice cream. Scandalously Delicious!

3-Point Leading

Bananas Foster . . . A Brennan creation and now World Famous! Bananas sauteéd in butter, brown sugar, cinnamon and banana liqueur, then flamed in rum. Served over vanilla ice cream. Scandalously Delicious!

4-Point Leading

Bananas Foster. . . A Brennan creation and now World Famous! Bananas sauteéd in butter, brown sugar, cinnamon and banana liqueur, then flamed in rum. Served over vanilla ice cream. Scandalously Delicious!

5-Point Leading

Bananas Foster . . . A Brennan creation and now World Famous! Bananas sauteéd in butter, brown sugar, cinnamon and banana liqueur, then flamed in rum. Served over vanilla ice cream. Scandalously Delicious!

FIGURE 4.5 Sample of Leading

Weight of Type

The *Weight of Type* on a menu refers to the lightness or heaviness of the print. Generally, *light print* looks gray and is difficult to read. Therefore, light print should never appear on a menu. *Medium print*, on the other hand, is darker than gray and is often utilized in books, magazines, and newspapers. Medium print should be applied to descriptive copy on the menu. *Bold print*, which is employed primarily to add emphasis, can be used for headings, subheadings, and menu items, but never for descriptive copy. Frequently, the name of a restaurant featured on the front cover is in bold print as well.

Uppercase and Lowercase Letters

Typeface can be set in either *uppercase*, capital letters (A, B, C), or *lowercase*, small letters (a, b, c). Uppercase is predominantly used for headings, subheadings, and menu items we wish to emphasize. When descriptive copy is employed on the menu, each sentence should begin with an uppercase letter, followed by lowercase letters. Also, when proper nouns are used on a menu, their first letter should be capitalized: Sauce Béarnaise or Shiitake mushrooms. On the other hand, lowercase letters are easier to read than uppercase letters and should be utilized for descriptive copy. Generally, it is advantageous to use both uppercase and lowercase type on the menu to ensure readability.

Describing Menu Items

When describing menu items, keep the explanation simple, and the number of sentences to a minimum. A longer sentence may cause customers to lose their place or their concentration. The length of a sentence should not be longer than 22 picas, or about three and two-thirds inches long.

Margins

Margins on the menu should be uniform from top to bottom, and left to right. One and one half inch margins are commonplace on menus. The key is to have well defined margins without crowding the descriptive copy. If overcrowding becomes an issue, additional pages can be added.

Color

Color also affects the readability of a menu. Black type on light-tinted paper (cream, ivory, tan, or white) is easy to read. Menus printed in colored ink or on colored paper are difficult to read. If type is printed in blue, brown, or red make sure that the print is dark and on white paper. Dark colored print on dark colored paper can also be problematic to read and should be avoided. Green print on red, or black on reddish orange paper also limits legibility. Copy in a light color on dark paper is difficult to read as well: white print on black, referred to as *reverse type*, should not be used.

Headings, subheadings, and menu items can be printed in a bold secondary color on the menu to distinguish them from medium colored type used for descriptive copy. Remember, the colors selected for the print and paper should complement the restaurant's decor. In a specialty restaurant with a nautical theme, blue print on white would be appropriate and easy to read.

Paper

Paper is made of a number of materials: wood pulp, fabric, chemical and fiber compounds. Generally, most papers that are utilized for menus are wood based and coated or treated with clay, pigment, varnish, or plastic. Most restaurants select paper based on menu usage. A menu that is designated for durability is usually printed on heavy, coated paper such as heavy cover, Bristol, or tag stock, which has been coated with clay, pigment, varnish, or plastic. These menus generally last an extended period of time, despite extensive customer usage, as they are extremely durable and easy to clean. On the other hand, a menu that changes daily is usually printed on lightweight, noncoated paper that is less expensive. In many cases, menus can be printed on more than one type of paper to curtail

Antique paper	Paper with a rough and textured surface
Bond paper	Paper utilized for forms, letterheads, and business correspondence
Book paper	Paper having attributes suitable for books, brochures, and magazines
Bristol	Cardboard which is 0.006 of an inch or more in thickness (index, mill, and wedding paper are examples of Bristol)
Coated	Paper or paperboard which has been treated with clay or some other pigment
Cover stock	A variety of papers utilized for the exterior cover of menus, booklets, catalogs, and magazines
Deckle edge	Paper with a feathered, uneven edge which is left untrimmed
Dull-coat	Paper coated with a low-gloss surface
Eggshell	Paper with a semi-rough exterior similar to the exterior of an egg
Enamel	Paper coated with a high-gloss surface
English finish	A book paper with a machine finish and uniform surface
Machine finish	A book paper with a medium finish, rougher then English finish, but smoother than eggshell
Matte coat	A coated paper with little or no glass surface
Offset paper	Coated or uncoated paper suitable for offset lithography printing
Vellum finish	A finish similar to eggshell, but from harder stock with a finer grained surface

FIGURE 4.6 Types of Paper Used for Menus

expenditures. A strong, heavy, coated paper might be employed for the menu cover, and a lighter weight and less permanent paper for the interior pages. The menu planner must keep in mind that paper represents 30% to 50% of the total menu cost.

When selecting the paper, take into consideration the following elements: texture, opacity, color, strength, weight, and grade. Textures can vary from very smooth or coated paper, to a slightly rough surface, such as antique eggshell, or vellum finish. Since customers generally hold the menu in their hands, the *texture* or "feel" is noteworthy. Another concern when selecting paper is opacity. The *opacity* of paper refers to the inability of light to penetrate through it. Maximum opacity is important regardless of the color of the paper. Paper colors can range from white and pastels to dark solids; but as mentioned earlier, light-tinted paper is the easiest to read.

The strength of the paper is the next consideration: paper with short pulp fibers is weaker and does not hold up well. The durability of paper also depends to a lesser degree on weight. Paper is manufactured and identified according to its *ream weight*: the weight in pounds for five hundred sheets in a basic size, for that appropriate grade. *Grade* is the name given to paper, based on its intended utilization. (Figure 4.6)

Cover

The cover is the symbol of a restaurant's identity. The cover should be carefully designed, attractive, and complement the restaurant's decor and style. A French classical menu might use leather or simulated leather with the restaurant's logo embossed in silver on the cover in order to reflect its more elegant and refined decor; whereas, a family style casual restaurant, or a dinner house, might decide on bright colors on a *laminated cover*, which is usually cardboard covered with a clear plastic coating to ensure longevity.

The selection of paper for the cover can be determined by how often the menu is used. If the menu is in the form of a place mat, light weight stock should be utilized. On the other hand, if the cover is permanent, heavy, cover stock, and Bristol or tag stock, are more appropriate. In some fine dining restaurants *padded covers* are popular. These permanent covers are protected with a durable plastic, or other materials such as leather, simulated leather, linen, silk, suede, or velvet. These materials are often laminated onto a light board or heavy cardboard, and then packed with material, resulting in a menu cover that has a padded appearance.

Once the menu cover has been chosen, the menu planner must decide what is acceptable to put on the front and back covers. Copy on the front can include the name of the restaurant or a *logo* (an identifying symbol unique to an operation). Other information such as the address, phone number, hours of operation, credit card acceptance, reservation policy, history of the operation, management's philosophy, catering and banquet information, and takeout information can be printed on the back cover. Whenever possible, avoid placing food or beverages on the back cover as many patrons tend to overlook those items.

Printing the Menu

There are a number of options available for printing the menu. These include: **professional printers, advertising agencies/artists designers,** and **desktop publishers**.

Professional Printers

The major advantage of having a menu professionally printed is the number of professionals on staff. These include: writers, artists or free-lance artists, production personnel, and designers who can assist the restaurateur in the layout and design of the menu. Once the layout and design is completed, the menu can be typeset into a computer system. The typesetting program then duplicates the type on photographic paper, or transparent film. The result is a copy of the type according to specifications, called the *proof* or the galley. The proof must be scrutinized for punctuation, misspelled words, and incorrect phrases. All corrections are made and then fed into the computer.

Advertising Agencies/Artists Designers

Occasionally, restaurants work with advertising agencies to help generate publicity. At times, these agencies also assist in the writing, layout, and design of the menu as well. Commercial artists or graphic designers, on the other hand, are generally responsible for just the layout and design of the menu, while the writing is left up to the menu planner or menu planning consultant.

Desktop Publishers

Printing the menu in-house on a computer and utilizing a laser color printer, has a number of advantages:

1. the wine list and menu can be changed on a daily basis to meet customer demand;

2. managers and chefs can react promptly to price fluctuations in the market place;

3. the chef can take advantage of regional and seasonal items by placing them on a menu at any time;

4. the restaurant is able to print special occasion and promotional menus when necessary;

5. desktop publishing saves money on overall menu costs such as typesetting; and

6. in-house publishing is convenient.

Review Questions

1. Select a particular restaurant concept. List and describe the type of headings, subheadings, and menu items you would use on your menu. Write the descriptive copy for each of the menu items. Choose the typeface, size of print, and color for the headings, subheadings, menu items, and descriptive copy. Select the paper for the inside and cover of the menu. Explain the cover and design in detail.

2. What are different options available for printing a menu?

3.   Define the following terms:

Serif Type	Set Solid
Sans Serif Type	Uppercase
Italic Printing	Lowercase
Letterspacing	Reverse Type
Wordspacing	Opacity
Leading	

Bibliography

Seaborg, Albin G. *Menu Design Merchandising and Marketing*. 4th ed. New York: Van Nostrand Reinhold, 1991.

Exploring Menus

objectives

Upon completion of this chapter, the student should be able to:

1. define the sales menu.
2. define the three types of menus: à la carte, semi à la carte, and prix fixe.
3. compare and contrast French, Russian, and American service.
4. differentiate among breakfast, luncheon, dinner, ethnic, specialty, special occasion, dessert, and wine menus.

key terms

À la Carte Menu
American Service
Cellar Master
Chef Du Rang
Club Section
Commis Du Rang
Continental Breakfast
Cross-Utilization

French Service
Guéridon
Menu
Prix Fixe Menu
Réchaud
Russian Service
Semi à la Carte Menu
Sommelier

Introduction

The main purpose of a menu is to provide a description of the food items available and their price. There are several types of menus used in the foodservice industry: the à la carte, semi à la carte, and prix fixe. Each menu type has its unique characteristics. In this chapter, we will examine these menu types and how they are used for: breakfast, luncheon, dinner, ethnic, specialty, special occasion, and wine menus.

Defining the Sales Menu

The term "menu" is a French word which means a detailed list. The menu is also referred to as a bill of fare. A bill is an itemized list, and a "fare" is a range of foods. A *menu* is, therefore, an itemized list of different foods that can be served at a meal.

Types of Menus

The à la Carte Menu

The "*à la carte menu*" prices each food item separately: the appetizer, soup, salad, entrée, accompaniment, and dessert. For this reason, an à la carte menu tends to be more expensive than a semi à la carte or prix fixe menu. Many patrons prefer the à la carte menu because it offers flexibility in choosing food items. (Figure 5.1)

The Semi à la Carte Menu

The *semi à la carte menu* prices appetizers, soups, and desserts separately. The entrées usually include a salad and the appropriate accompaniments. (Figure 5.2)

The "Prix Fixe" Menu

The term "prix fixe" comes from the French, meaning set price. The *"prix fixe" menu* charges a set price for a complete meal. A special occasion "prix fixe" menu, for example, might provide an appetizer, soup, salad, intermezzo, entrée, accompaniments, and dessert for one fixed price. A prix fixe dinner menu might offer a number of entrées from which to choose, as well as an appetizer, salad, entrée with the appropriate accompaniments, and dessert for a fixed price. (Figure 5.3)

Foodservice Menus

Breakfast Menus

A breakfast menu is usually inexpensive and includes food items that are cooked to order. The exception to this rule is the breakfast menu in upscale hotels where food items can be creative and labor intensive, and therefore, expensive. Most breakfast menus are either à la carte, continental, or club section. An à la carte menu offers items on a per item cost basis; a *continental breakfast* includes a choice of juice, beverage, and bakery items; and a *club section* generally provides a selection of juices, beverages, bakery goods, egg dishes, breakfast meats, and potatoes, for one set price.

Most breakfast menus have the following classifications: juices, fruits, cereals, specialty entrées, eggs, French toast, pancakes, waffles, bakery items, side orders, and beverages. Juices can be fresh or frozen and usually include apple, cranberry, grapefruit, orange, pineapple, tomato, and V-8®. Fruits can also be fresh or frozen, although fresh is preferred. Fruit offerings should be seasonal and might include: cantaloupe, honeydew, strawberries, peaches, or even fresh fruit kabobs. Cereals can be hot or cold and might include offerings such as: oatmeal with honey, and granola crowned with yogurt and fresh fruit. Specialty entrées should be imaginative and easy to prepare: a chourico, tomato, and spinach frittata, eggs provençale with sun dried tomato basil and hollandaise, an omelet with cheddar cheese, tomatoes, and black olives, eggs sardou, fruit crêpes, cinnamon French toast, and poached eggs over crabcakes. Eggs can be prepared a number of ways: boiled, fried, poached, scrambled, shirred, sunny-side up, and topped with various sauces. French toast, pancakes, and waffles should be served with

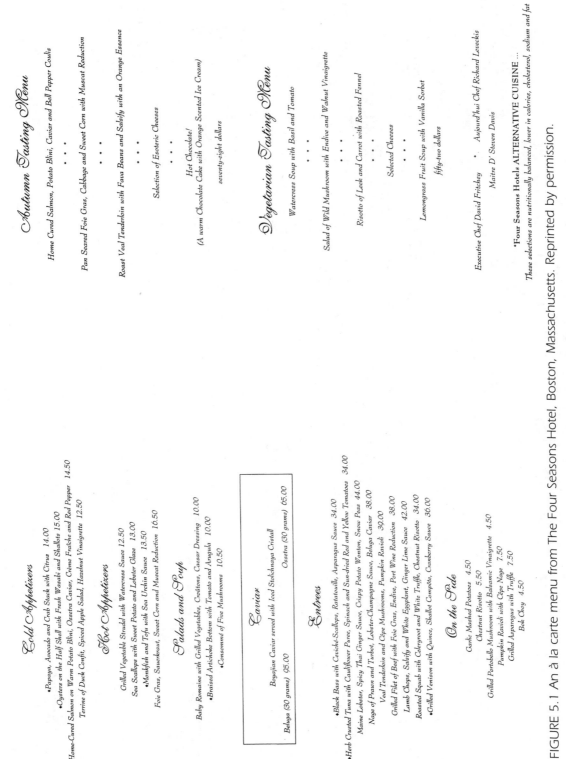

Autumn Tasting Menu

Home Cured Salmon, Potato Blini, Caviar and Bell Pepper Coulis

• • •

Pan Seared Foie Gras, Cabbage and Sweet Corn with Muscat Reduction

• • •

Roast Veal Tenderloin with Fava Beans and Salsify with an Orange Essence

• • •

Selection of Esoteric Cheeses

• • •

Hot Chocolate!
(A warm Chocolate Cake with Orange Scented Ice Cream)

seventy-eight dollars

Vegetarian Tasting Menu

Watercress Soup with Basil and Tomato

• • •

Salad of Wild Mushroom with Endive and Walnut Vinaigrette

• • •

Risotto of Leek and Carrot with Roasted Fennel

• • •

Selected Cheeses

• • •

Lemongrass Fruit Soup with Vanilla Sorbet

fifty-two dollars

Executive Chef David Fritchey   •   Aujourd'hui Chef Richard Levockis
Maitre D' Steven Davis

*Four Seasons Hotels ALTERNATIVE CUISINE…
These selections are nutritionally balanced, lower in calories, cholesterol, sodium and fat

Cold Appetizers

•Papaya, Avocado and Crab Stack with Citrus 14.00
Oysters on the Half Shell with Fresh Wasabi and Shallots 15.00
Home-Cured Salmon on Warm Potato Blini, Ossetra Caviar, Crème Fraîche and Red Pepper 14.50
Terrine of Duck Confit, Spiced Apple Salad, Hazelnut Vinaigrette 12.50

Hot Appetizers

Grilled Vegetable Strudel with Watercress Sauce 12.50
Sea Scallops with Sweet Potato and Lobster Glaze 13.00
•Monkfish and Tofu with Sea Urchin Sauce 13.50
Foie Gras, Sauerkraut, Sweet Corn and Muscat Reduction 10.50

Salads and Soup

Baby Romaine with Grilled Vegetables, Croûtons, Caesar Dressing 10.00
•Braised Artichoke Bottom with Tomato and Arugula 10.00
•Consommé of Five Mushrooms 10.50

Caviar

Beluga (30 grams) 95.00   Ossetra (30 grams) 65.00

Boyajian Caviar served with Iced Stolichnaya Cristall

Entrees

•Black Bass with Ceviche-Scallops, Ratatouille, Asparagus Sauce 34.00
•Herb Crusted Tuna with Cauliflower Puree, Spinach and Sun-dried Red and Yellow Tomatoes 34.00
Maine Lobster, Spicy Thai Ginger Sauce, Crispy Potato Wonton, Snow Peas 44.00
Nage of Prawn and Turbot, Lobster-Champagne Sauce, Beluga Caviar 38.00
Veal Tenderloin and Cèpe Mushrooms, Pumpkin Ravioli 30.00
Grilled Filet of Beef with Foie Gras, Endive, Port Wine Reduction 38.00
Lamb Chops, Salsify and White Eggplant, Ginger Lime Sauce 42.00
Roasted Squab with Celeryroot and White Truffle, Chestnut Risotto 34.00
•Grilled Venison with Quince, Shallot Compôte, Cranberry Sauce 36.00

On the Side

Garlic Mashed Potatoes 4.50
Chestnut Risotto 5.50
Grilled Portobello Mushroom with Balsamic Vinaigrette 4.50
Pumpkin Ravioli with Cèpe Nage 7.50
Grilled Asparagus with Truffle 7.50
Bok Choy 4.50

FIGURE 5.1 An à la carte menu from The Four Seasons Hotel, Boston, Massachusetts. Reprinted by permission.

HARBOR PORCHES DINNER MENU

Appetizers

FRESH MAINE SHRIMP RAVIOLI, 6.95
Fresh Maine Shrimp and Ricotta filled Ravioli,
cooked al Dente and topped with
a sauce of Heavy Cream, fresh Plum Tomatoes,
Basil, and Parmesan Cheese

GULF SHRIMP COCKTAIL, 7.95
Chilled Shrimp, served on a
bed of Romaine Lettuce, accompanied
by our Tangy Cocktail Sauce

BLACKENED MAINE CRAB CAKES, 6.95
Native Crabmeat Cakes, lightly sautéed
in Blackening Seasonings and
served with Spicy Remoulade Sauce

MAINE CLAM CHOWDER, 3.95
A House Specialty — Tender Clams,
simmered to perfection in a blend of
Homemade Broth and Heavy Cream

BAKED ONION SOUP GRATINÉE, 3.75
Tender Onions, simmered in a
rich Homemade Stock, topped with
a Crouton and melted Swiss Cheese

SOUP DU JOUR, 3.50
A hearty Selection,
prepared daily from
our Chef's Recipe Collection

SMOKED NORWEGIAN SALMON, 6.95
Served with Pumpernickel Toast Points
and Horseradish Cream Sauce
with Capers and Red Onion

PATÉ DE CAMPAIGNE, 5.50
A delicious Duck Liver and Veal Paté,
served with a
flavorful Orange Currant Cumberland Sauce

CRABMEAT-STUFFED PORTABELLO MUSHROOM, 7.95
Topped with crumbs, baked until
golden brown, and served with a
roasted Garlic and Red Pepper Coulis

Entrées

All Entrées are served with Your Choice of a Tossed Garden or Caesar Salad,
fresh Vegetable du Jour and Your Choice of Potato, Rice, or Pasta.
Seafood selections may be broiled, upon request.

FRESH SEAFOOD PASTA DU JOUR, 19.95
A selection of handmade pastas
and fresh, locally harvested seafood prepared daily

BOILED MAINE LOBSTER, Priced Daily
Served in the shell with Drawn Butter
and cracked for your convenience

BAKED-STUFFED MAINE LOBSTER, Priced Daily
Stuffed with Scallops, Shrimp, Crabmeat,
and Bread Crumbs, flavored with Sherry

GRILLED SEAFOOD MEDLEY, 19.95
Medallions of Salmon, Jumbo Shrimp
and Scallops served on Field Greens
with Raspberry Vinaigrette

GRILLED OR BLACKENED SWORDFISH, 19.95
with Black Bean and Smoked Corn Salsa
topped with Roasted Shallot and Cilantro Butter

GRILLED SCROD YORK HARBOR, 16.95
Served with braised Leeks and Mushrooms,
and Tomato-Caper-Lime Butter

SCALLOPS PORTOFINO, 18.95
Juicy Sea Scallops, sautéed with
Garlic, Sun-Dried Tomatoes and fresh Mushrooms
in White Wine and Olive Oil

FRESH MAINE SHRIMP RAVIOLI, 17.95
A generous portion of our popular appetizer...
Fresh Maine Shrimp and Ricotta filled Ravioli
cooked al dente, and topped with a sauce of Heavy Cream,
fresh Plum Tomatoes, Basil and Parmesan Cheese

SOLE MEUNIERE, 18.95
Sautéed in Butter with Lemon, Wine, and Parsley

SEAFOOD-STUFFED CHICKEN, 18.95
A succulent, skinless Chicken Breast,
stuffed with Lobster, Scallops and Shrimp,
and served with a Boursin Cheese Sauce

BONELESS DUCKLING, 17.95
Tender Duckling, roasted until its Skin is crispy,
topped with Your Choice of
Sauce a l'Orange
or fresh Raspberry Sauce

CHICKEN HARBOR PORCHES, 16.95
A boneless Breast of Chicken,
topped with a Dijon Garlic Glaze
and Sun-Dried Cranberries

VEAL OSCAR, 19.95
Tender medallions of Veal, sautéed
and served with Demi-Glace,
Asparagus, Crabmeat, and Sauce Bearnaise

VEGETARIAN PLATTER, 14.95
A medley of fresh, Seasonal Vegetables,
prepared in Your Choice of
Teriyaki-Style on Rice,
Alfredo-Style on Fettucini,
or Cajun-Style on Rice

NEW YORK SIRLOIN, 19.95
Grilled to Your Specifications
and served with Sherried Mushroom Caps

PEPPERCORN ENCRUSTED SALMON, 19.95
A luscious piece of Salmon, pan-seared
and served with warm Wild Mushroom Ragout
and Red Pepper Mayonnaise

BROILED FILLET OF SOLE, 18.95
Tender Fillets broiled to perfection

CHICKEN SCARPIELLA, 17.95
A plump, skinless Breast of Chicken,
sautéed with Garlic, Shallots, Scallions,
Basil, and Oregano then de-glazed with
White Wine and Demi-Glace

BROCHETTE OF LAMB, 18.95
Broiled to Your Liking and served
with Onions, Peppers, Tomatoes, and Mushrooms
with Demi-Glace on a bed of Rice

NEW YORK SIRLOIN AU POIVRE, 20.95
Coated with Five-Pepper Blend,
pan-seared and roasted, then served
with Madeira and Wild Mushroom Demi-Glace

Beverages, 1.50

Coffee, Decaffeinated Coffee,
Regular or Herbal Tea,
Iced Coffee, Iced Tea, or Milk

To help ensure everyone's dining pleasure, this is a non-smoking facility

EP96/97

FIGURE 5.2 A semi à la carte menu from the Stage Neck Inn, York Harbor, Maine. Reprinted by permisson.

Brennan's

Seasonal Dinner Specials

Four Course Prix Fixe
$35.00

Dinner at Brennan's without wine is like a day without sunshine!

Appetizers (Choice of one)

CREOLE ONION SOUP   OYSTER SOUP BRENNAN
CREOLE SEAFOOD GUMBO   NEW ORLEANS TURTLE SOUP
SOUP DU JOUR

Entrees

TROUT DUNCAN
Filet of fish poached in champagne and topped with crabmeat, roasted pecans and lemon butter sauce.

TROUT PECAN (Seasonal)
Filet of fresh trout sauteed and topped with roasted pecans and pecan butter.

REDFISH PEREZ (Seasonal)
Sauteed filet of redfish covered with lump crabmeat and shrimp and topped with Hollandaise sauce.

BRENNAN'S BLACKENED REDFISH (Seasonal)
Brennan's version of blackened redfish grilled to perfection with Brennan's own seasonings. Served with glazed carrots.

REDFISH WITH LUMP CRABMEAT JAIME (Seasonal)
An old favorite. Brennan-created. Filet of redfish topped with lump crabmeat in a fresh mushroom and red wine sauce.

GRILLED FILET OF SALMON AUDUBON
A zesty combination of Creole mustard, Hollandaise, shrimp and carrots served atop salmon.

BUSTER CRABS BEARNAISE (Seasonal)
Delicacy from Gulf waters - baby soft shell crabs sauteed in butter then topped with Bearnaise sauce.

SHRIMP CREOLE
Gulf shrimp in a traditional Creole sauce with parsley rice.

SHRIMP SAMANTHA WITH ANDOUILLE
Gulf shrimp and spicy Cajun sausage sauteed with fresh mushrooms, garlic, green onions, white wine, spices and served on a bed of parsley rice.

SHRIMP VICTORIA
Gulf shrimp sauteed in butter with fresh basil and fresh mushrooms served in a light cream sauce with parsley rice.

CRAWFISH SARDOU (Seasonal)
Deliciously spicy fried crawfish tails atop sliced artichoke bottoms nestled in a bed of creamed spinach and covered with Hollandaise sauce.

CHICKEN LAZONE
Breast of chicken sauteed in our own Brennan seasonings. served in a light cream sauce.

CHICKEN CORSICA
Chicken stuffed with fresh spinach and asparagus and poached in chicken stock with seasonings. Served with cream pasta in a light sauce.

BRENNAN'S HOT FRENCH BREAD

Salads

BRENNAN SALAD
Romaine lettuce with a tangy Creole dressing, grated Parmesan cheese and croutons.

TOSSED GREEN SALAD
Choice of French, Bleu Cheese, Jackson or Thousand Island dressings.

Desserts

BRENNAN'S LEMON CURD TARTELETTE
LOUISIANA CHOCOLATE PECAN PIE
CREOLE CHOCOLATE SUICIDE CAKE
BERRIES IN SEASON WITH DOUBLE CREAM
BRENNAN'S CHEESECAKE WITH BERRIES OF THE SEASON
CREOLE WHITE CHOCOLATE MOUSSE PIE

Coffee

Wines

Bottle

"J" JORDAN SPARKLING — 35.00
MIRASSOU CHARDONNAY — 19.75
VICHON CHARDONNAY — 30.00
MIRASSOU CHARDONNAY — 19.75
PIESPORTER — 17.50
MUSCADET — 19.75
JORDAN CHARDONNAY — 35.00
KOALA RIDGE CHARDONNAY — 19.75
FUMÉ BLANC — 19.00
KOALA RIDGE CHARDONNAY — 19.75
PINE RIDGE CHARDONNAY — 27.00
STAG'S LEAP CABERNET SAUVIGNON — 30.00
KENDALL-JACKSON VINTNER'S RESERVE CHARDONNAY — 25.00

Due to certain conditions we sometimes substitute fresh crawfish tails for lump crabmeat.

Due to certain conditions we sometimes substitute other fresh gulf or farm raised fish for redfish or trout.

Breakfast at Brennan's AND DINNER, TOO — our most recent cookbook and the story of our legacy — to purchase, ask your waiter or the hostess for information

417 ROYAL STREET NEW ORLEANS

FIGURE 5.3 A prix fixe menu from Brennan's, New Orleans, Louisiana. Reprinted by permission.

assorted fruit toppings and syrups. Bakery goods such as biscuits, coffee rolls, croissants, danish, doughnuts, fruit muffins, and scones, should be served with the appropriate jams, jellies, and preserves. Side orders are essential in increasing the overall check average and should encompass: toast, English muffins, potatoes, grits, ham, sausage, bacon, and corned beef hash. Finally, beverages might consist of: tea, coffee, espresso, cappuccino, hot chocolate, mineral water, smoothies, and specialty drinks, such as a Bloody Mary or a Mimosa. (Figure 5.4)

The Willard Room
Breakfast

---

*Inter*Continental Breakfast   11.50*
Includes Fresh Orange or Grapefruit Juice,
Apple, Tomato or Cranberry Juice,
Hot Beverage, and a selection of the "Willard Bakery
served with Butter, Preserves, and Honey

The Willard Breakfast   16.00
Includes the Inter-Continental Breakfast and
two eggs prepared any style, served with
Applewood Smoked Bacon, Country Sausage,
or Virginia Ham and Southern Grits

A La Carte

Granola or Cold Cereal with Milk   3.75

Granola or Cold Cereal with Fresh or Dried Fruit   5.00

Pink Grapefruit Segments topped with Grandmarnier Caramel Sauce   5.00

Fresh Raspberry Butter Milk Pancakes with Wild Flower Honey   6.75

Buck Wheat Pancakes with Pinneapple, Macadamia Nut and Coconut   5.50

Belgian Waffle with Warm Brandied Cherries in Syrup   6.25

Oatmeal with Fruit and Steamed Milk   7.00
Garnished with Seasonal Berries, Nuts, Fresh and Dried Fruit

Side Dishes
Southern Style Grits with Cracked Black Pepper   4.00
Canadian Bacon, Applewood Bacon, Sausage or Virginia Ham   5.00
Toast or English Muffins with Assorted Preserves   3.00

Beverages
Assorted Juices   3.50
Coffee, Tea or Brewed Decaffeinated Coffee   3.00
Espresso   3.50
Capuccino   3.75

FIGURE 5.4 A breakfast menu from the Willard Inter-Continental, Washington, D.C. Reprinted by permission.

Luncheon Menus

Luncheon menus are generally à la carte, but also offer combination items, such as soup and a salad, or a cup of soup and a sandwich. Luncheon menus also have the distinction of providing hot or cold sandwiches, and in most cases include daily specials such as soups, sandwiches, or pastas which can vary from day to day. Some luncheon menus also offer weekday specials that are cyclical. On Monday, the special might be baked breast of chicken, and on Friday, honey and soy glazed salmon. For the most part, luncheon menu items are also less expensive than dinner menu items because the portions are often smaller.

Luncheon menus usually have the following classifications: appetizers, soups, salads, entrées, sandwiches, accompaniments, and desserts. Some luncheon menus include side orders and beverages as well. It is imperative that each menu classification (beef, poultry, seafood, or fish), include a fairly diverse representation of offerings. Vegetarian items should also be included whenever possible.

Appetizers can be cold or hot, and might include: carpaccio of beef with mustard capers, red onions and shaved parmesan; smoked duck with mixed greens and cranberry compote; shrimp cocktail with sun-dried tomato cocktail sauce and foccacia. Soups could be clear, thick, "National" or "Specialty," as well as hot or cold and might include: chicken soup Southwestern style, seafood chowder, or vichyssoise. Salads can also be hot or cold and may encompass a bouquet of romaine lettuce with barbecued spareribs and garlic dressing; chicken Caesar salad; warm balsamic shrimp salad; and fresh spinach salad with shiitake mushrooms and croutons. Entrées might consist of: spiced charred flank steak with roasted garlic aioli; roasted chicken breast with boursin cheese and spinach; grilled swordfish steak with tomato capers black olive vinaigrette; and vegetarian lasagna. Sandwiches should be imaginative, and hot and cold selections should be available. A petite filet mignon served opened faced with a green pepper sauce; a grilled chicken breast; salmon salad sandwiches on marble rye bread; and vegetarian pockets are a few examples. Fresh accompaniments are also essential on a luncheon menu. There should be a choice of two vegetables and a rice, potato, or pasta, for instance, spicy stir-fried vegetables, braised Swiss chard with sweet blackberry ginger vinegar, cilantro pilaf, apple and potato pancakes, and penne with broccoli rabbi and spicy red pepper oil. Lastly, desserts should be fresh, creative, and extensive, and include: cakes, cobblers or crisps, fruits, ice creams, pies, puddings, sorbets, specialty items, and tarts. Angel food cake with lemon custard cream and strawberries, nectarine cobbler, an assortment of cheeses with fruit croutons, praline ice cream, peach and plum pie, sweet potato pudding, fruit sorbet, tiramisu, crème brulée, and orange marmalade tarts are always popular choices. (Figure 5.5)

Dinner Menu

The dinner menu generally has the same classifications as the luncheon menu including: appetizers, soups, salads, accompaniments, and desserts. In some fine dining restaurants the dinner service is *French service* and involves tableside cooking. French service is executed on a *guéridon*, or cart, which has a heating unit on it called a *réchaud*. In French service, all the food items are either semi-prepared, or uncooked, and are brought from the kitchen to the guéridon and served. All of the tableside cooking is prepared by the *chef du rang*, or captain. The chef du rang is aided by the *commis du rang*, or assistant, who brings all appropriate dishes, plates, and cutlery necessary for proper service. The commis du rang is also responsible for clearing after each course. In many cases, fine dining restaurants also have a *sommelier*, or wine steward, who will make wine recommendations, take the order, and serve the wine. When the meal is completed, the chef du rang presents the bill and collects all currency. Typical food items found in French service

Appetizers

Iced Shellfish

Oysters 1.75 ea.   Littlenecks 1.25 ea.   Gulf Shrimp 1.75 ea.

Sauté of Escargot   5.00
with fresh fennel, wild mushrooms and hot cherry peppers in an Absolut Pepper and tomato coulis

Tavern Gravlax   5.00
served with minced red onion, Hungarian liptauer cream and pumpernickel toast points

Sauté of Wild Mushrooms   5.00
in puff pastry with Marsala wine, sweet butter & fresh sage

Soups

Newport Clam Chowder   4.00

Soup of the Day   4.00

And special today...

Soup & Sandwich
changes daily

Pasta of the Day

Fresh Fish of the Day

Salads

Chicken Salad   9.00
diced chicken tossed in a sundried tomato & fresh dill mayonnaise and served over mixed field greens with crispy angel hair pasta

Chicken & Caesar Salad   9.50
classic Caesar preparation with grilled breast of chicken and French bread croutons

Warm Balsamic Shrimp Salad   10.00
sprinkled with toasted couscous and served over field greens with sweet red peppers and artichoke hearts

Grilled Duck Salad   11.00
served with arugula and mixed whole grains and topped with a dried cherry, port & fresh pear compote

Grilled Sirloin Strips   12.00
in a light tarragon dressing with red leaf lettuce, new potatoes & fresh asparagus

Sandwiches

Grilled Vegetable Pocket   8.50
grilled seasonal vegetables with ovendried tomatoes, shredded pepper jack cheese and walnut pesto

Tavern Burger   10.00
8 oz. of ground sirloin served with sautéed mushrooms, caramelized onions, marinated tomatoes, wilted spinach and Vermont cheddar on a sour dough roll

Club Sandwich   9.00
served on honey-wheat bread with smoked turkey, watercress mayonnaise, bacon, lettuce & tomato

Grilled Chicken Breast   9.00
on a bulkie roll with a lemon-tarragon vinaigrette, grilled portobello mushrooms and Provolone cheese

Baked Virginia Ham   9.50
topped with caramelized onions and served with maple syrup mayonnaise and Vermont Cheddar on grilled sour dough bread

Entrées

Vegetarian Lasagna   11.00
made with fresh pasta, assorted vegetables & sweet basil ricotta on a fire roasted red pepper coulis

Baked Fillet of Sole   12.00
topped with a fried onion and caper crust and served with mixed whole grains and a lemon-chive beurre blanc

Honey & Soy Glazed Salmon   14.00
served with Asian pickled beets, ginger risotto and grilled scallions

White Horse Tavern Bouillabaisse   17.00
a combination of lobster, scallops, mixed fish and shellfish in a fresh tomato and lobster broth

Sauté of Rock Shrimp & Scallops   13.00
served in a phyllo basket with spinach, ovendried tomatoes and calamata olives in a creamy tomato coulis

Baked Breast of Chicken   13.00
coated in herbed breadcrumbs and served with oven roasted garlic potatoes and sautéed vegetables over a whole grain mustard cream sauce

Tenderloin of Veal   17.00
sautéed and served over fresh pasta with arugula, mushrooms and roasted red peppers on a brandy and fresh thyme reduction sauce

Grilled Tournedos of Beef   16.00
served in a potato nest with whiskey glazed wild mushrooms and baby vegetables

Our dining rooms are smoke free.

FIGURE 5.5 A luncheon menu from the *White Horse Tavern*, Newport, Rhode Island. Reprinted by permission.

might include: Caesar salad, Châteaubriand, bouquetière of vegetables, sauce béarnaise, and crêpes suzette. French service is generally more time consuming than either. Russian or American service, and demands skilled employees. Furthermore, French service tends to be more labor intensive, as it utilizes additional equipment.

Russian service is used in many fine dining restaurants. Russian service food items are prepared in the kitchen and placed on silver or wooden platters, and then plated at the table. Russian service might be used to serve veal gulyas, stuffed cabbage, scampi à la hongroise, mushrooms, and stuffed sauerbraten.

American service, on the other hand, is more practical in quick-service restaurants where the turnover rate is significantly higher. In American service, all the food items are prepared and plated in the kitchen and then served in the dining room. American service also tends to be inexpensive and less labor intensive than both French and Russian service. Therefore, French and Russian service generally command a higher price for menu items. (Figure 5.6)

Ethnic Menus

The ethnic menu is a representation of cuisine from a particular country, such as France, Italy, Spain, etc. Chilled tomato consommé with Maine peeky toe crab; summer vegetables and herbs; roasted quail stuffed with foie gras; purple mission figs and prosciutto on a bed of spinach and young turnips; corn crêpes filled with chanterelles; farmers' market vegetables and chives; a salad of Summer mesclun and vegetables; or a crispy parmesan basket filled with seasoned fromage blanc, are all examples of ethnic menu offerings.

Ethnic menus are some of the most popular types of menus in the United States today due to the fact that people are more knowledgeable about food and are willing to experience various cuisines. Restaurants also continue to cater to an ever increasing multicultural market that is requesting diverse cuisine from around the world. In order to meet the needs of a more sophisticated clientele, some restaurants are fusing cuisines such as Asian and European.

Ethnic menus vary in price depending on the cuisine and type of restaurant. A French classical menu in a fine dining establishment commands a higher price for food items than an Italian restaurant that is part of a chain. Ethnic menu restaurants that provide French service also tend to be expensive due to additional labor, equipment, and skill level requirements.

For the most part, ethnic menus have the same classifications as the lunch or dinner menu. These classifications include: appetizers, soups, salads, entrées, accompaniments, and desserts. On a classical French menu, the salad course usually follows the entrée. An Italian menu might also include a pasta course.

To authenticate an ethnic menu, headings, subheadings, and menu listings should be in the original language. The descriptive copy, however, should be in English so that customers do not have to translate. A heading or classification on a French menu might read "ENTRÉES." Under the "Entrées," a subheading or subclassification which reads "Les Volailles et Viandes" followed by the menu listing "Le Carré d' Agneau Rôti à la Fleur de Thyme." Finally, the descriptive copy would read Roasted Rack of Lamb with Thyme. (Figure 5.7)

Chef Guillaume Burlion Presents The
Flood Tide Tasting Menu

Spring 2001
Truffle Menu

Amuse Bouche
Flood Tide Cocktail
★ ★ ★
Kobe Beef Carpaccio
★ ★ ★
1993 Martinez Bujanda Rioja "Gran Reserva"
★ ★ ★
Fricassee of lobster salad with Smoked Scallop Potatoes in a "12 year old" Balsamic Vinegar Sauce
1997 Newton Claret
★ ★ ★
Deer filet mignon Wellington in a Cabernet Reduction
1998 Geyser Peak Meritage
★ ★ ★
Crown of Fresh Seasonal Berries with a Marsala Sabayon
1997 Corte Rugolin Recioto della Valpolicella

★ Sixty Five Dollars for the complete dinner per person.
🍷 Ninety Five Dollars for the complete dinner with wine per person

3/24/01

Appetizers

Crepe filled with lobster Madeira
$12.00

Escargot Bourguignone
$9.00

Floodtide jumbo shrimp cocktail with a duo cocktail sauce
$9.00

Timbale of Langoustine, Peeky-toe crab and Smoked Salmon with a celery root salad & a caviar vinaigrette
$11.00

Black Truffle scrambled eggs served in the shell with shaved Langoustine and Foie Gras
$10.00

Watch Hill oysters with mignonette, and fresh horseradish
$10.00

Tartar of Black Angus beef with Roasted Tomato Couscous in a fresh tarragon sauce
$10.00

Tower of foie Gras and marinated white peach in a red port reduction
$12.00

Soups

New England Clam Chowder
$6.00

Chef's Soup of the Day
$6.00

Salads

Mesclun greens with Monterey marinated artichokes in a sherry and walnut dressing
$6.00

Parma Prosciutto and Romaine Heart with Parmesan Tuile in a Calamata Olive Emulsion
$7.00

Yellowfin Tuna and Diver Scallop ceviche with herb salad and ginger vinaigrette in a scallop shell
$8.00

Caesar salad prepared table side for two or more
$8.00 per person

Table Side Classics

Chateaubriand for two or more.
$36.00 per person.

Old fashion mustard encrusted Rack of Lamb slowly braised in a cabernet and mint infused sauce for two
$36.00 per person

Main Course Offerings

Slow cooked center cut of Copper River King Salmon with day boat diver scallops over pesto risotto
$24.00

Pistachio dusted filet of Chilean sea bass with a spinach fondue in a rasberry infused sauce.
$26.00

Roasted whole local lobster with provencale ratatouille vegetables and saffron rice in a crustacean reduction.
$32.00

Crown of Dayboat Diver scallops with acini de pepe in a farsi bean sauce
$26.00

Grilled boned Colorado rack of lamb with creamy shallot polenta and a roasted goats' cheese galette in a cabernet wine reduction
$27.00

Slowly braised honey and orange marinated duck breast with confit over wild mushrooms in an Armagnac infused sauce.
$25.00

Grilled Black Angus filet mignon with a clam shell mushroom tarte in a roasted bone marrow sauce
$28.00

FIGURE 5.6 A dinner menu from the FloodTide Restaurant, Mystic, CT.

daniel

*These very special tasting menus and classic dishes can be ordered for your entire table with **one week's advance notice**. Our sommelier will be very happy to suggest wines to complement your meal.*

LES MENUS SUR UN THÈME

Les crustacés et poissons de l'Atlantique
North Atlantic seafood menu
$96

La Provence
A menu inspired by the flavors of Southern France

La tomate
A menu composed of a variety of summer tomatoes
$95

Le foie gras en quatre services
A selection of four foie gras preparations

LES PLATS CLASSIQUES

Le loup de mer farçi de coquillages
Roasted whole sea bass stuffed with shellfish
(for four to six people)

Le foie gras entier aux raisins
Whole foie gras roasted with grapes, hazelnuts and spinach
(for four to six people)

Les petits farcis comme en Provence
An assortment of Provençal stuffed vegetables

Le poulet rôti en croûte de sel
Free range chicken roasted in a sea salt crust with herbs
(for two people)

La bouillabaisse de poissons et crustacés
A classic fish and shellfish bouillabaisse

APPETIZERS

La soupe glacée de maïs et homard au coulis de corail et cerfeuil
Chilled soup of summer corn with lobster, zucchini and a coral and chervil coulis
$13

Le velouté glacé de crevettes et de melon à la citronelle et basilic violet
Chilled velouté of gulf shrimp and summer melon flavored with lemon grass, lime leaves and purple basil
$16

Le tartare de thon au curry, vert de céleri et radis roses
Curried tuna tartar with pink radishes and a celery coulis
$18

Le crabe du Maine à la mangue et au concombre, vinaigrette de coriandre et menthe
Maine Peeky Toe crab with mango, cucumber and a lime, coriander and mint dressing
$19

La salade de homard au pistou, avocat, haricots du marché et olives niçoises
Lobster salad with avocado, local summer beans, pine nuts and black olives in a pesto dressing
$19 / $35

Le filet de maquereau grillé à l'aubergine et aux piments doux, vinaigrette de sesame
Grilled filet of mackerel with eggplant, tomato confit, sweet pimentos and a sesame seed dressing
$16

La salade de mesclun au croustillant de fromages
Salad of summer mesclun and vegetables
And a crispy parmesan basket filled with seasoned fromage blanc
$15

Les rillettes fermières aux cerises et aux noisettes
Rillettes of duck, squab, quail, rabbit, and foie gras with cherries and hazelnuts
$21

Le Caviar Beluga et blinis
$115 (1½ oz)

A CELEBRATION OF SUMMER TOMATOES

La gelée de tomate et crabe du Maine aux légumes d'été et pluches d'herbes
Chilled tomato consommé with Maine Peeky Toe crab, summer vegetables and herbs
$19

Les tomates du marché au fromage de chèvre mariné, olives noires et pourpier
Salad of farmer's market tomatoes with marinated goat cheese, black olives and purslane
$16

Les raviolis de neuf herbes au coulis de tomates fraîches et aux chanterelles
Ravioli of nine herbs with a tomato coulis, chanterelles and sheep's milk ricotta
$17 / 29

There will be a $7.00 cover charge for guests ordering one course only.

MAIN COURSES

La paupiette croustillante de sea bass
Roasted black sea bass in a crisp potato shell on a bed of leeks with a red wine sauce
$36

Le thon de Montauk poivré à l'échalote aigre-douce, raisins et amandes
Peppered Montauk tuna with a spinach purée, shallot confit, raisins, capers, almonds and a vinegar jus
$34

Le bar rôti au fenouil et à la Suze, courgette, artichaut frit et tomates cerises au balsamic
Roasted Atlantic striped bass with dried fennel, gentian , zucchini, fried artichoke
And tomato confit with balsamic vinegar
$36

La truite du Vermont farçie de blettes et trompettes de la mort, lard de campagne et sauge
Roasted Vermont trout stuffed with Swiss chard, wild mushrooms, country bacon,
Artichokes, black trumpets with sage and a port wine glaze
$33

Le cabillaud rôti à l'ail et au persil, coques, calamar, pommes nouvelles et tomate fondante
Roasted cod with olive oil, garlic, parsley, cockles, stuffed squid, new potatoes and tomatoes
$35

La caille farçie de foie gras et figues violettes sur pousses d'épinards et jeunes navets
Roasted quail stuffed with foie gras, purple mission figs and prosciutto
On a bed of spinach and young turnips
$36

Le râble de lapin rôti aux olives et cuisse effilochée aux raviolis à l'ail doux et à l'origan
Roasted saddle of rabbit stuffed with olives
And braised rabbit legs with summer vegetables, sweet garlic ravioli and an oregano jus
$32

La côte et le ris de veau rôti à la camomille avec une douzaine de légumes d'été
Roasted veal chop and sweet bread studded with fresh chamomile served with a dozen summer vegetable
$36 per person (for two)

Le contre-filet poêlé aux oignons "Saucier" confit au vin rouge, racines aux pousses vertes
Roasted Black Angus sirloin with cipoline onions glazed in red wine,
Spinach watercress, nettles and summer root vegetables
$36

L'agneau cuisiné de deux façons au thym citronné, gratin de courgettes à la polente de maïs
Roasted lamb chops and braised lamb shank with a lemon-thyme jus, young root vegetables,
And a zucchini and fresh corn polenta gratin
$35

A CELEBRATION OF CHANTERELLES
Appetizer or Side Dish

Les fleurs de courgettes farçies de chanterelles, foie gras et truffes d'été
Zucchini flowers filled with chanterelles, foie gras and summer truffles
$24

La fricassée de chanterelles et trompettes aux pois gourmands et au romarin
Fricassee of chanterelles and black trumpets with pea pods and rosemary
$17

Les crêpes de maïs aux chanterelles et légumes d'été à la ciboulette
Corn crepes filled with chanterelles, farmers'market vegetables and chives
$16

FIGURE 5.7 An ethnic menu from Restaurant Daniel, New York, New York. Reprinted by permission.

The Specialty Menu

The specialty menu offers an extensive selection of a particular type of food such as: seafood and fish, beef, or chicken. If the specialties of the restaurant are seafood and fish, beef and/or chicken items might also be offered as an alternative. Some patrons dislike seafood or fish while others have an allergic reaction to such foods. Alternatives might be, aged New York sirloin, garlic roasted Amish chicken, and filet mignon with sauce béarnaise.

Generally, restaurants that specialize in seafood and fish display their specialty throughout the menu for two primary reasons: to cross-utilize, and to showcase their signature items. *Cross-utilization* enables the chef to offer a product prepared in a variety of ways on the menu. For example, crab could be used in a crab and lobster quiche entrée and in a crabcake appetizer. Effective cross-utilization is paramount when dealing with seafood or fish because the product is highly perishable and expensive. If cross-utilization is restricted on the menu, the impact on the restaurant's overall food cost can be considerable. On the other hand, showcasing signature items for which the restaurant is known can aid in promotion and increase revenue.

Non Smoking —Section— Available | All Seafood Is —Subject to Season, Weather— And Fishing Conditions | Gift —Certificates— Available

—DAILY SPECIALS—
August 8, 1996

TODAY'S HALF SHELL OYSTERS

Elfin Cove (Crassostrea gigas) Alaska . . . . 1/2 doz 8.95
Coromandel (Crassostrea gigas) New Zealand . . . . . 1/2 doz 8.95
Rilan Bay (Crassostrea gigas) Chile . . . . 1/2 doz 8.95
Chiloe (Ostrea chilensis) Chile . . . . 1/2 doz 8.95
Umpqua (Crassostrea gigas) Oregon . . . . 1/2 doz 7.95
Oyster Sampler . . . . (2 each) 13.95

APPETIZERS	SALADS/SIDES
Steamed Greenlip Mussels, Provencal . **6.95**	Green Bean & Cherry Tomato Salad . . . 4.95
Sauteed Virginia Soft Shell Crab 7.95	Vidalia Onion Vinaigrette
Steamed Manila Clams, Wine & Garlic . 6.95	Duchess Potatoes 2.95
Seared Mussels, Garlic & Parsley 6.95	Steamed Local Sweet Corn 1.50
Steamed Blue Mussels, Provencal 6.95	Fried Great Lakes Smelt 4.95

FRESH FISH & SEASONAL SPECIALS

VIRGINIA SOFT SHELL CRABS, Lemon, Garlic or Amandine . . (2) 18.95 (3) 25.95

—GRILLED—

ALASKAN HALIBUT 18.95
   Sauteed Summer Vegetables and Chipotle Pepper Mayonnaise
HALF MOON BAY KING SALMON 18.95
   Braised Fennel and Leeks with Port Plum Sauce
GULF YELLOWFIN TUNA, PEPPER CRUSTED 19.95
   Fried Red Onions and Diable Sauce
ECUADORIAN MAHI MAHI 17.95
   Wild Rice and Chanterelle Mushroom Sauce
NANTUCKET STRIPED BASS 19.95
   Roasted Yukon Gold Potatoes, Cipollini Onions and Roasted Garlic Vinaigrette

—SAUTEED—

SHRIMP & MEDITERRANEAN MUSSELS ON PENNE PASTA 15.95
   Summer Vegetable Tomato Sauce
CANADIAN WALLEYE 17.95
   Pistachio & Almond Crust, Green Beans and Lemon Butter

—ROASTED—

ALASKAN HALIBUT STEAK 23.95
   Sauteed Summer Vegetables and Chipotle Pepper Mayonnaise

CHICAGO'S 1996 RESTAURANT CELEBRATION
Chicago'96
1 lb. Steamed Whole Maine Lobster with Red Potatoes & Cole Slaw, ... 19.96
Cup of Soup or House Salad & Fresh Fruit Sorbet

CRAB AND LOBSTER

Whole Cracked Alaskan Dungeness Crab 29.95
Crab Combination 26.95
  Maryland Style Crab Cake, Alaskan King Crab Legs, Jumbo Virginia Soft Shell Crab
Whole Maine Lobster: 1½ to 2½ Pounds . . . . (per pound) 19.95
Stuffed Maine Lobster: 1½ to 2½ Pounds . . . . (per pound) 24.95
New Zealand Twin Lobster Tails 38.95
Texas Stone Crab Claws . . . . (per pound) 28.95
Alaskan King Crab Legs . . . . (per 1¼ pounds) 29.95

SHAW'S SPECIALTIES	SHRIMP PLATTERS
Planked Lake Superior Whitefish 14.95	Shrimp, Spinach, Tomatoes on Linguine . 13.95
Sauteed Yellow Lake Perch 17.95	French Fried Shrimp 13.95
Shaw's Crab Cakes (2) 16.95	Shrimp DeJonghe 14.95
Sauteed Frog's Legs 11.95	Griddled Garlic Shrimp 14.95
Seasonal Vegetable Platter 12.95	Baked Stuffed Shrimp 14.95
Sauteed Sea Scallops 16.95	Shaw's Seafood Platter 18.95
Lemon Or Garlic Butter	Griddled Garlic Shrimp, Crab Cake & Sauteed Sea Scallops

Whole Key Lime Pies —Available— To Take Home | Lunch & Dinner —Reservations— Available | 16% Gratuity Will be —Added To Parties of— Six or Larger

---

Soft Shell Crabs —From Virginia— May 15—Sept. 15 | Royster With the Oyster —Oyster Hour: 4:00-6:30, Mon-Fri— Blue Crab Lounge | Private Party —Facilities Available— See Manager

FRESH OYSTERS

On The Half Shell 7.95
  Cold Water Varieties, Shucked to Order
Oysters Rockefeller 6.95
Pan Fried Pacific Oysters 6.95

OYSTER ACCOMPANIMENTS

Oyster-Friendly Wines
A selection of dry, crisp, clean-finishing wines are available by the glass or bottle to complement Shaw's oysters. Or try a malty beer from our beverage list on the back cover of the menu.

OYSTER GEOGRAPHY

Oysters are traditionally marketed by the name of their growing area.
—For Today's Selections—
See Daily Specials on opposite page

Eastern (Crassostrea virginica)
Long Island Sound . . . . Connecticut
Malpeque . . . . Prince Edward Island, Canada
Caraquet . . . . . . New Brunswick, Canada
Dutch Island . . . . Rhode Island
Wellfleet . . . . Massachusetts
Pemaquid . . . . Maine

European Flats (Ostrea edulis)
Westcott Flats . . . . Washington
Umpqua Flats . . . . Oregon
Totten Flats . . . . Washington

Olympia (Ostrea lurida)
Grown in the Bays of Southern Puget Sound

Kumamoto
(Crassostrea gigas var. kumomoto)
Grown in Northern California & Washington

Pacific (Crassostrea gigas)
Totten Inlet . . . . Washington
Malaspina . . . . British Columbia
Fanny Bay . . . . Vancouver Island, Canada
Hamma Hamma . . . . Washington
Hog Island . . . . California
Netarts Bay . . . . Oregon
Sund Creek . . . . Washington
Shoalwater Bay . . . . Washington
Coromandel . . . . New Zealand
Trail's End . . . . Washington
Eagle Creek . . . . Washington
Quilcene . . . . Washington
Tenass Pass . . . . Alaska
Rilan Bay . . . . Chile

Chilean (Ostrea chilensis)
Chiloé . . . . Chile

SEAFOOD AT SHAW'S

Commitment to quality is a source of pride at Shaw's. We fly in seasonal seafood daily from the Atlantic, Gulf and Pacific Coasts. To preserve flavor, fish is filleted on premise as needed, never in advance.
  Shaw's actively supports the management of America's fisheries to preserve fish and water quality for future generations.

PROPRIETORS	MANAGMENT SUPERVISOR
Chef Yves Roubaud	Ginna Shannon
Kevin Brown	**GENERAL MANAGER**
Stephen LaHaie	Tod Barber

COLD APPETIZERS

Topneck Clams, Half-Dozen 5.95
Blue Crab Fingers 7.95
Charred Sashimi Tuna 7.95
Shrimp Cocktail (in shell) 7.95
Spicy Shrimp 7.95
Smoked Salmon 7.50

HOT APPETIZERS

Escargot, Garlic Butter 5.95
Herbed-Cheese Mushrooms 5.95
French Fried Calamari 6.50
Popcorn Shrimp 6.95
Baked Clams Casino 6.50
Shaw's Crab Cake 8.50

SEAFOOD APPETIZER PLATTERS
—per person—

Cold Combo—Shrimp, Oysters,
  Clams, & Blue Crab Fingers 7.95
Hot Combo—Mini Crab Cake,
  Popcorn Shrimp, & Calamari 7.50

SOUPS
                    CUP/BOWL

Seafood Gumbo 2.75/3.95
New England Clam Chowder 2.75/3.95
Lobster Bisque 2.95/4.25

SALADS

Shaw's Caesar Salad 4.25
House Mixed Greens 3.75
House Mixed Greens/Blue Cheese 3.95
House Mixed Greens/Boursin Cheese . . . 4.25
Tomato & Onion 3.75
Cole Slaw 1.95
Iceberg Wedge 3.25

VEGETABLES
—serves two—

Creamed Spinach 2.95
Steamed Fresh Broccoli 2.75
Steamed Green Beans 2.50
Green Beans and Mushrooms 2.75

POTATOES & RICE
—serves two—

Hashed Browns 3.25
Hashed Browns w/Onions. 3.50
Au Gratin Potatoes 3.50
Boiled Red Potatoes 2.50
Cajun Rice 2.50
Four Grain Wild Rice 2.95
—single—
Charred Baked Potato. 2.75

CHICKEN & PRIME BEEF

Whole Roasted Amish Chicken 13.95
Garlic Roasted Amish Chicken 14.95
Aged New York Sirloin 28.95
Filet Mignon, Sauce Béarnaise 25.95
Filet Mignon/Lobster Tail 36.95

Cigar and Pipe —Smoking— In Bar Only | All Major —Credit Cards— Accepted | Live Jazz and Blues —Blue Crab Lounge— Tuesday & Thursday

---

FIGURE 5.8 A specialty menu from shaw's Crab House, Chicago, Illinois. Reprinted by permission.

The specialty menu generally has: appetizers, soups, salads, entrées, accompaniments, and desserts. In some cases, the entrée section might also be divided into a number of different sections consisting of: grilled, braised, sautéed, and roasted items. A typical specialty restaurant specializing in fish might have the following selections: grilled half moon bay king salmon with braised fennel and leeks with port plum sauce; sautéed shrimp and Mediterranean mussels on penne pasta with summer vegetables tomato sauce, and roasted Alaskan halibut steak with sautéed summer vegetables and chipotle pepper mayonnaise. A restaurant specializing in beef might include: grilled Porterhouse steak with seasoned onion rings; broiled filet mignon with sauce béarnaise; and rack of lamb with a pistachio crust. (Figure 5.8)

The ultimate success of a specialty restaurant depends on how fresh the food product actually is when served to the customer. Some restaurants back their commitment to quality by stating right on the menu that all their seasonal product is flown in daily.

The Special Occasion Menu

The special occasion menu revolves around a distinctive event or holiday: a wedding reception, bas mitzvah, Christmas, New Year's, etc. For the most part, special occasion menus are prix fixe, and include a choice of appetizer, soup, salad, entrée, accompaniment, and dessert. In some cases, special occasion menus also offer a complimentary glass of wine with dinner. Whether formal or informal, the special occasion menu should be imaginative and well planned. The cover and graphics on the menu should also match the occasion or theme; for example, a Thanksgiving menu cover could depict an autumn scene with a turkey in the background. The food selections on a special occasion menu should be suitable for that occasion as well. Thanksgiving menu course choices might encompass the following: Maine crabcakes with almond crust, or duck proscuitto with chanterelles and tomatoes. Purée of butternut squash and apple soup or roasted garlic soup with shiitake mushrooms; fresh Romaine lettuce sprinkled with stilton cheese, red bell peppers and a garlic crouton with garlic vinaigrette dressing, or pan-seared sesame and peppercorn-crusted tuna salad. Carved turkey with apple raisin stuffing and cranberry sauce; baked ham with honey and thyme demi-glace, or roasted salmon with sautéed spinach and glazed yams, butternut squash, and potatoes au gratin. Assorted fresh baked bread, rolls and muffins, and pumpkin pie or pecan caramel upside down pie, and assorted fruit and cheese to complete the selections. (Figure 5.9)

Dessert Menu

One of the major objectives of any restaurant is to serve well-known and imaginative desserts to their patrons. This can be done in a variety of ways: by tray or cart, on the main menu, or on a separate dessert menu. An effective strategy that many restaurants employ is a combination of both the dessert tray or cart and a separate dessert menu. Using a tray or cart allows the restaurant to focus on its signature baked goods and gives the customer a visual presentation of the desserts being served. This is a very effective way of merchandising. Since all desserts cannot be served on a tray or cart, a separate menu is also used. A separate dessert menu gives each dessert listing adequate space to allow for descriptive copy. Dessert offerings should be fresh, creative, and extensive. Cakes, cobblers or crisps, fruits, ice cream, pies, puddings, sorbets, specialty items, and tarts should be included. Dessert offerings might include: Black Forest cake, peach and plum crisp, assorted fruit and cheese, butterscotch ice cream, banana-coconut cream pie, crème brulée, rice pudding with an almond madeleine, fresh fruit sorbets with biscotti cookies, Grand Marnier soufflé, and a lemon tart garnished with seasonal fruits.

Some dessert menus also provide specialty coffees, teas, and after dinner drinks. Cappuccino, espresso, and café latté, English breakfast tea, vintage Darjeeling, Earl Grey, and Chamomile, and ports, single malt scotch, cognac, and Armagnac are all possible offerings. Remember, not every customer wants a dessert after a heavy meal, so coffee, tea, or an after dinner drink might be considered in place of dessert. With these additions on the dessert menu, the average check is often increased. (Figure 5.10)

The Wine menu

Wine can be displayed in a variety of ways on the menu. Wines can be incorporated into the liquor menu if there are only a few selections; wines can be placed on the main menu paired with entrées; or finally, a separate wine list of domestic and foreign wines might be offered. A separate wine list is recommended if the restaurant has more than 20 wine selections. The first two ways of displaying wines are used in many restaurants, however, they are not as popular as the wine list. For out purpose, the separate wine list is discussed in detail in this chapter.

Everglades Grand Ballroom
New Year's Eve Gala
December 31, 1996
7 pm - 1 am

Las Vegas-Style Revue Featuring Levi John...All Diverse Music
From the '20's Right on up to Today's Popular Tunes

** New Year's Eve Favors **

7 pm - Cocktail Reception
Hors d'Oeuvres and Open Bar

8 pm - Dinner and Wine Service

Seared Ahi Tuna Loin
Maine Lobster Carpaccio served with Winter Baby Mixed Greens
Floridian Orange Sorbet
Sauteed Salmon with Tomato and Shallot Compote and
Roasted Veal Loin with Basil and Roasted Garlic Demi-Glace
Trio of Hazelnut Napoleon, Chocolate Bittersweet Mousse and Crispy Apple Tarte
Coffee, Teas and Decaffeinated Coffee

Complimentary Wine served with Dinner
Cash Bar Available

Midnight Festivities
Champagne, Light Show, Balloon Drop, Ball Drop from Times Square

Black Tie Optional

$99.00 per person plus tax and gratuity

Call 466-4000 extension 2380 for reservations

FIGURE 5.9 *A special occasion menu from Sanibel Harbour Resort & Spa, Fort Myers, Florida. Reprinted by permission.*

The *cellar master* is usually the person responsible for composing the wine list. The cellar master often has years of experience in the wine field and is extremely knowledgeable in wine and food pairing. On the wine list, each wine is identified by a bin number. The bin number is also written on the label of each bottle of wine in the bin. The bin system makes inventory more accurate and service more effective. The wine list should encompass both white and red wines, domestic and foreign. The range of domestic and foreign wines offered has a direct correlation to the geographical location of the restaurant, the accessibility of the product, and customer preference. Domestic wines might include both red and white offerings from California, Oregon, Washington State, and Virginia. There should also be a good showing of European reds and whites. France, Italy, Germany, and Spain are the most popular producers of wines; however, Australian wines have gained respect in the wine world over the last few years. European wines are generally classified into reds and whites, and when appropriate, also divided by wine regions. French wines are divided into the following regions: Bourgogne, Rhone, Provence, Languedoc, and Bordeaux. Whether the wine is domestic or foreign, it should be classified as an apéritif, dinner wine, or dessert wine. Wines should be described on the menu according to their style: light, soft, silky, smooth, crisp, dry or medium dry, rich or full-bodied, vigorous, robust, hearty or full. It is also recommended that the vintage year be listed next to each wine, as the vintage has a direct bearing on the price. Wines should also be presented on the menu by bottle, half bottle, or "by the glass."

LAURA CHENEL'S "CABECOU" GOAT CHEESE
Marinated in Olive Oil and Thyme, Served with Honey
$10.50

✩✩ DESSERTS ✩✩

GRAND MARNIER "CREPE BRULEE"

STRAWBERRY PIE WITH CREME FRAICHE

"TARTE AU CITRON" WITH ORANGE SAUCE
(FRENCH LEMON MERINGUE PIE)

FLOATING ISLAND
WITH CARAMEL, ALMONDS AND VANILLA CUSTARD

THIN APPLE TART
WITH CARAMELIZED PISTACHIO ICE CREAM

FRESH FRUIT SORBETS WITH BISCOTTI COOKIES

HOT "GOOEY" CHOCOLATE CAKE
WITH VANILLA ICE CREAM

BANANA-COCONUT CREAM PIE "BRULÉE"

WARM CHOCOLATE FEUILLETÉ WITH STRAWBERRY ICE CREAM

RICE PUDDING WITH ALMOND MADELEINE

ALL DESSERTS
$7.00
✩✩✩✩

CRYSTAL GEYSER	$4.50
EVIAN	$5.50
NAVARRO VARIETAL GRAPE JUICES	$2.50
Gewurztraimer • Pinot Noir	

"THE TEA COMPANY" TEAS   Two Cup Pot $4.00
Keemun Mao Feng • Green Oolong • Jasmine Pearl • Four Treasures

✩✩✩✩

PHILIPPE JEANTY
EXECUTIVE CHEF

CHANDON

FIGURE 5.10 A dessert menu from Domaine Chandon, Yountville, California. Reprinted by permission.

Although many customers still follow certain rules when pairing food and wine, for the most part, the stringent rules of food and wine pairing have somewhat dissipated over the last decade. Red wines do not necessarily have to accompany red meats, nor do white wines have to accompany seafood or fish. (Figure 5.11)

Some wine lists are fairly extensive when domestic and imported wines are both well represented. (Figure 5.12)

Menu Listing	Wine Recommendations
Appetizers	Dry white, sherry, or Champagne
Entrée of:	
Beef	Vigorous, robust, full-bodied, hearty or spicy red
Chicken	Crisp, full-bodied white, or silky, soft red
Duck	Crisp, full-bodied white, or silky, soft red
Fish	Dry white, medium dry white
Ham	Rosé, dry white, medium dry white
Lamb	Vigorous, robust, full-bodied, hearty or spicy red
Pheasant	Vigorous, robust, full-bodied, hearty or spicy red
Pork	Rosé, dry white, medium dry white
Seafood	Dry white, medium dry white
Turkey	Crisp, full-bodied white, or silky, soft red, or Champagne
Veal	Crisp, full-bodied white, or silky, soft red
Venison	Vigorous, robust, full-bodied, hearty or spicy red
Desserts	Sweet wine or semisweet sparkling wine

FIGURE 5.11 A Food and Wine Pairing Chart.

WHITE WINES

OREGON

1	(Blush) Pinot Noir Blanc, Shafer, 1993 Willamette Valley	$12
3	Dry White Riesling, Argyle, 1993 Willamette Valley, Reserve	$15
4	White Riesling, Tualatin, 1995 Willamette Valley	$12
6	Dry – Gewurztraminer, Elk Cove, 1993 Willamette Valley, Reserve Exceptional	$20
7	Dry – Gewurztraminer, Tyee, 1994 Willamette Valley	$16
8	Pinot Blanc, WillaKenzie, Estate 1995	$25
9	Pinot Bianco, Cameroni, Bricco Abbazia, 1995	$20
11	Pinot Gris, Eyrie, 1995 Willamette Valley	$28
12	Pinot Gris, Willamette Valley Vineyards, 1995 Willamette Valley	$25
13	Pinot Gris, Erath, 1994/95 Willamette Valley	$22
14	Pinot Gris, WillaKenzie, Estate, 1995	$25
15	Pinot Gris, Cooper Mountain, 1995 Willamette Valley	$22
16	Pinot Gris, Hinman, 1994/95 Willamette Valley	$22
17	Pinot Gris, Silvan Ridge, 1994 Willamette Valley	$27
18	Pinot Gris, King Estate, 1994 Oregon, Reserve	$27
19	Fume Blanc, Valley View, 1995 Rogue Valley	$20

OREGON (continued)

21	Chardonnay, Cameron, 1994 Willamette Valley, Clos Electrique	$45
22	Chardonnay, Eyrie, 1992 Willamette Valley, Reserve	$45
23	Chardonnay, Argyle, 1990 Willamette Valley, Reserve	$30
24	Chardonnay, King Estate, 1993 Oregon	$25
25	Chardonnay, Cooper Mountain, 1992 Willamette Valley, Reserve	$35
26	Chardonnay, Evesham Wood, 1994 Willamette Valley	$25
27	Chardonnay, Sokol Blosser, 1992 Yamhill County, Redland	$35
28	Chardonnay, Elk Cove, 1993 Willamette Valley, Reserve Exceptional	$30
29	Chardonnay, Bethel Heights, 1994 Willamette Valley, Reserve	$30
31	Chardonnay, Tualatin, 1993 Willamette Valley, Reserve	$30
32	Chardonnay, Valley View, 1994 Rogue Valley, Anna Maria	$30
33	Chardonnay, Adelsheim, 1993 Willamette Valley, Reserve	$35
34	Chardonnay, Chehalem, 1994 Ridgecrest Vineyard	$30

WASHINGTON

40	Sauvignon Blanc, Caterina, 1994 Columbia Valley	$20
41	Chardonnay, Canoe Ridge Vineyards, 1994/95 Columbia Valley	$25
44	Chardonnay, Covey Run, 1993 Yakima Valley, Reserve	$25
45	Chardonnay, Barnard Griffin, 1994 Columbia Valley, Reserve	$35
46	Chardonnay, Chateau Ste. Michelle, 1994 Columbia Valley, Canoe Ridge Vineyard	$40
47	Chardonnay, Woodward Canyon, 1995 Walla Walla Valley	$45
48	Chardonnay, Columbia, 1994 Yakima Valley, Wyckoff Vineyard	$30

CALIFORNIA

50	Sauvignon Blanc, Frog's Leap, 1995 Napa Valley	$25
51	Sauvignon Blanc, Mondavi, 1994 Napa Valley, Stags Leap District	$35
52	Meritage, Langtry, 1994 Guenoc Valley	$30
53	Chardonnay, Guenoc, 1994 Lake County, Geneviere Magoon Reserve	$35
54	Chardonnay, Peter Michael, 1994 Napa Valley, Clos du Ciel	$55
55	Chardonnay, Stonestreet, 1994 Sonoma County	$40
56	Chardonnay, Hanzell, 1993/94 Sonoma Valley	$50
57	Chardonnay, Ferrari–Carano, 1994 Alexander Valley	$40
58	Chardonnay, Sonoma—Cutrer, 1993 Les Pierres Vineyard	$45
59	Chardonnay, Matanzas Creek, 1994 Sonoma Valley	$45
60	Chardonnay, Kistler, 1993 Sonoma Valley, McCrea Vineyard	$60
61	Chardonnay, Franciscan, 1993/94 Napa Valley, Cuvee Sauvage	$50
62	Chardonnay, Chateau Montelena, 1994 Napa Valley, Estate	$40
63	Chardonnay, Joseph Phelps, 1993/94 Carneros	$30
64	Chardonnay, Mount Eden Vineyards, 1994 Santa Cruz Mountains	$60
65	Chardonnay, Chalone, 1994 The Pinnacles, Monterey County	$45
66	Chardonnay, Bernardus, 1994 Monterey County	$25
67	(Dry) Chenin Blanc, Chappellet, 1994 Napa Valley	$20
68	Pinot Blanc, Chalone, 1993/94 The Pinnacles, Monterey County	$40
69	Viognier, Joseph Phelps, 1994 Napa Valley, Vin Du Mistral	$45

–2–

–3–

FIGURE 5.12 A wine list from The Heathman Hotel, Portland, Oregon. Reprinted by permission.

FRANCE

LOIRE

72	Vouvray, Champalou, Cuvee des Fondraux, 1994	$25
73	Sancerre, Domaine Vincent Pinard, Cuvee Flores, 1994	$30

ALSACE

75	Pinot Blanc, Weinbach, Reserve, 1994	$30
77	Pinot Auxerrois, Josmeyer, Cuvee 'H', Villes Vignes, 1993	$40
78	Riesling, Meyer–Fonne, Vielles Vignes, 1990	$30
79	Riesling, F. E. Trimbach, Cuvee Frederic Emile, 1990	$55
80	Tokay Pinot Gris, Kuentz–Bas, Reserve Personnelle 1993	$35
81	Pinot Gris, F.E. Trimbach, Reserve, 1993	$30
83	Gewurztraminer, Hugel, Jubilee, Reserve, 1990	$50
84	Chasselas, Domaine Schoffit, Vielles Vignes, 1993/94	$25

PROVENCE

85	(Rose) La Deesse, Domaines Ott, 1994	$30

BORDEAUX

87	Chateau Couhins–Lurton, Cru Classe De Graves, 1990	$50

BOURGOGNE

88	Chablis, Louis Michel, 1993	$30
89	Chablis, J. Moreau & Fils, Vaudesir, Grand Cru, 1988	$60
91	Corton–Charlemagne, 1993 Domaine Bonneau du Martray, Grand Cru	$100
93	Chassagne–Montrachet, Marquis de Laguiche, 1994 Joseph Drouhin, Premier Cru	$60
94	Puligny–Montrachet, Domaine Leflaive, 1990	$90
96	Meursault, Domaine Joseph Matrot, 1994	$45
97	Auxey–Duresses, Louis Jadot, 1993	$30
99	Pouilly–Fuisse, Chateau Fuisse, Le Clos, 1994	$65

GERMANY

101	Riesling, Kabinett, Mosel–Saar–Ruwer, 1994 Josephshofer, Von Kesselstatt	$25
102	Riesling, Spatlese, Mosel–Saar–Ruwer, 1993 Piesporter Goldtropfchen, J. Selbach	$30
103	Riesling, Auslese, Mosel–Saar–Ruwer, 1993 Urziger Wurzgarten, Joh. Jos. Christoffel	$35

–4–

OREGON

126	Pinot Noir, Cooper Mountain, 1993 Willamette Valley, Reserve	$40
127	Pinot Noir, King Estate, Oregon, 1993	$35
128	Pinot Noir, St. Innocent, 1994 Select Vineyard	$40
129	Pinot Noir, Chehalem, 1993 Ridgecrest Vineyard	$35
130	Pinot Noir, Panther Creek, Reserve, 1994	$45
131	Pinot Noir, Ken Wright Cellars, 1994 Carter Vineyard	$55
132	Pinot Noir, Erath, 1993 Yamhill County, Reserve	$40
133	Pinot Noir, Sokol Blosser, Single Cask 1993	$60
134	Pinot Noir, Rex Hill, 1993 Archibald Vineyard, Reserve	$40
135	Pinot Noir, Cristom, 1993/94 Willamette Valley, Reserve	$40
136	Pinot Noir, Autumn Wind, 1994 Estate, Reserve	$40
137	Pinot Noir, Domaine Serene, 1993 Willamette Valley, Evenstad Reserve	$50
138	Pinot Noir, Bethel Heights, 1994 Estate, Southeast Block Reserve	$60
139	Pinot Noir, Evesham Wood, 1993 Willamette Valley, Cuvee "J"	$50
140	Pinot Noir, Torii Mor, 1994 Yamhill County	$90
141	Pinot Noir, La Boheme Vineyard, 1993 Willamette Valley	$45
142	Pinot Noir, Tualatin Vineyard, 1994 Willamette Valley, Reserve	$30
144	Pinot Noir, Adelsheim, 1993 Estate, Elizabeth's Reserve	$60
145	Pinot Noir, Domaine Drouhin, 1993 Laurene, Reserve	$25
146	Pinot Noir, Henry Estate, 1990 Umpqua Valley, Winemaker's Reserve	$30
147	Pinot Noir, Bridgeview, 1992 Cave Junction, 10th Anniversary	$35

–5–

OREGON (Continued)

150	Merlot, Valley View, 1992 Rogue Valley, Anna Maria	$35
151	Merlot, La Merleausine, 1993 Applegate Valley	$30
152	Merlot, Bridgeview, 1994 Cave Junction, Black Beauty	$25
153	Merlot, Seven Hills, 1993 Columbia Valley, Seven Hills Vineyard	$35
154	Cabernet Sauvignon, Seven Hills, 1992 Columbia Valley, Seven Hills Vineyard	$35
155	Reserve Red, Valley View, 1992 Rogue Valley, Anna Maria	$35

WASHINGTON

159	Merlot, Woodward Canyon, Columbia Valley, 1994	$45
160	Merlot, Columbia, 1993 Red Willow Vineyard, Milestone	$35
161	Merlot, Barnard Griffin, Columbia Valley, 1994	$30
162	Merlot, Covey Run, Columbia Valley, Reserve 1993	$35
163	Merlot, Caterina, Columbia Valley, 1994	$30
165	Syrah, Columbia, 1992 Yakima Valley, Red Willow Vineyard	$35
166	Red Wine, Cana's Feast, Columbia Valley, 1992	$45
167	Cabernet Sauvignon, Columbia Crest, 1992 Columbia Valley, Barrel Select	$30
168	Cabernet Sauvignon, Woodward Canyon, 1993 Columbia Valley, Barrel Select	$45
169	Cabernet Sauvignon, Woodward Canyon, 1992 Columbia Valley	$50
170	Cabernet Sauvignon, Andrew Will, 1993 Washington	$50
171	Cabernet Sauvignon, Hogue Cellars, 1991 Washington, Reserve	$35
172	Cabernet Sauvignon, Columbia, 1992 Otis Vineyard, David Lake	$40
173	Cabernet Sauvignon, DiStefano, 1993 Columbia Valley	$40
174	Cabernet Sauvignon, Chateau Ste. Michelle, 1993 Columbia Valley, Cold Creek Vineyard	$40

–6–

FIGURE 5.12 A wine list from *The Heathman Hotel, Portland, Oregon (continued)*

CALIFORNIA

175	Merlot, Havens, Napa Valley, 1994	$35
176	Merlot, Merryvale, Napa Valley, 1993	$45
177	Merlot, Ferrari–Carano, Sonoma County, 1993	$40
178	Merlot, Dry Creek Vineyards, Sonoma County, 1994	$30
179	Marinus, Bernardus, Carmel Valley, Estate, 1993	$40
180	Insignia, Joseph Phelps, Napa Valley, 1991	$80
181	Reserve Alexandre, Geyser Peak, 1993 Alexander Valley	$45
182	Mount Veeder Winery, Napa Valley, Reserve, 1992	$60
183	Cabernet Sauvignon, Chateau Montelena, 1992 Napa Valley, Estate	$55
184	Cabernet Sauvignon, Guenoc, 1992 Napa Valley, Beckstoffer Vineyard	$65
185	Cabernet Sauvignon, Sterling, 1990 Napa Valley, Reserve	$55
186	Cabernet Sauvignon, Groth, Napa Valley, 1993	$35
187	Cabernet Sauvignon, Stag's Leap Wine Cellars, 1992 Napa Valley, S.L.V.	$55
188	Cabernet Sauvignon, Hess Collection, 1992 Napa Valley, Mount Veeder	$50
189	Cabernet Sauvignon, Deloach, Russian River, OFS, 1992	$50
190	Cabernet Sauvignon, Jordan, Alexander Valley, 1992	$50
191	Cabernet Sauvignon, Mount Eden Vineyards, 1993 Santa Cruz Mountains, Estate	$35
193	Mataro (Mourvedre) Ridge, 1994 Bridgehead Vineyard, Contra Costra County	$35
194	Shiraz, Geyser Peak, Alexander Valley, Reserve, 1992	$50
195	Petite Sirah, Ridge, 1992 Napa Valley, York Creek Vineyard	$35
196	Pinot Noir, Elude, Carneros, 1994	$45
197	Zinfandel, Ridge, 1994 Sonoma County, Lytton Springs Vineyard	$40
198	Zinfandel, Sky, Napa Valley, 1987	$50
199	Zinfandel, Storybook Mountain, 1991/92 Napa Valley, Reserve	$45

VIRGINIA

200	Norton, Horton Vineyards, Orange County, 1993	$20

-7-

FRANCE

BOURGOGNE

(Cote de Nuits)

201	Chambertin, Clos de Beze, 1992 Domaine Pierre Damoy, Grand Cru	$100
203	Clos des Lembrays, Domaine Clos Lembrays, 1993 Grand Cru	$80
204	Vosne–Romanee, Clos Des Reas, 1988 Domaine Jean Gros, Premier Cru	$90
205	Nuits St. Georges, Hauts Pruliers, 1993 Domaine Daniel Rion, Premier Cru	$95

(Cote de Beaune)

206	Bourgogne Rouge, Domaine La Farge, 1993	$35
207	Corton Rouge, Domaine Bonneau Du Martray, 1990 Grand Cru	$70
209	Pommard, Domaine Joillot, 1993	$60
210	Auxey–Duresses, Clos Du Val, 1988 Domaine Michel Prunier, Premier Cru	$50
212	Volnay, Caillerets, 1988 Domaine Michel Prunier, Premier Cru	$60

(Beaujolais)

214	Beaujolais–Villages, Georges Duboeuf, 1995	$20

RHONE

215	Gigondas, Edmond Burle, Les Pallieroudas, 1993	$30
216	Chateauneuf–du–Pape, Vieux Telegraphe, 1993	$45
217	Hermitage, Paul Jaboulet, Pied De La Cote, 1991	$50

PROVENCE

218	Domaine Trevallon, 1988	$50

LANGUEDOC

219	Mas de Daumas Gassac, Grand Cru (Organic), 1992	$35

-8-

FRANCE
(continued)

BORDEAUX

220	Chateau La Mission Haut Brion, 1983 Cru Classe, Graves	$125
221	Chateau Les Ormes De Pez, St. Estephe, 1989 Grand Cru Bourgeoise	$60
222	Chateau Ducru Beaucaillou, St. Julien, 1983 Second Growth	$110
223	Chateau La Tour De Mons, Margaux, 1990 Cru Bourgeois	$65
225	Chateau De Sales, Pomerol, 1989	$50
227	Chateau Grand Puy Lacoste, 1989 Pauillac, Fifth Growth	$70
229	Chateau St. Georges, St. Emilion, 1990 Grand Cru Classe	$45

ITALY

230	Chianti Classico, Riserva, 1990 Castello di Cacchiano	$35
231	Cepparello, Isole e Olena, 1989	$30
232	Brunello di Montalcino, Caprili, 1990	$45
233	Brunello di Montalcino, Castello Banfi, 1988	$60
234	Brunello di Montalcino, Fornacina, 1990	$65
235	Barbaresco, Pora, 1989 Produttori del Barbaresco, Riserva	$50
236	Barbaresco, Gaiun Martinenga, 1990 Marchesi Di Gresy	$85
238	Barolo, Giacomo Conterno, 1985	$100
239	Barolo, Aldo Conterno, Bussia Soprana, 1989	$75

WINES OF THE WORLD

240	Bin 389, Cabernet–Shiraz, Penfold's, 1992 South Australia	$40
241	Grange, Shiraz, Penfold's, 1991 South Australia	$165
243	Rioja, Conde de Valdemar, Gran Reserva, Spain, 1987	$30
244	Quinta Do Crasto, Vintage Porto, Portugal, 1985	$50
245	Croft, Vintage Porto, Portugal, 1963	$150

-9-

FIGURE 5.12 A wine list from The Heathman Hotel, Portland, Oregon (continued)

HALF BOTTLES

OREGON WHITE WINES

251	Pinot Gris, Eola Hills, 1994	$12
252	Chardonnay, Cristom, 1994	$15
254	Chardonnay, Ken Wright, Celilo, 1995	$16

OREGON RED WINES

255	Pinot Noir, Rex Hill, Reserve, 1993	$20
257	Pinot Noir, Kramer, Estate, 1993	$20
258	Pinot Noir, Domaine Drouhin Oregon, 1994	$30

WASHINGTON WINES

260	Chardonnay, Woodward Canyon, Reserve, 1994	$30
263	Merlot, Hyatt Vineyards, 1994	$15

CALIFORNIA WHITE WINES

265	Sparkling—Blanc de Blancs, Schramsberg, 1990	$25
266	Chardonnay, Steele, 1994	$20
267	Chardonnay, Far Niente, 1994	$30
268	Fume Blanc, Dry Creek Vineyards, 1994	$12

CALIFORNIA RED WINES

270	Cabernet Sauvignon, Shafer, 1993	$25
271	Cabernet Sauvignon, Far Niente, 1993	$45
272	Cabernet Sauvignon, B.V., Georges De Latour, 1991	$40
274	Merlot, Pine Ridge, 1994	$20
275	Zinfandel, Storybook Mountain, 1992	$20

–10–

HALF BOTTLES

CHAMPAGNES

276	Brut, Billecart—Salmon, N.V.	$30
277	Brut, Taititinger, La Francaise, N.V.	$30
278	Demi—Sec, Veuve Clicquot, White Label, N.V.	$30
279	Extra Dry, Moet & Chandon, White Star, N.V.	$30

FRENCH WHITE WINES

280	Riesling, F.E. Trimbach, Clos Ste. Hune, 1990	$60
281	Gewurtztraminer, F.E. Trimbach, Ribeaupierre, 1990	$30
282	Sancerre, Reverdy, 1993	$20
283	Pouilly Fuisse, Louis Jadot, 1994/95	$20
284	Puligny—Montrachet, Sauzet, 1993	$40
285	Beaune, J. Drouhin, Clos des Mouches, Premier Cru, 1993	$50
286	Chablis, Duplessis, Monte de Tonnere, Premier Cru 1990	$25

FRENCH RED WINES

288	Chateauneuf—du—Pape, Chateau Beaucastel, 1993	$30
289	Bandol, Domaine Tempier, 1993	$25
291	St. Estephe, Chateau De Pez, Cru Bourgeois 1990	$25
292	St. Julien, Chateau Gruaud Larose, Second Growth, 1986	$45
293	Mercurey, Maurice Protheau, Clos des Corvees, 1990	$20
294	Beaune, J. Drouhin, Clos des Mouches, Premier Cru, 1990	$55

SPANISH RED WINE

296	Rioja, Muga, Reserva, 1990	$15

SWEET WINES

321	Pinot Gris, Pierre Sparr, Vendage Tardive, 1989	$35
322	Riesling, Auslese Gold Kap, Oberemmler Karlsberg, 1989 Von Kesselstatt	$35
323	Late Harvest Riesling, Henry Estate, 1987	$15
325	Late Harvest Semillon, Chateau Ste. Michelle, 1992	$30
326	Select Late Harvest Riesling, Arrowood, 1994	$50
327	Sauternes, Chateau Rieussec, 1986	$50
328	Tokaji Aszu, 5 Puttonyos, Diszhoko, (500 ml) 1988	$30
329	Vintage Porto, Gould Campbell, 1980	$30

–11–

SPARKLING WINES

OREGON

300	Blanc de Blanc, Argyle, 1987 Methode Champenoise, Oregon	$35
302	Rose, Argyle, 1987 Methode Champenoise, Oregon	$35
304	Brut, Laurel Ridge, N.V. Methode Champenoise, Oregon	$25

CALIFORNIA

305	Brut, Reserve, Domaine Chandon, N.V. Methode Champenoise, Napa Valley	$35
306	Brut, "J" Jordan, 1991 Methode Champenoise, Sonoma County	$45
307	Brut, Roederer Estate, N.V. Methode Champenoise, Anderson Valley	$35

FRANCE

CHAMPAGNE

310	Brut, Bollinger, Special Cuvee, NV	$60
311	Brut Premier, Roederer, N.V.	$60
312	Brut, Yellow Label, N.V. Veuve Clicquot	$60
313	Brut, Krug, Grand Cuvee, N.V.	$150
314	Brut, Dom Perignon, 1988 Moet & Chandon	$150
318	Brut, Pol Roger, 1986	$65
319	Rose, Billecart—Salmon N.V.	$75

SPAIN

320	Brut Zero, Castellblanch, 1991	$15

–12–

FIGURE 5.12 A wine list from The Heathman Hotel, Portland, Oregon (continued)

Review Questions

1. Compare and contrast the à la carte, semi à la carte, and prix fixe menus. Explain which types of foodservice establishments would use each of these.

2. What are the classifications patrons would expect to find on a breakfast and luncheon menu?

3. What are some significant elements to consider when developing an ethnic menu?

4. Why is cross-utilization important on a specialty menu?

5. What strategies should be implemented when merchandising desserts?

6. Explain in detail the factors that should be considered when developing a wine menu.

Bibliography

Sandbach, Nancy E., Frank A. Terranova, and Bradley J. Ware. *New Paradigm Cooking*. Nashville, TN: Favorite Recipes Press, 1996.

Menus Included

Brennan's, New Orleans, LA.
Domaine Chandon, Yountville, CA.
FloodTide Restaurant, Mystic, CT.
Four Seasons (The), Boston, MA.
Heathman Hotel (The), Portland, OR.
Restaurant Daniel, New York, NY.

Sanibel Harbour Resort & Spa, Fort Myers, FL.
Shaw's Crab House, Chicago, IL.
Stage Neck Inn, York Harbor, ME.
White Horse Tavern (The), Newport, RI.
Willard Inter-Continental (The), Washington, D.C.
Reprinted by permission

List of Figures

The Cycle of Cost Control

The Big Picture: Income Statement

objectives

Upon completion of this chapter, the student should be able to:

1. state the purpose of an income statement.
2. prepare an income statement.
3. define and calculate sales, Cost and Cost %.
4. define and calculate gross profit.
5. define and distinguish between controllable and non-controllable costs.
6. define and distinguish between variable and semi-variable costs.

key terms

Controllable Expenses	*Sales*
Cost of Sales	*Seating Capacity Method*
Fixed Expenses	*Semi-variable Expenses*
Forecast	*Turnover rate*
Gross Profit	*Variable Expenses*
Non-Controllable Expenses	

Introduction

The concept and the menu are the basis of all costs control measures taken by a foodservice operation to insure that the foodservice operation is successful. This chapter is designed to give an overall picture of how a business operates. Dollars brought in (sales), minus the dollars paid out to operate the business (costs), determine how much money the foodservice operation makes (profit). A review of an operation's income statement provides a picture of its financial condition.

Income Statement

The income statement, also referred to as the profit and loss statement, is a financial report that lists the amount of revenue (sales) that has been taken in and the expenses (costs) that have been paid out to operate a foodservice operation over a period of time. Typically, the period of time is a year or a month, and is expressed as "for the year ending . . ." or "for the month ending . . .". The income statement provides management with a summary of profits earned over a specific period of time.

Components of the Income Statement

The income statement is composed of three parts: sales, expenses, and profit.

Sales

Sales refers to the dollars (or revenue) generated from the sale of food and beverages. As will be further discussed in Chapter 12, the tracking of sales begins when the server records an order on the guest check. Sales are usually tracked in two categories: food sales and beverage sales. *Food sales* is the total dollar amount brought in through the sale of food items. *Beverage sales* is the total amount brought in through the sale of beverage items. Total sales is the combination of both food and beverage sales and is the total dollar amount the business has to pay its expenses and ultimately to generate a profit. Total sales may also include other types of sales such as merchandise, take-out, banquet, room service, etc.

Expenses (Costs)

An expense (cost) is the total dollar amount spent by the foodservice operation to purchase goods or to provide a service to its customers. Foodservice managers classify expenses (costs) into four categories: food, beverage, labor, and overhead. *Food cost* is the total dollar amount spent to purchase food and beverage items needed to produce the food menu items sold. *Beverage cost* is the total dollar amount spent to purchase alcoholic beverages, non-alcoholic beverages, and food items needed to produce a beverage sale. The combination of food and beverage cost is defined as Cost of Sales. *Labor cost* is the total dollars spent on employees' wages, salaries, and benefits. *Overhead costs* are all costs that are not food, beverage, or labor costs. The combination of labor and overhead costs is known as operating expenses. Chef/managers analyze these costs by identifying the percent of sales that each represents. This is just one way chef/managers can identify how their business is performing.

Analyzing Costs and Their Relationship to Sales. Foodservice managers also identify and analyze costs in relation to sales. Expenses (costs) are often classified as fixed, variable, or semi-variable. A fixed cost is a cost that does not fluctuate in direct relation to the increase or decrease of sales. It is a cost that remains constant regardless of an increase or decrease in sales. An example of a fixed cost would be the chef's salary. No matter how much money the foodservice operation brings in, management will know that the chef will always be earning the same amount each week. Also included in fixed costs are: mortgage, real estate taxes, insurance, etc.

A variable cost is a cost that fluctuates in direct proportion to an increase or decrease in sales. As sales increase, the amount of money spent to purchase goods to produce those sales increases. Food and beverage costs (Cost of Sales) are variable costs. Even though the cost of goods fluctuates as sales fluctuate, the relationship between food cost and food sales (the food cost %) should remain the same if effective control procedures are in place.

A semi-variable cost is a cost that fluctuates within limits in relation to sales. As sales increase or decrease, so does the semi-variable cost increase or decrease until it reaches a maximum or minimum expenditure. When the cost reaches a maximum expenditure, sales may increase but the cost no longer does. When sales decrease, there is a point where the minimum expenditure is realized, and at that point, the cost can go no lower. A foodservice operation must expend at least the minimum cost to operate. An example of a semi-variable cost is employees' wages. A minimum number of employees is always needed to "open the doors." As sales grow, chef/managers have to increase the number of employees to effectively handle the amount of business. A foodservice operation with a full staff reaches its maximum cost in wages.

Analyzing Cost to Management's Ability to Control. Foodservice managers classify costs as controllable or non-controllable. A controllable cost is a cost that management can reduce. Food and beverage costs are controllable costs. Chef/managers can control food and beverage costs by implementing portion control devices and through proper production forecasting (Chapter 11). The wages paid employees are also controllable. These costs are controlled by forecasting staffing needs and preparing a weekly work schedule (Chapter 13).

A non-controllable cost is a cost that cannot be controlled by management. It is a cost that cannot be changed over a short period of time. Chef/managers often have the opportunity to set original costs, but once established, managers can do nothing to reduce the waste of that cost. Examples of non-controllable costs are salaries, mortgages, and real estate taxes. Fixed costs are similar to non-controllable costs, while variable and semi-variable costs are usually controllable. The terms fixed, variable, semi-variable, controllable, and non-controllable costs will be utilized throughout the cycle of cost control.

Profit

Profit is the goal of a commercial foodservice operation. It is the amount of money a foodservice makes. A direct relationship exists between sales and expenses, and profit.

1. When sales are greater than expenses there is a profit.

2. When sales are less than expenses there is a loss.

3. When sales are equal to expenses, this is called the break-even point. *Break-even* means that there is neither a profit nor a loss. A knowledge of the break-even point assists managers in proactively managing sales and expenses. When a chef knows that he/she has to serve 25 customers for sales to pay for expenses (break-even point), it is rather evident that 50 buffet reservations produce a profit. If there are only 10 reservations, the chef should take steps to increase the numbers. The process of calculating the break-even point is discussed in Chapter 12.

Preparing an Income Statement

STATEMENT OF INCOME

THE NAME OF THE RESTAURANT

Month/year Ending _____31, 20____

SALES		
Food	$1,550,000	78.9%
Beverages	$ 414,000	21.1%
Total Sales	**$1,964,000**	**100.0%**
COST OF SALES		
Food	$ 527,000	34.0%
Beverages	$ 91,080	22.0%
Total Cost of Sales	**$ 618,080**	**31.5%**
GROSS PROFIT	$1,345,920	68.5%
OPERATING EXPENSES		
Salaries and Wages	$ 549,920	28.0%
Employee Benefits	$ 98,200	5.0%
Direct Operating Expenses	$ 157,120	8.0%
Music and Entertainment	$ 19,640	1.0%
Marketing	$ 49,100	2.5%
Utilities Services	$ 68,740	3.5%
Repairs and Maintenance	$ 29,460	1.5%
Occupancy Costs	$ 137,480	7.0%
Depreciation	$ 39,280	2.0%
General and Administrative Fees	$ 58,920	3.0%
Total Operating Expenses	**$1,207,860**	**61.5%**
Operating Income	**$ 138,060**	**7.0%**
Interest	$ 7,856	.4%
Income Before Taxes	**$ 130,204**	**6.6%**

FIGURE 6.1 Income Statement

Analyzing Sales

Businesses usually analyze sales and costs using percentage analysis. In order to calculate what percentage of sales each expense (or cost) represents, the chef/manager must have a sound understanding of basic mathematical operations. Knowledge of addition, subtraction, multiplication, division, and percentages is a must for successful foodservice employees. Although most people are comfortable with the first four operations, calculation of percentages is sometimes misunderstood. If you do not have a sound understanding of how to use percentages, Appendix B provides a tool to help you to succeed in percentage analysis. This tool, the Percentage Formula Triangle, is referred to throughout the next.

Sales is the revenue generated by selling food and beverages to customers. Foodservice operations often analyze their sales by evaluating the percent of revenue derived from food sales and/or beverage sales. The formula to calculate the food sales percentage and beverage sales percentage is as follows:

Food Sales	÷	**Total Sales**	=	**Food Sales %**
$1,550,000	÷	$1,964,000	=	78.9%
Beverage Sales	÷	**Total Sales**	=	**Beverage Sales %**
$414,000	÷	$1,964,000	=	21.1%

Determining Cost of Sales

Cost of Sales is the total dollar amount spent to purchase the food and beverages needed to produce total sales. Cost of Sales includes two costs: food cost and beverage cost. *Food cost* is the total dollar amount spent to purchase items needed to produce the food menu items. Food cost may include beverage item costs as well as food item costs if the beverage item is required in the standard recipe for a food item. For example, brandy is used to produce a sauce for a filet or Chambord® is used in a raspberry parfait.

Beverage cost is the total dollar amount spent to purchase alcoholic beverages, non-alcoholic beverages, and food items needed to produce a beverage sale. Alcoholic beverages consist of distilled spirits, wine, and beer. Non-alcoholic beverages include bottled water, carbonated drinks, juices, non-alcoholic beer, and wine. The food items that are added in beverage cost are those used in a beverage's standard recipe, such as strawberries in a strawberry daiquiri, or a fruit or vegetable used for garnish.

When preparing an income statement, food cost and beverage cost are calculated by using the cost of sales formula. The cost of sales formula is perpared for food cost and then again for beverage cost. The two primary components of the cost of sales formula are inventories and purchases. Prior to business on the first of each month, an actual count (physical inventory) of all food (or beverage) items is made and their costs determined. (Chapter 10) Foodservice operations usually also develop a system to track and total all food and beverages purchased during the month. The equation to calculate the *Cost of Food Sold* (Food Cost) and the *Cost of Beverages Sold* (Beverage Cost) is found in Chapter 9.

The combination of the Cost of Food Sold (food cost) and the Cost of Beverages Sold (beverage cost) is the total *Cost of Sales*.

Cost of Food Sold	+	Cost of Beverages Sold	=	Total Cost of Sales
$527,000	+	$91,080	=	618,080

Foodservice operations analyze their food and beverage costs using percentage analysis. The Food Cost % is calculated by dividing the cost of food sold (food cost) by the food sales.

Cost of Food Sold	÷	Food Sales	=	Food Cost %
$527,000	÷	$1,550,000	=	34.0%

The Beverage Cost % is calculated by dividing the cost of beverages sold (beverage cost) by the beverage sales.

Cost of Beverage Sold	÷	Beverage Sales	=	Beverage Cost %
$91,080	÷	$414,000	=	22.0%

The Total Cost of Sales % is calculated by dividing the Total Cost of Sales by Total Sales.

Total Cost of Sales	÷	Total Sales	=	Cost of Sales %
$618,080	÷	$1,964,000	=	31.5%

Gross Profit is the difference between Sales and Cost of Sales. Foodservice operations often calculate the gross profit for food and beverage items separately. The gross profit for food results when the cost of food sold is subtracted from food sales. Beverage's gross profit results when the cost of beverages sold is subtracted from beverage sales. The combination of food's gross profit and beverage's gross profit is total gross profit. Total gross profit is the total dollar amount left to pay all operating expenses.

To calculate the Food Gross Profit %:

Food Gross Profit $	÷	Food Sales	=	Food Gross Profit %
$1,023,000	÷	$1,550,000	=	66.0%

To calculate the Beverage Gross Profit %:

Beverage Gross Profit $	÷	Beverage Sales $	=	Beverage Gross Profit %
$322,920	÷	$414,000	=	78.0%

To calculate the Total Gross Profit %:

Total Gross Profit $	÷	Total Sales $	=	Total Gross Profit %
$1,345,920	÷	$1,964,000	=	68.5%

Operating Expenses

Operating expenses are the combination of all labor and overhead costs. As defined and explained in Chapter 13, *labor cost* is the total dollars spent to pay employees' wages, salaries, and benefits. *Overhead costs* can be defined as all costs that are not food, beverage, or labor costs. Foodservice operations often use the Uniform Systems of Accounts for Restaurants Chart of Accounts (Appendix D) to categorize and track operating expenses that are then posted to the income statement and totaled.

Operating income is the difference between Gross Profit and Operating Expenses. Interest paid on all borrowed capital is then subtracted from operating income to arrive at Income Before Taxes.

Operating Income	−	Interest	=	Income Before Taxes
$138,060	−	$7,856	=	$130,204

To calculate the percentage of sales represented by the operating expenses and profit, divide the expense (or profit) by total sales. For example, to calculate the Salaries and Wages percentage:

Salaries and Wages	÷	Total Sales	=	Salaries and Wages%
$549,920	÷	$1,964,000	=	28.0%

To calculate the Income Before Taxes %:

Income Before Taxes	÷	Total sales	=	Income Before Taxes %
$130,204	÷	$1,964,000	=	6.6%

Forecasting Sales

Foodservice managers often forecast sales. One way to forecast sales is to use the actual expense method. The actual expense method may employ the feasibility study prepared for investors to determine the operation's projected expenses, or the prior year's income statement to help *forecast* (predict) the upcoming year's sales and expenses. A forecasted income statement:

1. projects targeted profits, expenses, and sales.

2. is used by management as an operating budget to compare the actual sales and expenses with the forecasted sales and expenses.

3. allows management to be proactive rather than reactive in managing food, beverage, labor, and expense budgets.

Another method used to **forecast** sales is the *seating capacity method*. The seating capacity method is based on the foodservice operation's seating and is calculated using one meal period. If a foodservice operation offers three meal periods (breakfast, lunch, and dinner), the annual sales for each meal period is calculated separately and the three are then added together. There are four steps to the seating capacity method. These are illustrated in the following example:

Calculating Annual Sales for the Dinner Meal Period

Example:

Capacity	80
Turnover Rate	1.5
Additional Customers	20
Average Sale/Cover	$18.00
Days Open Per Year	313

Step 1: Seating Capacity × Turnover Rate Per Meal = Customers Per Meal Period

$$80 \quad \times \quad 1.5 \quad = \quad 120$$

Using the seating capacity method, the chef/manager must first determine the number of seats that occupy the dining room (example: 80 seats) and the average turnover rate. The *turnover rate* is the number of times guests are seated in a dining room in a given meal period. Due to variations in business, Saturday nights are usually busier than Tuesday nights, so an average turnover rate must be used. If the turnover on Friday, Saturday, and Sunday is 2 times, and Monday through Thursday is only 1 time, the average turnover rate would be approximately 1.5 times.

Step 2: Customers Per Meal Period + Additional Customers = Total Customers Served

$$120 \quad + \quad 20 \quad = \quad 140$$

Additional customers would include those not occupying a dining room seat, diners at the bar, take-out customers, etc.

Step 3: Total Customers Served × Average Sale/Cover = Daily Dinner Sales

$$140 \quad \times \quad \$18.00 \quad = \quad \$2,520.$$

The average sale per cover is the amount of money each person spends dining at a restaurant. When this average is multiplied by the total number of customers, the foodservice manager can estimate potential sales for that meal period. If dinner is the only meal period a foodservice operation serves, then the annual sales would be calculated as follows:

Step 4: Daily Sales × Number of Days Open Per Year = Annual Sales

$$\$2,520 \quad \times \quad 313 \quad = \quad \$788,760.$$

This foodservice operation, which is only open for dinner, would have annual sales equaling $788,760. If this same operation also offered lunch, the annual lunch sales would be calculated in the same fashion and then added to the annual dinner sales to forcast Total Annual Sales.

Calculating Annual Sales for the Lunch Meal Period

Example:

Capacity	80
Turnover Rate	2.0
Additional Customers	15
Lunch Check Average	$8.50
Days Open Per Year	313

Step 1: Seating Capacity × Turnover Rate = Customers Per Meal Period

$$80 \quad \times \quad 2 \quad = \quad 160$$

Step 2: Customers Per Meal Period + Additional Customers = Total Customers Served

$$160 \quad + \quad 15 \quad = \quad 175$$

Step 3: Total Customers × Average Sale/Cover = Daily Lunch Period Sales

$$175 \quad \times \quad \$8.50 \quad = \quad \$1,487.50$$

Step 4: Daily Sales × Number of Days Open Per Year = Annual Lunch Sales

$1,487.50 ×   313   = $465,587.50

The foodservice operation's annual sales equal $1,254,347.50 (the sum of the Annual Lunch Sales $465,587.50 + Annual Dinner Sales $788,760.00).

Annual sales for different meal periods should be kept separate. The seating capacity and the number of days open per year are usually the same for all meal periods, while the turnover rate, additional customers, and check average usually vary. Recording food and beverage sales separately allows management to easily identify which sales category needs more attention when total sales are below the Forecasted targeted sales. Tracking the two types of sales facilitates management's task in clearly identifying problem areas.

Review Questions

1. Explain the difference between sales and expenses.

2. Businesses often classify costs in relation to sales and management's ability to control. Define and identify the similarities of variable, semi-variable, fixed, controllable, and non-controllable costs.

3. Use the Seating Capacity Method to forecast sales using the following information.

	a.	**b.**	**c.**
Capacity	120	75	300
Turnover Rate	4	2	3
Additional Customers	35	10	0
Average Sale/Cover	$32.00	$65.00	$18.50
Days Open per Year	363	260	313

4.   Using the Statement of Income form in Appendix F and the following information, complete Statements of Income for each of the three examples.

	a.	b.	c.
Food Sales	$250,000	$276,250	$348,500
Beverage Sales	$ 50,000	$ 48,750	$ 75,750
Food Cost	$ 90,000	$ 96,687	$111,520
Beverage Cost	$ 11,500	$ 12,188	$ 16,665
Salaries/Wages	$ 75,000	$ 75,250	$108,750
Employee Benefits	$ 21,500	$ 22,650	$ 25,455
Direct Operating	$ 18,550	$ 22,750	$ 33,940
Music/Entertainment	$ 7,000	$ 6,500	$ 5,000
Marketing	$ 6,000	$ 8,125	$ 11,935
Utilities/Services	$ 15,000	$ 13,000	$ 16,900
Repairs/Maintenance	$ 6,000	$ 5,000	$ 8,485
Occupancy Costs	$ 17,000	$ 19,500	$ 27,570
Depreciation	$ 1,500	$ 5,400	$ 1,300
General/Admin	$ 12,000	$ 16,250	$ 14,850
Interest	$ 900	$ 1,300	$ 2,100

Bibliography

Deloitte & Touche LLP. *Uniform Systems of Accounts for Restaurants*, 7th ed. Washington DC: National Restaurant Association, 1996.

Determining Portion Costs and Selling Prices

objectives

Upon completion of this chapter, the student should be able to:

1. define standards, standard recipe, standard yield, standard portion, and standard plate cost.
2. define the terms "As Purchased" and "Edible Portion" when used to cost recipes
3. determine Standard Portion Cost using the methods of Cost per Unit, Yield Test, Cooking Loss Test, and Recipe Costing.
4. calculate and use Cost Factors.
5. calculate a Preliminary Selling Price using methods of "Desired Cost %" and "Pricing Factor."
6. set the selling price of a menu item to insure a profit as well as to maintain customer satisfaction.

key terms

As Purchased
Cooking Loss Test
Cost Factor
Desired Beverage Cost %
Desired Cost %
Desired Food Cost %
Edible Portion
Edible Yield %
Mark up
Menu Selling Price

Preliminary Selling Price
Pricing Factor
Q Factor
Standard Plate Cost
Standard Portion Cost
Standard Recipe
Standard Yield
Standards
Yield Test

Introduction

Everyone Enjoys Celebrating

The party begins at 8:00 p.m. sharp so don't be late! The best thing of all is that the party is at my favorite restaurant. Every time I have eaten at this restaurant the food has been great, . . . every time! How do they serve excellent food all the time?

They have standards. The chefs, cooks, servers, bartenders, managers, and all the other employees are knowledgeable about, and execute, quality standards. A *standard* is a rule, policy, or statement written by management, which results in employees performing quality tasks, producing quality products, and providing excellent service.

When purchasing food and beverages, preparing meals, writing recipe cards, answering the telephone, greeting the customer, serving customers, taking inventory, performing yield tests, determining portions, deciding on plate presentations, closing out the cash register, cleaning and sanitizing, and hiring and training employees, standards should be used.

When there are no set performance standards, there is no consistency in the quality of how tasks are performed. The customer is always left wondering how good the food and service are going to be. Customers want to be assured that the food and service are great every time they dine.

The most common standard used in the foodservice industry is a standard recipe. A standard recipe is a written formula used to produce a food or beverage item that uses the same quantity and quality of product and the same method of preparation each time the product is made. Using a standard recipe promotes consistency in product and ultimately leads to customer satisfaction. There is nothing worse than going to a restaurant and enjoying a fabulous meal and returning the next week to repeat the experience only to find that the product is completely different. Having standard recipes and properly training staff to follow the standard recipe in preparation will prevent inconsistency.

Standard recipes should be written in edible portion form. Products should be measured or weighed after they are rid of trim components such as the core and skin of an apple, or the fat and trim of a filet. If a recipe is prepared using the same quality and quantity of ingredients in their edible form and using a prescribed method of preparation, a standardized and consistent product will always result. A *standard yield* is the expected quantity of food that results from a standard recipe. It can be stated in the total quantity of food the recipe produces, such as 3 gallons of clam chowder, or by the number of portions it produces, such as 48–8 oz. bowls.

A *standard portion* is the consistent quantity of product served to each person each time it is served. Maintaining a standard portion through portion control tools such as scoops, ladles, a standard serving bowl, or count promotes consistency and customer satisfaction, and aids in insuring a business' profit. Methods of standardizing portion sizes are discussed in Chapter 11.

Determining the Standard Portion Cost

The process of calculating the *Standard Portion Cost* of a menu item is used by foodservice operations to determine how much the prepared menu item actually cost the business to purchase and to present on a plate. Prior to setting a selling price for a menu item, it is extremely important that the chef/manager know exactly how much the food or beverage item cost the business to prepare. As defined in Chapter 6, "Food Cost" is the total dollar amount spent to purchase the products needed to produce a food item to be sold. "Beverage Cost" is the total dollar amount spent to purchase the products needed to produce a beverage item to be sold. Food and Beverage Costs combined are referred to as "Cost of Sales." How does a chef determine the cost of preparing a menu item when some items are made from scratch using standard recipes, and other items are purchased ready to sell? A combination of both of these practices is also used at times. There are four methods that can help the chef/manager to calculate Standard Portion Costs of both food and beverage menu items. The four methods of determining a standard portion cost are:

1. Cost per Unit Method
2. Yield Test
3. Cooking Loss Test
4. Standard Recipe

One, two, three, or all four of these methods can be used to determine a standard plate cost. A *standard plate cost* is the total cost of the product needed to produce a menu listing.

The "Cost per Unit" Method

Due to the improvement of product processing and the preparation of food and beverage items by suppliers, an increasing number of products are now purchased in ready to use, edible portion form. *Edible portion* is defined as the form in which the product is served. Little or nothing needs to be done to prepare a product in its edible portion form. Purchasing a prepared cheese cake that needs only slicing; a case of 6 oz. chicken breasts needing only to be cooked; or a case of 24–10 oz. bottles of sparkling water that need only to be opened; are examples or edible portion. These products are already in their "edible portion", servable form. The only procedure the chef needs to perform to "make ready" this product is to portion the product, cook the product, or perhaps open and serve the product.

The formula to determine the portion cost of a prepared item purchased in its edible portion form using the Cost/Unit method is:

PURCHASE UNIT COST ÷ NUMBER OF PORTIONS = STANDARD PORTION COST

Example: The chef purchases a prepared cheesecake for $12.50. Using the 12-slice portion marker, the *Standard Portion Cost* is calculated as follows:

Purchase Unit Cost	÷	Number of Portions	=	Standard Portion Cost
$12.50	÷	12	=	$1.04

Example: The chef purchases a case of twenty-four, 6 oz. boneless chicken breasts that costs $26.50. The Standard Portion Cost of each chicken breast is determined as follows:

Purchase Unit Cost	÷	Number of Portions	=	Standard Portion Cost
$26.50	÷	24	=	$1.10

Example: The bar manager purchases a case of twenty-four, 10 oz. bottles of sparkling water at a cost of $12.00. The Standard Portion Cost is calculated in this way:

Purchase Unit Cost	÷	Number of Portions	=	Standard Portion Cost
$12.00	÷	24	=	$0.50

With the use of advanced processing technology, purchasing prepared food and beverage products is becoming commonplace within many different types of foodservice operations. Restaurants often purchase products in an edible portion form, and use the product as an ingredient in their Standard Recipes. Using the Cost per Unit method to determine the standard portion cost of a prepared item within a standard recipe is often just one step in the process of recipe costing. The process of determining the Standard Portion Cost of a Standard Recipe will be more thoroughly explained later in this chapter.

The Yield Test

A *yield test* is a process in which raw product purchased in an "As Purchased" form is broken down into edible product and waste. *As Purchased* is defined as the form of the purchased product that needs some preparation before it is ready to be served in its edible portion form. The preparation needed is usually that of trimming waste from the product and separating it from the usable product. Although yield tests are usually performed on raw product, they may also be used on prepared products. A cooking loss test, which is a similar method of breaking product into edible product and waste, is used to determine the "Standard Portion Cost" of products that need to be cooked before portioning. The purpose of a yield test is to determine the yield, the cost per pound, and the cost per portion of a product purchased in an "As Purchased" form.

A yield test can be performed on a variety of food and beverage items: fresh produce (a case of green beans), poultry (a turkey), seafood or meat (a 10 lb. beef tenderloin), as well as canned (#10 can chopped tomatoes), bottled (14 oz. artichoke hearts), and frozen items (5 gallons ice cream) that have been prepared prior to purchasing. Many of these products are not 100% usable as they include some waste. The purpose of the yield test is to break down the product into useable product and non-usable waste.

Preparation of the Yield Test Form

The information required to perform a yield test is the As Purchased Cost (the cost of the product when purchased), the As Purchased Weight (the weight of the product when purchased), and the Standard Portion Size (the size of the serving in ounces). The Standard Recipe and appropriate purchasing documents can supply this information. Figure 7.1 illustrates how a yield test would be performed on a 25 lb. case of fresh green beans.

As Purchased Cost per Pound

The process to calculate the As Purchased Cost per Pound is:

Formula:

AS PURCHASED COST	÷	AS PURCHASED WEIGHT	=	AS PURCHASED COST PER POUND
Green Beans: $18.00	÷	25 lb.	=	$0.72/lb.

YIELD TEST STANDARD PORTION COST FORM			MENU LISTING: Accompaniment				
PRODUCT: Green Beans			STANDARD PORTION SIZE IN OZ.: 3				
AS PURCHASED COST: $18.00		AS PURCHASED WEIGHT IN LB.: 25			AS PURCHASED COST/LB.: $0.72		
PRODUCT USE	WEIGHT	YIELD %	NUMBER OF PORTIONS	EDIBLE COST/LB.	EDIBLE COST/PORTION	COST FACTOR PER LB.	COST FACTOR PER PORTION
	LB.						
TOTAL WEIGHT:	25	100.0%					
TRIM LOSS:	3	12.0%					
EDIBLE PRODUCT:	22	88.0%	117	$0.82	$0.15	1.139	0.208

FIGURE 7.1 Yield Test Form: Case of Green Beans

Product Break Down

Although a yield test is normally performed in a kitchen or laboratory setting, the resulting information is also used by management to both cost and purchase product. Once the product is broken down into edible product and waste, the edible yield % for the specification of the product can be determined.

Edible Yield %

The *Edible Yield* % represents the part of the product that is useable. If the chef/manager maintains quality standards when purchasing, the edible yield should remain fairly consistent. The Edible Yield % is important in both the costing and purchasing processes.

The formula to calculate the Edible Yield % is:

Formula:

$$[(\text{EDIBLE WEIGHT} \div \text{AS PURCHASED WEIGHT}) \times 100] = \text{EDIBLE YIELD \%}$$

Example:

Green Beans: [(22 lb.   ÷   25 lb.)   × 100] = 88%

As indicated in the break down of the case of green beans, the case of green beans was not 100% useable. The chef needs to separate the waste from the edible product to be able to determine, not only how many portions the case of green beans will yield, but also to be able to determine a "true portion cost." The chef must be certain that all waste and the edible yield % have been taken into consideration in order to insure adequate product and profit.

Number of Portions

After the product has been broken down and the edible yield has been determined, the number of edible portions can be determined. The case of green beans delivered 22 lb. of edible product. If the chef were to serve the Standard Portion of 3 oz., how many portions would be available? Determining the number of portions is a two-step process:

Step A

Formula:

POUNDS OF EDIBLE WEIGHT	×	16 OZ.	=	TOTAL OUNCES
Green Beans: 22 lb.	×	16 oz.	=	352 oz.

Step B

Formula:

TOTAL OUNCES	÷	PORTION SIZE	=	NUMBER OF PORTIONS
Green Beans: 352 oz.	÷	3 oz.	=	117 (117.333)

Step A illustrates that the case of green beans yields 352 ounces of edible product. Step B illustrates that if the chef were to serve 3 oz. portions, the case of green beans should provide 117 portions of product.

The Edible Cost per Pound

It is important that the chef/manager calculate the Edible Cost per Pound. The Edible Cost per Pound is how much each pound of edible product costs the foodservice operation to purchase when it is purchased in the As Purchased (AP) form. For example, if the chef/manager determines that the process of cleaning and trimming a case of fresh green beans is too labor intensive, he/she may consider purchasing green beans in a frozen, prepared form, where no cleaning and trimming is needed.

When looking at the "As Purchased Cost" of $18.00 for the case of Green Beans and the "As Purchased Weight" of 25 lb., we can determine an "As Purchased Cost per Pound" of $0.72 per Pound. However, as identified in the product breakdown, the case of green beans does not yield an edible yield of 25 lb., it only yields 22 lb. due to "waste". The formula for calculating the Edible Cost per Pound is:

AS PURCHASED COST ÷ EDIBLE WEIGHT = EDIBLE COST PER POUND

Green Beans: $18.00 ÷ 22 lb. = $0.82/lb.

The chef/manager can now compare the Edible Cost per Pound of $0.82 to the $0.88 cost per pound for green beans in the frozen, prepared form. This is form of "cost analysis." Once the "cost analysis" has been done, the chef/manager must also consider quality of product and preparation time. The Edible Cost per Pound provides the chef/manager with the information necessary to make important food cost decisions.

The Edible Cost per Portion

The Edible Cost per Portion is the cost of each portion when the product has been purchased in AP form. As previously determined, the Edible Cost per Pound tells the chef/manager how much 1 lb. (1 lb. = 16 oz.) of the edible product costs the business to purchase. However, since the chef is selling the green beans in 3 oz. portions rather than 16 oz. portions, he/she must calculate the cost per 3 oz. portion. To calculate the Edible Cost per Portion, the chef uses the number of portions determined previously.

Formula:

AS PURCHASED ÷ NUMBER OF = EDIBLE COST
COST PORTIONS PER PORTION

$18.00 ÷ 117 = $0.15/portion

By preparing a yield test on a case of fresh green beans, we determine that a 3 oz. portion costs $0.15 to prepare.

Cost Factors

A *cost factor* is a ratio that illustrates the relationship between the "Edible Cost" and the original "As Purchased" price. The Cost Factor can be illustrated either in decimal or percentage form. There are two types of cost factors: the Cost Factor per Pound and the Cost Factor per Portion.

The *Cost Factor* per Pound illustrates the relationship between the Edible Cost per Pound and the As Purchased Cost per Pound.

Formula:

EDIBLE COST	÷	AS PURCHASE	=	COST FACTOR
PER POUND		COST PER POUND		PER POUND

Example:

Green Beans: $0.82   ÷ $0.72   =   1.139 (113.9%)

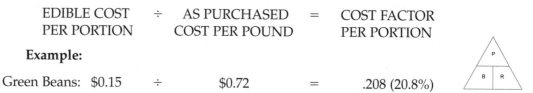

This means that the Edible Cost per Pound is 1.139 times greater than the As Purchased Cost per Pound, or that the Edible Cost per Pound is 113.9% of the As Purchased Cost per Pound.

The *Cost Factor per Portion* illustrates the relationship between the Edible Cost per Portion and the As Purchased Cost per Pound

Formula:

EDIBLE COST	÷	AS PURCHASED	=	COST FACTOR
PER PORTION		COST PER POUND		PER PORTION

Example:

Green Beans: $0.15   ÷ $0.72   =   .208 (20.8%)

The Edible Cost per Portion is 0.208 times the original As Purchased Cost per Pound, or the Edible Cost per Portion is 20.8% of the original As Purchased Cost per Pound. It is understood that the "As Purchased Costs" increase and decrease on a regular basis, due to a change in season, supply and demand, the popularity of the products, etc. It is therefore impossible to prepare a yield test on a case of green beans every time the As Purchased Cost fluctuates. It is important to understand the relationship between the "Edible Cost" and the "As Purchased Cost" originally paid, to be able to recalculate the new Edible Cost, without performing a new yield test whenever the "As Purchased Cost" changes.

Using the Cost Factors

Another case of green beans is purchased at a new price of $20.00 per case. Using the calculations derived in Figure 7.1 and changing the "As Purchased Cost per Pound" to $0.80 per pound ($20.00 ÷ 25 lb.), determine the new Edible Cost per Pound and the new Edible Cost per Portion. The formula to calculate the new Edible Cost per Pound is:

COST FACTOR   ×   NEW AS PURCHASED   =   NEW EDIBLE COST
PER POUND   COST PER POUND   PER POUND

Green Beans: 1.139   × $0.80   = $0.91/lb.

The formula to calculate the new Edible Cost per Portion is:

COST FACTOR   ×   NEW AS PURCHASED   =   NEW EDIBLE COST
PER PORTION   COST PER POUND   PER PORTION

Green Beans: 0.208   × $0.80   = $0.17/lb.

Even though the increase in cost may only be a few cents, these few cents represent money that foodservice operators once found in the profit column. The chef/manager needs to pay attention to the effect that the increase or decrease of As Purchase Costs has on the foodservice operation's food cost. Cost Factors are tools to help the chef/manager determine changes without having to perform additional yield tests.

The Cooking Loss Test

Unlike the yield test where the number of portions and the costs are determined prior to the restaurant's cooking process; the cooking loss test is performed on products that need to be cooked before portioning and serving. *Cooking Loss Tests* are most often prepared on whole roasts (lamb, beef, pork) and poultry (turkey, chicken). The breakdown of the number of portions and their costs are determined after the cooking process. The actual procedure of the cooking loss test is performed in a kitchen or laboratory setting. The information is then provided to the chef/manager to allow him/her to determine the edible yield %, the number of portions, the Edible Cost per Pound, the Edible Cost per Portion, and the cost factors of the cooked product. Most of the steps in preparing the Cooking Loss Test are very similar to those applied in preparing a Yield Test.

Preparation of the Cooking Loss Test Form

First examine the required information given in the Standard Recipe and the purchasing information provided. Additional information concerning cooking time is also needed when preparing a cooking loss test. Many chefs will perform several tests on the same type of product, cooking them at different temperatures and for different lengths of time, in order to evaluate the product yield. Figure 7.2 illustrates the results of a Cooking Loss Test performed on a 9 lb. leg of lamb.

As Purchased Cost per Pound

The As Purchased Cost per Pound refers to how much the product costs per pound. The following formula is used to calculate the As Purchased Cost per Pound:

COOKING LOSS STANDARD PORTION COST FORM

MENU LISTING: Roasted Lamb with Rosemary

PRODUCT: Leg of Lamb

STANDARD PORTION SIZE IN OZ.: 6

AS PURCHASED COST: $20.25 | AS PURCHASED WEIGHT IN LB.: 9

AS PURCHASED COST/LB.: $2.25

PRODUCT USE	WEIGHT IN LB.	YIELD %	NUMBER OF PORTIONS	EDIBLE COST/LB.	EDIBLE COST/PORTION.	COST FACTOR PER LB.	COST FACTOR PER PORTION
TOTAL WEIGHT	9.00	100%					
TRIM LOSS	3.50	39.0%					
PRE-COOKED WEIGHT	5.50	61.0%					
LOSS IN COOKING	1.50	16.7%					
TRIM AFTER COOKING	0.25	2.8%					
EDIBLE PRODUCT:	3.75	42%	10	$5.40	$2.03	2.4	0.902

FIGURE 7.2 Cooking Loss Standard Portion Cost Form

Formula:

AS PURCHASED COST	÷	AS PURCHASED WEIGHT	=	AS PURCHASED COST PER POUND
Leg of Lamb: $20.25	÷	9 lb.	=	$2.25/lb.

Product Breakdown

The Product Breakdown consists of weighing, trimming and cooking, and weighing and trimming again after cooking to achieve the edible product weight.

Edible Yield %

The *Edible Yield* % is the percent of the product that is servable. When looking at the total cost and weight of the leg of lamb, we are led to believe that the 9 lb. leg of lamb is going to yield 9 lb. of edible product. But as we have identified in Figure 7.2, after the leg of lamb is boned, trimmed, and cooked, it only yields 3.75 lb. of servable product. The chef can only use just about one third of the product's "As Purchased Weight" in the preparation of the menu item. The formula to calculate the Edible Yield % for the Leg of Lamb is:

Formula:

EDIBLE WEIGHT IN POUNDS	÷	AS PURCHASED WEIGHT	=	EDIBLE YIELD %
Lamb: 3.75 lb.	÷	9 lb.	=	0.42 (42%)

The Edible Yield % listed in the specification of the product purchased will usually aid the chef/manager to determine how much product is needed to feed a prescribed number of customers.

Number of Portions

Once it is known that the 9 lb. Leg of Lamb produces 3.75 lb. of edible product, the next step is to determine the number of portions derived from the Leg of Lamb. A 6 oz. Standard Portion size is used in the following example. There are two steps to this process.

Step A

Formula:

POUNDS OF EDIBLE WEIGHT	×	16 OZ.	=	TOTAL OUNCES
Lamb 3.75 lb.	×	16 oz.	=	60 ounces

Step B

Formula:

TOTAL OUNCES	÷	PORTION SIZE	=	NUMBER OF PORTIONS
60 ounces	÷	6 oz.	=	10 portions

The Edible Cost per Pound

The Edible Cost per Pound is derived by dividing the "As Purchased Cost" of the product by the edible weight. Knowing the Edible Cost per Pound helps the chef/manager to determine whether or not the "As Purchased" form of the product is the most cost effective from to purchase.

Formula:

	AS PURCHASED COST	÷	EDIBLE WEIGHT	=	EDIBLE COST PER POUND
Lamb:	$20.25	÷	3.75 lb.	=	$5.40/lb.

The Edible Cost per Portion

A knowledge of the Edible Cost per Portion ensures that the chef/manager knows exactly how much each portion of product served costs to prepare. To calculate the Edible Cost per Portion, the chef divides the As Purchased Cost by the Number of Portions.

Formula:

	AS PURCHASED COST	÷	NUMBER OF PORTIONS	=	EDIBLE COST PER PORTION
Lamb:	$20.25	÷	10	=	$2.03 per portion

When determining the standard portion cost of a menu item, be sure to take into consideration all waste and cooking loss.

Cost Factors

Cost Factors show the relationship between the Edible Cost per Pound or the Edible Cost per Portion and the original As Purchased Cost per Pound. Since the costs of products fluctuate, determining Cost Factors can help the chef/manager to adjust costs as needed.

The Cost Factor per Pound illustrates the relationship between the Edible Cost per Pound and the As Purchased Cost per Pound.

Formula:

EDIBLE COST PER POUND	÷	AS PURCHASED COST PER POUND	=	COST FACTOR PER POUND
Lamb: $5.40	÷	$2.25	=	2.4 (240%)

The Edible Cost is 2.4 times greater than the original As Purchased Cost per Pound. In other words, the boneless lamb's Edible Cost per Pound is 240% of the As Purchased Cost per Pound.

The Cost Factor per Portion illustrates the relationship between the Edible Cost per Portion and the As Purchased Cost per Pound.

Formula:

EDIBLE COST PER PORTION	÷	AS PURCHASED COST PER POUND	=	COST FACTOR PER PORTION
Lamb: $2.03	÷	$2.25	=	.902 (90.2%)

This means that the Edible Cost/Portion is .902 times the original As Purchased Cost per Pound, or that the Edible Cost per Portion is 90.2% of the As Purchased Cost per Pound.

Using the Cost Factors

If the chef/manager purchases another Leg of Lamb weighing 9.5 lb. with an As Purchased Cost of $21.85, the new As Purchased Cost per Pound can be determined at $2.30 per pound ($21.85 ÷ 9.5 lb.). Using the Cost Factors previously determined, the chef/manager can calculate the new Edible Cost per Pound and the new Edible Cost per Portion. The formula to determine the new Edible Cost per Pound follows.

Formula:

COST FACTOR PER POUND	×	NEW AS PURCHASED COST PER POUND	=	NEW EDIBLE COST PER POUND
Lamb: 2.4	×	$2.30/lb.	=	$5.52/lb.

The new Edible Cost per Pound can then be used to perform a cost analysis when purchasing other cuts of lamb. The formula to determine the new Edible Cost per Portion is:

COST FACTOR PER PORTION	×	NEW AS PURCHASED COST PER POUND	=	NEW EDIBLE COST PER PORTION
Lamb: 0.902	×	$2.30/lb.	=	$2.08/portion

By using Cost Factors, the chef/manager can quickly identify any changes in portion costs and can adjust menu prices as needed.

Recipe Costing

Most foodservice establishments have developed *standard recipes* for the menu items they offer for sale. These recipes include the name of the menu item, the standard yield, the standard portion, the name, and quantity of ingredients needed, and the standard procedures involved in preparing the recipe. Because most recipes include several ingredients, it is often a time consuming process to calculate how much a recipe costs to prepare. But the process is necessary, especially for the inexperienced foodservice worker.

Recipe Costing is a way the chef/manager can determine the Standard Portion Cost of a menu item. By knowing the entire cost of the recipe, the business can determine the standard portion cost and an adequate selling price, in order to insure that all costs in preparing that recipe are covered and that a profit is realized. Figure 7.3 illustrates the Standard Costing form for a side order of Three Bean Salad. The recommended steps to determine the Standard Portion Cost of a Standard Recipe follow:

Step 1: Readying the Costing Form

Fill in the required information such as the name of the recipe, standard yield, standard portion and the ingredients (including garnishes), and their exact quantities from the standard recipe. The latest "As Purchased Cost" of each ingredient should be posted in the Invoice Cost per Unit column.

Step 2: Calculate the Individual Ingredient Cost

The "individual ingredient cost" informs the chef/manager of the price of each ingredient within the standard recipe. By knowing the cost of each ingredient, the chef/manager can identify the high cost items that need special tracking. The formula to calculate the Individual Ingredient Cost is:

Formula:

INGREDIENT QUANTITY × PRICE = INDIVIDUAL INGREDIENT COST

As illustrated, calculating the "Individual Ingredient Cost" is a simple multiplication process; however, there are several procedures to thoroughly consider before performing the calculation.

Standard Recipe Cost Card

RECIPE NAME: Three Bean Salad						STANDARD PORTION: 6 oz.				
STANDARD YIELD: 30						PORTION CONTROL TOOL: #6 scoop				
RECIPE		EY%	AS PURCHASED			INVOICE		RECIPE		INDIVIDUAL INGREDIENT COST
QTY	UNIT		QTY	UNIT	INGREDIENT	COST	UNIT	COST	UNIT	COST
3	lb.	88.0%	3.50	lb.	Beans, fresh yellow	$ 0.80	lb.	$0.80	lb.	$ 2.80
3	lb.	88.0%	3.50	lb.	Beans, fresh green	$18.00	25 lb.	$0.72	lb	$ 2.52
2	lb.	100.0%	2.00	lb.	Beans, red kidney	$ 2.05	#10	$0.32	lb.	$ 0.64
1	lb.	80.0%	1.25	lb.	Peppers, red	$ 2.25	lb.	$2.25	lb.	$ 2.81
4	hd.	100.0%	4.00	hd.	Lettuce, green leaf	$18.80	24hd.	$0.78	hd.	$ 3.12
2	qt.	100.0%	2.00	qt.	Olive oil	$14.75	gal.	$3.69	qt.	$ 7.38
1	qt.	100.0%	1.00	qt.	Vinegar, red wine	$10.60	4 gal.	$0.66	qt.	$ 0.66
4	oz.	100.0%	4.00	oz.	Sugar, granulated	$20.20	50#	$0.03	oz.	$ 0.12
1	bun.	100.0%	1.00	bun.	Basil	$14.40	12 bun.	$1.20	bun.	$ 1.20
1	bun.	100.0%	1.00	bun.	Oregano	$ 1.00	bun.	$1.00	bun.	$ 1.00
0.5	tsp.	100.0%	0.50	tsp.	Marjoram	$ 2.20	12 oz.		tsp.	Q
3	clv.	100.0%	3.00	clv.	Garlic	$ 1.75	lb.		clv.	Q
1	tsp.	100.0%	1.00	tsp.	salt	$ 0.42	26 oz.		tsp.	Q
1	tsp.	100.0%	1.00	tsp.	Pepper	$ 3.59	lb.		tsp.	Q

Garnish:

Method of Preparation:

Total Ingredient Cost:	$ 22.25
Q Factor %: 5.0%	$ 1.11
Recipe Cost:	$ 23.36
Portion Cost:	$ 0.78
Additional Cost:	
Additional Cost:	
Additional Cost:	
Total Plate Cost:	$ 0.78
Desired Cost %:	30.0%
Preliminary Selling Price:	$ 2.60
Actual Selling Price:	$ 2.75
Actual Cost %:	28.4%

Equipment Required:

FIGURE 7.3 Three Bean Salad Costing Form

WebCOM™

Edible Yield %

It is important to understand that most standard recipes are written in an edible portion form. In order to achieve the correct *standard yield* using the stated standard portion size, the quantity of ingredients listed must be measured in edible portion form (not in As Purchased form). Writing Standard Recipes in edible portion form ensures a consistent product. Let us examine the recipe in Figure 7.3 that calls for 3 lb. of green beans. Please note that it is calling for 3 lb. of green beans that have already been cleaned and snipped. Knowing that the Standard Recipes are written in edible portion quantities will insure the standard yield and the standard portion. Three pounds of edible product is 3 lb. of edible product, no matter who prepares the recipe. When calculating the Individual Ingredient Cost, the chef/manager must decide whether to use the Edible Yield % to determine the actual "As Purchased amounts." At this point, it should be quite obvious that 3 lb. of As Purchased green beans do not yield 3 lb. of edible green beans. It would take more. But, how much more?

This is where a yield test can be valuable. Although time consuming, it is possible to prepare a yield test for every ingredient in a recipe. However, the more familiar the chef becomes with preparing the ingredients, the more familiar the chef will become with how much edible product is derived from an "As Purchased" product. The chef may also acquire the edible yield % from the purveyors who supply their products or from published guidelines prepared by the US Department of Agriculture. Appendix C provides a partial list of recommended Edible Yield %s from the USDA.

In the yield test example, we broke down a 25 lb. case of green beans into edible product and waste. We also illustrated how to calculate an edible yield %. An edible yield % is that part of an "As Purchased" product which is actually edible. The edible yield % of 88% was previously determined in the yield test in this chapter by dividing the 22 lb. of usable product by the 25 lb. total weight.

Once it is determined that an edible yield % is needed for an ingredient, post it to the Edible Yield % column. The process now is to determine how much product must be purchased to yield the quantity of product stated in the original recipe. It is important to understand that the "As Purchased" quantity should be used to calculate the Individual Ingredient cost of each recipe ingredient. The foodservice operation will need to purchase that amount to achieve the necessary amount of edible product.

As Purchased Quantity

The following formula is used to determine how many pounds of green beans are needed to yield the 3 lb. required by the recipe.

Formula:

RECIPE AMOUNT	÷	EDIBLE YIELD %	=	AS PURCHASED QUANTITY
Green Beans: 3 lb.	÷	88%(.88)	=	3.5 lb. (3.41)

The 3 lb. originally called for in the recipe are only part of the whole amount needed to produce a 3 lb. yield. In order to obtain the yield and portion size of the standard recipe, it must be understood that the Recipe Quantity is stated in the edible portion form. The chef would need to purchase 3.5 lb. of green beans to yield the 3 lb. called for in the recipe.

Invoice Cost per Unit

Post the purchase price and unit of each ingredient to the Invoice Cost per Unit column. Most foodservice operators use the current market price of ingredients in this column. These prices are normally taken from the invoice that accompanies the order when delivered (Chapter 9), and are based on the purchase unit stated on the product specification (Chapter 8).

Recipe Cost per Unit

Before calculating the "Individual Ingredient Cost," the preparer should be certain that the quantity needed and price of each ingredient are stated in the same unit. If the quantity and the price are in the same unit of measure, multiply these two numbers to derive the Individual Ingredient cost. In Figure 7.3 for example, both the Recipe Quantity and the Invoice Cost of the Yellow Beans are stated in the same unit of measure. Simply multiply 3.5 lb.×$0.80 per pound = $2.80.

If the quantity and cost are not stated in the same unit, the preparer can use the Recipe Cost per Unit column to convert the Invoice Cost per Unit to the Recipe Unit that is called for in the Standard Recipe. The Recipe Cost per Unit column is only used when the Invoice Cost per Unit is different than the Recipe Quantity per Unit. To convert the Invoice Cost per Unit to the Recipe Cost per Unit, the chef/manager must be familiar with measurement equivalents in weight and volume including container sizes. (Appendix C)

If the Invoice Cost per Unit is $18.00 per 25 lb. case, and the recipe quantity per unit is also in pounds, merely calculate the cost per pound.

Formula:

INVOICE COST	÷	INVOICE QUANTITY	=	RECIPE COST PER UNIT
Green Beans: $18.00	÷	25 lb.	=	$0.72/lb.

Post the new Recipe Cost per Unit and proceed to solve the Individual Ingredient Cost by multiplying the As Purchased Quantity by the Recipe Cost per Unit.

Formula:

AS PURCHASED QUANTITY PER UNIT	×	RECIPE COST PER UNIT	=	INDIVIDUAL INGREDIENT COST
Green Beans: 3.5 lb.	×	$0.72/lb	=	$2.52

Now let us examine the example of Red Kidney Beans that come in a #10 can. The chef/manager must know the yield of the product from the different size cans. (Appendix B) Normally a #10 yield between 6.0 and 7.5 lb. of product. To solve for the Recipe Cost per Unit, the chef/manager would take the invoice cost divided by the invoice quantity.

Formula:

INVOICE COST	÷	INVOICE QUANTITY	=	RECIPE COST PER UNIT
Red Kidney Beans: $2.05	÷	6.5 lb.	=	$0.32/lb

Now the chef/manager can multiply the Recipe Quantity, which is 2 lb. in this recipe, by the Recipe Cost per Unit, to get the Individual Ingredient Cost for Red Kidney Beans.

Formula:

$$\text{RECIPE QUANTITY} \times \begin{array}{c}\text{RECIPE COST}\\\text{PER UNIT}\end{array} = \begin{array}{c}\text{INDIVIDUAL INGREDIENT}\\\text{COST}\end{array}$$

Red Kidney Beans: 2 lb. $\times$ $0.32 Per Pound = $0.64

Remember that if the Recipe Amount per Unit is in the same unit as the Invoice Cost per Unit, a figure is not needed in the Recipe Cost per Unit column.

Individual Ingredient Cost: The Last Step

To calculate the Individual Ingredient Cost simply multiply the Ingredient Quantity (Recipe Quantity or As Purchased Quantity if needed), by the Cost (Invoice Cost per Unit or Recipe Cost per Unit if utilized). When calculating the individual ingredient cost, it is important to understand that both quantity and cost must be in the same unit of measure. An Individual Ingredient Cost cannot be determined for all ingredients.

Calculating the Individual Ingredient Cost calls for a great deal of knowledge about food products. Although a time consuming effort, it is extremely important to determine the Individual Ingredient Cost to guarantee that a foodservice operation is charging an adequate price to cover product cost.

Step 3: Totaling the Individual Ingredient Costs

Once the individual ingredient costs are calculated, total the Individual Ingredient Cost column. The Total Ingredient Cost is the total cost of all the ingredients for which the chef/manager is able to determine a cost.

Step 4: Calculating the "Q Factor" (the Questionable Ingredient Factor)

There are certain ingredients to which an actual cost cannot be assigned due to the small quantity used. In fact, in some cases, the ingredients are actually immeasurable. It is in these situations that a "Q Factor" should be utilized. A *Q Factor* is an immeasurable ingredient cost. It is assigned to the cost of the Standard Recipe to cover the costs of ingredients which are impossible, or too time consuming, to calculate. It must be realized that even though an individual ingredient cost cannot be determined, the ingredient still costs the business money to purchase and to use. It is a cost that needs to be accounted for even if it is an estimated cost.

A "Q Factor" can be utilized in the following cases:

1. when pinches, dashes, or "to taste" type of measurements are needed;

2. if a recipe ingredient (such as salt) calls for a very small quantity (.25 tsp.). This quantity is measurable, however salt is a low cost item. It is difficult to calculate an actual cost for such a small quantity, so chefs and managers will cover their costs by including them in the Q Factor. The purchase of salt costs the business money, and that cost must be considered so that it may be passed on to the consumer.

3. to cover excessive costs caused by an incorrect measurement, or even to absorb some of the costs due to seasonal fluctuations.

4. to account for the cost of condiments used. Condiments are often included in the Q Factor rather that in the Individual Ingredient Cost. Since condiments are often placed on tables for customer use, it is much more practical to use the Q Factor than to determine how much each customer uses and what the cost per portion of each condiment is to the foodservice operation.

The "Q Factor" is usually calculated based upon a percentage of the Total Ingredient Cost of those costs that are measurable. Normally, chef/managers will choose a percentage between 1% and 15% of the Total Ingredient Cost. The more accurate the calculation of each ingredient cost, the lower the percentage usually added to the recipe. The less accurate the calculation, the higher the percentage used. Some chefs elect not to determine the individual ingredient cost of spices and herbs in a recipe. Instead they increase the Q Factor % to compensate. Other chefs think this outrageous and take the time to determine the exact cost of all small ingredients. The choice of using the Q Factor percentage is up to the chef/manager costing the recipe. The Q Factor is used to insure that the costs of all ingredients are covered while maintaining a fair price for the customer.

It is common practice to include a Q Factor in the cost of the Recipe even if there are no immeasurable ingredients within the recipe. Some foodservice operations will use the same Q Factor % for every recipe, while others will assign a Q Factor % based on the individual ingredients within each standard recipe.

The Q Factor is calculated by multiplying the Total Ingredient Cost by the Q Factor % chosen. In Figure 7.3, a Q factor of 5% has been selected. The Q Factor $ amount would be calculated as follows:

Formula:

$$\text{TOTAL INGREDIENT COST} \times \text{Q FACTOR \%} = \text{Q FACTOR \$ AMOUNT}$$

Three Bean Salad: $22.25 $\times$ 5%(.05) = $1.11

The Q Factor $ can range from a few cents to a few dollars, depending upon the Q Factor Cost % and the Standard Yield of the recipe. Including a Q Factor in the recipe costing process rarely increases a Standard Portion Cost by more than a few cents, but those "few cents" add up to a noticeable overall food cost increase.

Step 5: Calculating the Recipe Cost

The Recipe Cost is the total cost of measurable ingredients and the estimated immeasurable ingredients. It is an educated estimate of how much the Standard Recipe costs the foodservice operation to prepare.

Formula:

$$\text{TOTAL INGREDIENT COST} + \text{Q FACTOR DOLLARS} = \text{RECIPE COST}$$

Three Bean Salad: $22.25 + $1.1 = $23.36

Step 6: Calculating the Standard Portion Cost

In Step 5 (Calculating the Recipe Cost), we illustrated how much it costs the restaurant to prepare the entire recipe. However, since it is unusual to sell menu items by the recipe as a whole, we must also calculate the Standard Portion Cost of a Standard Recipe.

Formula:

$$\text{RECIPE COST} \div \text{STANDARD YIELD} = \text{STANDARD PORTION COST}$$

Three Bean Salad: $23.36 $\div$ 30 = $0.78

It is these six major steps that are needed to determine the Standard Portion Cost of a standard recipe. Once each of the Standard Portion Costs have been determined, the Additional Portion Cost can be used to total Standard Portion Costs to get the *Standard Plate Cost* (Total Cost) of the Menu Item.

As the chef sets the Standard Plate Cost of each menu item listed, he/she may very well utilize all of the previously mentioned costing methods within one sales menu item. Example: A menu item of boneless Leg of Lamb is accompanied by scalloped potatoes, fresh green beans, and applesauce. The chef has to perform a cooking loss test to determine the portion cost of the leg of lamb; cost out a recipe to determine the portion cost for the scalloped potatoes; perform a yield test to get a portion cost for green beans; and calculate the cost per unit of the applesauce.

It is important in Menu Costing that thought be given to each and every item provided to the customer. The cost of rolls, butter, and garnishes must be included. The more the chef/manager uses the prescribed methods, the more expertise he/she will attain in costing menu items.

Setting the Preliminary Selling Price

It is extremely important and strongly recommended that before setting a selling price for a menu item, that one of the aforementioned Standard Portion Costing methods be utilized. If the Standard Portion Cost of a product or menu item is unknown, it is nearly impossible to successfully set a Menu Selling Price that insures a profitable menu and a successful foodservice operation. Once the Standard Portion Cost of a menu item is calculated, then and only then, should the chef/manager start to consider how much to charge for the menu item.

In order to determine the actual selling price to be stated on the menu, we must first determine the "Preliminary Selling Price." The *Preliminary Selling Price* is the least amount of money that a foodservice operation should charge for a menu item in order to guarantee that all costs are covered (food, beverage, labor overhead, profit). There are several mathematical approaches that one might use in setting the Preliminary Selling Price. Two of these methods will be discussed.

Desired Cost %

The *Desired Cost %* is the overall cost percentage that a restaurant is striving to achieve (by setting control standards throughout the cycle of food and beverage cost control). It is the ideal cost percentage attainable when all standards have been maintained and the purchase prices have remained constant. Normally, the Desired Cost Percentage can be 2 to 4 percentage points below the Actual Cost Percentage. The Actual Cost Percentage is the cost percentage that is determined by implementing the Cost of Sales formula. The Desired Cost Percentage can be looked at as a goal of the restaurant operation.

When setting the Preliminary Selling Price for a food item the *Desired Food Cost %* is used. When setting the Preliminary Selling Price for a beverage item, the *Desired Beverage Cost %* is used. Often, restaurateurs will have different Desired Cost % for the different categories of menu items. They may want all their Soups at a 20% Desired Food Cost %, and their Entrées at 28% Desired Food Cost %. The Desired Cost % to strive for is derived from the foodservice operation's historical data as well as the knowledge and experience of the chef/manager.

The examples below include Standard Portion Costs that have been previously determined in the costing explanation in this chapter. These costs will be used to illustrate the Desired Cost % method of calculating a Preliminary Selling Price. The formula for setting the Preliminary Selling Price using the Desired Cost % method is:

Formula:

STANDARD PORTION COST ÷ DESIRED COST % = PRELIMINARY SELLING PRICE

Example: If a side order of Three Bean Salad has a portion cost of $0.78 to prepare, and the Desired Food Cost % is 30%, the Preliminary Selling Price for the 3 oz. portion would be $2.60.

The price is determined as follows:

Formula:

STANDARD PORTION COST	÷	DESIRED FOOD COST%	=	PRELIMINARY SELLING PRICE
Three Bean Salad: $0.78	÷	30%(.3)	=	$2.60

Example: If a slice of cheesecake has a Standard Portion Cost of $1.04 and the chef wants to maintain a 25% Desired Food Cost, the Preliminary Selling Price for the slice of cheesecake would be $4.16.

Formula:

STANDARD PORTION COST	÷	DESIRED FOOD COST%	=	PRELIMINARY SELLING PRICE
Cheesecake: $1.04	÷	25%(.25)	=	$4.16

How does the Desired Cost % method insure that all of our costs are covered? An example and explanation follow.

Three Bean Salad	One Sold	10 Sold	100 Sold
Sales	$2.60	$26.00	$260.00
Food Cost	$0.78	$ 7.80	$ 78.00
Gross Profit	$1.82	$18.20	$182.00

When breaking down the sales price into Food Cost and Gross Profit, (Labor, Overhead, Profit), we conclude that every portion of Three Bean Salad sold contributes $2.03 to the Gross Profit of the foodservice operation. Gross Profit is the amount of money remaining after the business pays the Cost of Sales (Food and Beverage Cost). Although the Gross Profit from one menu item may not seem like much money, the gross profit from the sale of 100 portions or from the total menu items is sizable. It is a simple concept to ensure that all the costs are covered. Remember, in order to make this work, cost control standards must be in place.

		Desired Food Cost %		Pricing Factor
100%	÷	40%	=	2.5
	÷	38%	=	2.632
	÷	36%	=	2.778
	÷	35%	=	2.857
	÷	34%	=	2.941
	÷	32%	=	3.125
	÷	30%	=	3.333
	÷	28%	=	3.571
	÷	26%	=	3.845
	÷	25%	=	4.0
	÷	24%	=	4.167
	÷	22%	=	4.545
	÷	20%	=	5.0
	÷	18%	=	5.556
	÷	16%	=	6.25
	÷	15%	=	6.667

FIGURE 7.4 Pricing Factors

Pricing Factor

The second method used to determine the Preliminary Selling Price is called the *Pricing Factor*. Divide 100% by the Desired Food Cost % to arrive at the Pricing Factor. (Figure 7.4)

Using the previous examples, we see that the Three Bean Salad generates a 30% Desired Food Cost % and the Cheesecake a 25% Desired Food Cost %. The formula for determining the Pricing Factor for each of the Desired Food Cost %s previously stated is:

Formula:

	100%	÷ DESIRED FOOD COST %	=	PRICING FACTOR
Three Bean salad:	100% ÷	30%	=	3.333
Cheesecake:	100% ÷	25%	=	4.000

In a restaurant that wishes to maintain a 30% or 25% Desired Food Cost, the chef/manager would multiply the Standard Portion Cost by the 3.33 or 4 pricing factor to arrive at a preliminary selling price.

Formula

	STANDARD PORTION COST	×	PRICING FACTOR	=	PRELIMINARY SELLING PRICE
Three Bean Salad:	$.78	×	3.333	=	$2.60
Cheese Cake:	$1.04	×	4	=	$4.16

The Pricing Factor provides the foodservice operator with the same Preliminary Selling Price as does the Desired Food Cost % method. Some chef/managers find the Pricing Factor method easier to work with. The Preliminary Selling Price is the smallest amount a business might charge to reach its Desired (Food or Beverage) Cost %, assuming again that all cost control standards are met.

Determining the Menu Selling Price

Once the chef/manager has determined the Preliminary Selling Price, it is time to set the price that will be stated on the menu. The *Menu Selling Price*, unlike the Preliminary Selling Price, is not only determined mathematically. Considerations as to potential profit and customer price acceptance are also evaluated. The chef/manager wants to charges as much as possible so that the business makes a maximum profit from every menu item sold.

When a manager says that a restaurant is maintaining a 30% food cost, it must be understood that not every menu item is working at a 30% food cost. The overall menu average is 30%. Some menu items may generate a 20% food cost, while others may be at 35% or 40%. The Preliminary Selling Price guarantees that the Desired Cost % is achieved. Menu items have different cost %s due to the *mark up* (or mark down) that takes place after the Preliminary Selling Price has been determined.

Chef/managers must select a Menu Selling Price that insures a profit, without crossing the line of fairness to customers. Charging prices that are too expensive for the target market will cause customers to go elsewhere. On the other hand, a price decrease might mean an inadequate Gross Profit to pay expenses.

When setting a Menu Selling Price, there are many considerations to evaluate: labor, competition, clientele, atmosphere, location, etc.

Labor

Chef/managers will often make-up the Preliminary Selling Price of menu items that are labor intensive. Products that are labor intensive require more time, care, and skill in preparation than the average product. A good example of a labor intensive item is a Caesar's Salad prepared table side. If the chef were to cost the ingredients of a Caesar's Salad, it would be determined that the ingredients of the salad are not any more expensive than any other salad on the menu; possibly less expensive. So why do restaurants charge so much for a Caesar's Salad prepared table side? It takes more time, labor, and skill to prepare. People enjoy watching the table side preparation of the Caesar's Salad and therefore will be willing to pay more.

Competition

Competition is good. Do not let anyone tell you otherwise. Foodservice operators will often review the menus of competitors to see what they are charging for similar items. This can be a way of helping to lock in a Menu Selling Price, however, it should not be the only method utilized. Although competitors often appear to have similar menu items, be careful to examine the quality of ingredients and the portion sizes. Use competitors' prices only as a guide.

Clientele

The clientele of a foodservice operation plays an important part in setting the Menu Selling Price. Foodservice operators who accept credit cards and who have a large percentage of customers who pay with credit cards will often mark up the Menu Selling Prices to pay for service charges. Foodservice operations that cater to the business professional often charge more than those that cater to families. The business professional is thought to have more disposable income or an expense account that may be drawn upon.

Atmosphere

The more formal the style of the foodservice operation, the higher the prices they charge due to Product Differentiation. Product Differentiation refers to the uniqueness of a product. A local pub may be serving a 13 oz. New York Sirloin for $15.50, while a fine dining restaurant just next door offers a 13 oz. New York Sirloin for $24.95. Chances are that the cost of the New York Sirloin is the same to both restaurants, but each has developed its own product differentiation. Traditionally, fine dining foodservice operations charge more than family style dining operations.

Location

Location can play a part in marking up Menu Selling Prices. Various cities and regions of the country have different cost of living standards. Foodservice operations located in a city can charge more for a product than those in a rural community due to increased disposable income and competition.

Psychology of Pricing

The Psychology of Pricing refers to how a customer reacts to the prices on a menu. How does the customer react to a price of $4.95 as compared to one of $5.00? When chef/managers raise their selling prices, they often hesitate to move into a new dollar category. A price of $13.95 raised to $14.25 has a bigger increase perception than one of $14.25 raised to $14.75, even though the first increase is only $0.30 while the second is $0.50. Start the Menu Selling Prices on the lower end of the dollar category, so that when prices have to be adjusted, they can be adjusted once or maybe twice without entering into the next dollar category. A starting price of $12.25 can go to $12.50, $12.75, or $12.95 before entering a new dollar category.

The most important aspect in setting a menu item's selling price is covering the costs of operating the business. First use one of the mathematical methods presented to set the Preliminary Selling Price. Once the Preliminary Selling Price has been determined, adjust the selling price to make sure that it is contributing to the profit of the business and that the price is fair and reasonable to the customer.

Determining a Standard Portion Cost is important to the success of foodservice operations. Using the methods of Cost per Unit, the Yield Test, the Cooking Loss Test, and Recipe Costing, the chef/manager can determine how much the products cost the foodservice operation to produce. Once the Standard Portion Cost is determined, then and only then, can the chef/manager create a Menu Selling Price. The Menu Selling Price must 1) cover all costs, 2) contribute to the profit of the business, and 3) be fair to the customer. The determination of a Standard Portion Cost and the setting of a Menu Selling Price are major components of the cycle of cost control. They form the basis of every other function in the cycle (Purchasing, Receiving, Storage/Inventories, Production, Sales, and Analysis).

Review Questions

1. Determine the Standard Portion Cost using the Cost per Unit Method.

   a. The chef/manager purchases a case of 84–3 oz. fruit filled Danish for $46.25.

   b. The chef/manager purchases a case of 100 Maine Baking potatoes for $8.50 per case.

   c. The chef/manager purchases a pound of bacon at $1.89 per pound. The pound of bacon has sixteen slices, what is the cost per slice?

2A. Using the information given and the Yield Test Form in Appendix F, perform a Yield Test to calculate the following.

   Beef Tenderloin, No. 189

As Purchased Cost:	$38.00	Portion Size: 8 oz.
As Purchased Weight	10 lb.	
Edible Weight (lb.):	8.5 lb.	
Waste:	1.5 lb.	

   (Trim, Cutting Loss)

   a. As Purchased Price per Pound

   b. Edible Yield %

   c. Number of Portions

   d. Edible Cost per Pound

   e. Edible Cost per Portion

   f. Cost Factor per Pound

   g. Cost Factor per Portion

2B. If another beef tenderloin is purchased at an As Purchased Cost of $3.95 per pound, how would we calculate the following?

   a. New Edible Cost per Pound

   b. New Edible Cost per Portion

3A. Post the following information to the Cooking Loss Form in Appendix F, and perform a Cooking Loss Test using the following information:

   Turkey

As Purchased Cost:	$22.25	Portion Size: 5 oz.
As Purchased Weight:	25 lb.	
Edible Weight after Cooking:	10 lb.	
Waste:	15 lb.	

   (Trim, bones)

Calculate:

   a. As Purchased Cost per Pound

   b. Edible Yield %

   c. Number of Portions

   d. Edible Cost per Pound

e.   Edible Cost per Portion

f.   Cost Factor per Pound

g.   Cost Factor per Portion

3B.   A second turkey was purchased at an As Purchased Cost of $0.59 per pound, determine the:

a.   New Edible Cost per Pound

b.   New Edible Cost per Portion

4.   Make three copies of the Standard Recipe Costing Form in Appendix F, and post each of the following recipes on the form. Determine the Standard Portion Cost for these three recipes. Use the Edible Yield % as given, and use a 3% Q Factor for each recipe. Round off Purchase Amounts up to the next whole purchase unit, and round costs to the nearest cent.

Recipe #1: Baked Scrod with Lemon Butter Yield: 50 Standard Portion: 6 oz.

Qty./Unit	Edible Yield %	Ingredient	Invoice Cost per Unit
19 lb.		Scrod fillets	$4.25/lb.
As Needed		Fish Stock	n/c
1/2 cup		Wine, White	$30.54/cs. 4–1.5 liters*
1/4 cup		Lemon Juice	$1.10/qt.
2 1/2 lb.	67%	Clarified Butter	$1.75/lb.
2 1/2 lb.		Bread Crumbs	$0.60/lb.
1 bunch		Fresh Parsley	$0.55/bun.
9		Fresh Lemons	$16.74/case-140
To taste		Salt	$0.46–26 oz.
To taste		White Pepper	$4.50/lb.

*1 liter = 33.8 ounces

Recipe #2: White and Wild Rice with Mushrooms Yield: 10 Standard Portion: 4 oz.

Qty./Unit	Edible Yield %	Ingredient	Invoice Cost per Unit
6 oz.	67%	Clarified Butter	$1.75/lb.
6 oz.	88%	Onions	$10.00/50 lb.
6 oz.		Wild Rice	$7.10/28 oz.
10 oz.		White Rice	$3.80/2 lb.
1 qt.		Chicken Stock	n/c
1		Bay Leaf	$5.00/lb.
10 oz.	98%	Mushrooms	$1.10/lb.
1/2 bunch		Parsley	$0.40/bunch
To Taste		Salt	$0.46/26 oz.
To Taste		Pepper	$5.68/lb.

Recipe #3: Ratatouille Yield:20 Standard Portion: 6 oz.

Qty./Unit	Edible Yield %	Ingredient	Invoice Cost per Unit
8 oz.		Oil	$1.30/qt.
8 oz.	88%	Onions	$10.00/50 lb.
2 lb.	80%	Green Peppers	$0.62/lb.
1 lb.	99%	Tomatoes	$18.00/25# case
1.5 lb.	81%	Eggplant	$18.00/24# case
1.5 lb.	94%	Zucchini	$0.69/lb
1.5 lb.	88%	Green Beans	$22.95/25# case
8 oz.		Tomato Puree	$16.50/6–# 10 cans
2 oz.		Garlic	$0.98/lb.
To Taste		Salt	$0.46/26 oz.
To Taste		White Pepper	$4.50/lb.

5. Assuming that the Standard Portion Costs in Question #4 are from an à la carte menu, calculate the Preliminary Selling Price using a Desired Food Cost % of 30%. Round out your answer to the nearest cent.

6. Assuming that the Standard Portion Costs in Question #4 are from a table d'hôte menu, total the Standard Portion Costs and calculate the Preliminary Selling Price using the price factor for maintaining a 28% Food Cost. Round out your answer to the nearest cent.

7. List and explain the considerations described in the text to help the chef/manager set the Menu Selling Price. What other considerations might also play a part in setting the Menu Selling Price?

8. Using a spreadsheet package of your professor's choice, create a work sheet to calculate a yield test.

9. Using a spreadsheet package of your professor's choice, create a work sheet to calculate a cooking loss test.

10. Using a spreadsheet package of your professor's choice, create a work sheet to determine the standard portion cost of a Standard Recipe.

Bibliography

Dittmer, Paul R. and Gerald G. Griffin. *Principles of Food, Beverage, and Labour Cost Controls*, 5th ed., New York, NY: Van Nostrand Reinhold, 1994.

Drysdale, John A. *Profitable Menu Planning*, Englewood Cliffs, NJ: Prentice-Hall Career & Technology Prentice-Hall Inc., 1994.

Keister, Douglas C. *Food and Beverage Control*, Englewood Cliffs, NJ: Prentice-Hall, Inc., 1977.

Kotschever, Lendal H. and Marcel R. Escoffier. *Management by Menu*, 3d. ed. The Educational Foundation of the National Restaurant Association, 1994.

Sackler, Warren and Samuel R. Trapani. *Foodservice Cost Control Using Lotus 1–2–3*, New York, NY: John Wiley and Sons, Inc., 1995.

Schwartz, William C. "Eliminating Poor Receiving Habits", *Nation's, Restaurant News*, April 9, 1984.

Stefanelli, John M. *Purchasing: Selection and Procurement for the Hospitality Industry*, 3d. New York, NY: John Wiley and Sons, Inc., 1992.

Purchasing Controls

objectives

Upon completion of this chapter, the student should be able to:

1. identify the person who is responsible for the purchasing function within different size foodservice operations.
2. perform the three steps of decision making in the purchasing function: the identification of the product and service; the determination of how much to purchase; and the procurement decisions.
3. organize and prepare specification forms to be utilized in the purchasing function.
4. perform the steps in choosing the best purveyor to meet operational needs.
5. differentiate among the methods of procurement and when each should be utilized.
6. calculate how much to purchase based on business needs and customer demands.
7. develop and set up business forms necessary in purchasing controls.

key terms

Cash and Carry
Contract Buying
Edible Portion per Purchase Unit
Identification
Large Independent
Lead Time
Maximum Par
Medium Independent
Minimum Par
Multi-Unit Operation
Non-competitive Procurement
One Stop Shopping

Par Stock System
Procurement
Purchase Order
Purchase Unit
Purveyor Bid Sheet
Shelf-Life
Small Independent
Specification
Standing Order
Stock Out
Stockless Purchasing

Introduction

When a novice thinks of the purchasing function, it is in reference to the process of buying products from a supplier. Although buying is a very important part of the purchasing function, it is not the entire picture. Purchasing is:

1. the identification of the quality and quantity of product or service needed by the foodservice operation;

2. the determination of the quantity of purchase units needed to order; and

3. the procurement of the product/service at the most favorable price.

The *Identification* stage is when the chef/manager indentifies the quality and quantity standards of a product or service. It is the step at which the decision concerning which product/service best meets the needs and standards of the business operation is made. Determining the quantity of purchase units needed is based on usage, delivery times, and the space available to store the product. Procurement is the process in which a supplier is identified, and the order is placed with the purveyor who offers the best priced products or service.

There are many decisisons to be made within the purchasing function. **Who** should make the buying decisions and perform the purchasing function is the first question to answer. Once the business identifies the Purchasing Agent, the decisions concerning **what** to buy, **where** to buy, **how much** to buy, and **when** to buy, follow. The answers to each of these questions are discussed in detail within this chapter.

Who Should Do the Purchasing?

The person who has the responsibility and the authority for the purchasing function is the Purchasing Agent. The style and size of a business operation will determine who actually performs this task.

John M. Stefanelli, in his book *Purchasing: Selection and Procurement for the Hospitality Industry*, suggests that foodservice operations be divided into two classifications: independent operations and multi-unit/chain operations. Most foodservice operations fit into variations of these two classifications.

The Independent Foodservice Operation

The Independent operation can be divided into three categories depending upon the size and volume of the business. Stefanelli classifies the independent foodservice operations as: the Small Independent, the Medium Independent, and the Large Independent.

A *Small Independent* Operation can be thought of as a restaurant business that seats less than 75 customers. The purchasing function is usually performed by a single individual who often owns the foodservice operation. In many small independent operations, the owner not only owns the business, but also works within the business either as the General Manager or Chef. The owner/general manager is the person who makes the purchasing decisions about what to buy, how much to buy, and from whom to buy. He/she not only identifies the products needed but also determines which purveyors the restaurant will utilize.

A *Medium Independent* Operation can be thought of as a restaurant business that seats between 75 to 150 customers. With the increased size of medium independent operations, the business is organized into departments such as kitchen, dining room, and beverage. The responsibility of the purchasing function lies with department heads, the Dining Room Manager, Bar Manager, or Executive Chef (regardless of their actual titles). The Department Head is responsible for the identification of the product needed, as well as for placing orders with purveyors. The Chef is responsible for the identification and procurement of food items. The Beverage Manager is responsible for the identification and procurement of beverage items. Each department head must identify the product/service needed within his/her department and then procure the products or services from the purveyor.

A *Large Independent* Operation is a foodservice operation that seats more than 150, and is often accompanied by banquet facilities. Many hotel operations with multiple dining facilities, and single, high volume restaurants, fall within this category. In this type of foodservice operation, a full time Purchasing Agent is usually employed. This person may have the title of Purchasing Agent or may hold a more management specific title such as Food and Beverage Director, or Food and Beverage Controller. Within a large, independent foodservice operation, the decisions in the identification stage are still made by the department heads; however with such a high volume of sales and customers, the procurement of the products and the task of dealing with purveyors is left to the full time Purchasing Agent.

The Multi-Unit Foodservice Operation

In *multi-unit operations*, the purchasing function is normally directed from corporate headquarters. The individual stores are organized with managers and department heads, and most products are purchased through the regional central warehouse system. At times, the decision may be made by the store manager to purchase some products from local purveyors. If the decision is made to use local purveyors, the products purchased must still meet the standards of the corporate office. In most multi/unit foodservice operations, individual stores will control how much product to order; but the identification of the actual products needed and the setting of standards are determined by the corporate office.

"Who" should do the purchasing in the multi-unit operation depends upon the size of the foodservice operation. The size of the foodservice operation will also affect the two other areas of the purchasing function. From this point on, we will refer to the person having the responsibility and authority to perform the purchasing function as the Purchasing Agent.

Identification of the Product Needed

The Purchasing Agent has the responsibility of identifying the quality and quantity of the products/services that need to be purchased to meet the standards of the foodservice operation. It is in this decision making process that the Purchasing Agent decides which product available best meets the needs of the Standard Recipe and of other operational functions such as the skill level of employees.

Product Name: Green Beans	Name: Shrimp
Intended Use: Three Bean Salad	Intended Use: Shrimp Scampi
Purchase Unit: case/25 lb.	Purchase Unit: lb

Quantity/Packaging Standards:
  Desired Edible Yield: 88%
	Quantity/Packaging:
	  U-16/20

Quality Standards:
  fresh
  USDA Grade No. 1
  Whole Bean: 2 sieve
	Quality Standards:
	  fresh. peeled and
	  deveined (shell and black sand vein have
	  been removed.)

Special Requirements:	Special Requirements:

FIGURE 8.1 Specification Cards

Strong competition exists between different food and beverage products because there are many options of products and services available to foodservice operators. Products are available fresh, frozen (bulk or IQF), bottled, canned, in bulk quantities, or in individual PC (portion control) units, just to name a few. It is up to the Purchasing Agent to decide what form of product best meets the foodservice operation's standards. This decision is based on the type of menu and the sales volume of the operation. Once the quality and quantity characteristics have been identified, the information is recorded on a document known as a specification. A *Specification* is a detailed description of the product or service being purchased. It is a brief yet specific statement which describes the desired quality and quantity characteristics of the product or service. It is important that adequate information be included in the specifications. The term "adequate " information will vary depending upon the product being purchased. The Purchasing Agent must be certain that the specification is written explicitly enough to insure the quality standards of the product. It is recommended that a business organize its specifications using headings identical to or similar to those listed in Figure 8.1.

Exact Name of the Product

When creating a specification, it is important to be as precise as possible when naming the product needed. If you are purchasing lettuce, it is not enough to say "lettuce," due to the many different types of lettuce that are available. Instead, be specific as to the exact name of the lettuce product being purchased, using Green Leaf, Romaine, or Iceberg. When purchasing peppers, use Green, Yellow, or Red.

Intended Use or Menu Requirement

In addition to knowing the exact name of the product, it is important to know the intended use of the product. If a foodservice operation is offering an appetizer Shrimp Cocktail, and an entrée Shrimp Scampi; the Shrimp Cocktail appetizer might call for size U-10/12 shrimp (10 to 12 shrimp per pound) while the Shrimp Scampi entrée calls for size U-16 shrimp (16 shrimp per pound). On a very busy evening, if the operation runs out of the shrimp used in the Shrimp Cocktail appetizer, the chef simply has to leave the manager a memo to this effect. The manager refers to the specification listed for that particular menu item, and places the order. The specification sheet is a communication tool. In most situations, the purchasing agent would know the size shrimp needed for each menu item, but for the novice or the trainee, this document is invaluable.

Purchase Unit

The *Purchase Unit* is the weight or size of the item to be purchased, stated in units of measure such as pound (of chicken), gallon (of 1% milk), or quart (of heavy cream). The purchase unit can also be stated in the size of the container in which the product comes: a #10 can of chopped tomatoes, a loaf of bread, or a 14 oz. bottle of ketchup. Often the Purchase Unit of a product is a case. If the business is purchasing by the case, it is important to state the number and size of units within the case. When purchasing ketchup, for example, make sure that you specify if it is a case of twenty-four 14 oz. bottles, or one thousand 1 oz. P.C. (portion control) packets. Be specific as to the purchase unit to insure that the product desired is ordered and received.

It is important when determining the size of the purchase unit that the Purchasing Agent take into consideration the size of purchase unit which is most cost effective for the foodservice operation. The Purchase Unit selected often goes hand-in-hand with the intended use(s) of a product. The unit price of a product is usually less when the quantity of the purchase unit is larger. For example, a 3 gallon tub of ice cream costs the foodservice operation $25.00. The price per oz. of that 3 gallon tub is $0.07 per oz. The same ice cream purchased in a smaller quart unit costs $5.25 per qt., for a price per ounce of $0.16 per oz. The smaller the container, usually the higher the unit price. But be careful, if the use of the product is limited, a lower price does not necessarily guarantee a better buy for the restaurant. If the only use of ice cream is to serve it as a dollop on top of a piece of pecan pie, and the business only sells 8 pieces of pie every evening, then perhaps the better buy is a quart of ice cream. The 3 gallon drum could develop ice crystals long before it is used up. When developing specifications, don't be drawn in by unit price alone. Once you decide upon a purchase unit, be certain to monitor large quantities of product that are left in walk-ins and reach-ins for long periods of time. It is good practice to evaluate the standard purchase units on a regular basis to avoid waste.

Quantity and Packaging Standards

Depending upon the type of product being purchased, it may be important to state weight, product size, portion size, edible yield, count requirements, and packaging standards. When the Purchasing Agent is purchasing a case of greenhouse tomatoes, it is important that he/she state how they are packed (5 × 6, or slab 100 count). It is also important that the Purchasing Agent consider how items are packaged, individually or in bulk. The greater the detail supplied the purveyor, the better the chance that the purveyor will deliver products meeting the desired standard. Often a business will prefer a specific type of container: a 12 oz. bottle of Coors Lite® as compared to a 12 oz. can; or a paper/cardboard half gallon of Tropicana® Orange Juice in lieu of a plastic container. Packing decisions are important to quality and food costs. Does the business want to purchase 5 lb. tubs of Cole Slaw, or individual 4 oz. portion control size units of the same product? Is cheese purchased in 5 lb. blocks, or sliced and individually wrapped? Remember that generally the closer a purchase unit is prepared to edible portion size, the higher the unit cost of the product.

Quality Standards

Quality standards are criteria used to indicate a level of "goodness" of a product or service. The most widely known quality standard is the grading system used by the United States Department of Agriculture. The USDA has assigned government grades, based on visual testing, to well over one hundred different food products.

The USDA also has certain recommendations of Edible Yield % for a variety of products (Appendix C). These recommendations give the Purchasing Agent a sound idea of what percent of the product being purchased is actually usable as compared to what is waste. Edible Yield % was explained in Chapter 7 and will be important when determining how much to buy.

Another quality standard used regularly in the foodservice industry is Brand Names. Although Brand Names do not have to meet governmental guidelines, they do indeed make a quality statement. When we hear Grey Poupon®, or Perdue® Chicken, a guarantee of quality is definite. Knorr® sauces; Nabisco's Ritz Crackers®; Hobart® mixers, etc., just scream out quality. It is common that Brand Name items are more expensive, however many foodservice operations believe that the guaranteed consistency in quality found in Brand Name items outweighs the additional expense.

Specific Product Information

If the purchasing agent has failed to be precise within the previous categories, the area of specific product information needs to be expanded upon. Specific Product Information includes some or all of the information concerning a product.

Point of Origin

Where does the product come from? Is it a Maine Lobster? Idaho Potato? Maryland Crab? If the origin of the product is important to the quality of the item being purchased, it should be stated. This is also very important in upholding Truth-in-Menu standards. *Age.* What is the vintage of the wine? Has the beef been aged for a stated length of time? Is the degree of ripeness of the produce item important?

Preservation Method

The Preservation Method refers to the state of the product when purchased. Is it fresh? Previously frozen? Frozen bulk? IQF (individually quick frozen)? Dried? Smoked? All of these preservation methods are important in maintaining product consistency within the menu. If the foodservice operation normally uses a smoked turkey breast for the preparation of a popular sandwich, and forgets to specify a smoked product when purchasing, the product served will be different.

Price Indicator

Often with seasonal products, prices will rise and fall as the product's season begins and ends. Purchasing Agents will regularly include the maximum price per unit that they are willing to spend for a product on the specification sheet. This price indicator reminds the purveyor to contact the purchasing agent prior to filling the purchase order, if the prescribed price per unit is surpassed. Please note, desired unit prices should not be stated on the specification, only the maximum unit price the foodservice operation is willing to pay.

When writing specifications, it is important to be exact in the description of the product to guarantee receipt of the item ordered. However, be careful not to overstate your requirements. Demanding a higher quality than actually needed will increase the cost of the product and may also complicate its acquisition. On the other hand, a lack of detail can leave the door wide open to the receipt of lower end product quality. Writing specifications can be time consuming, but in the long run, specifications may save the business a great deal of time and money.

Although developing a specification system is a time consuming process, it is one that is basic to all cost controls within the foodservice operation. Specifications should be organized into a standardized form (Figure 8.1), and should be on file in multiple copies, so that individuals involved in the purchasing function have a copy available to them. Copies should be available for the Purchasing Agent to insure that the proper product is being purchased. The receiving clerk should have a copy to guarantee that the item received is indeed the product that was ordered. A copy should be sent to all the potential purveyors to inform them of the quality and quantity standards that the foodservice operation requires. This is especially important when the foodservice operation is using several purveyors and those purveyors are in price competition.

As more foodservice operations become computerized, the actual business document is being replaced by computer programs. Instead of having a book of specifications, or a card file, businesses often have the specifications on disc so that any department can access them when needed.

Determining the Quantity of Purchase Units Needed

Determining how much to buy can often be a process of trial and error. Some Purchasing Agents find the task routine, while others find themselves constantly over or under purchasing. Experience and good record keeping are essential for success. The better the Purchasing Agent is at keeping records of product usage and purveyor delivery schedules, the better he/she will be at determining the correct quantity to purchase. The foodservice operation must also take into consideration the time needed to perform the purchasing function as well as the space required to store the products purchased. There are two ways to simplify the ordering task: the Par Stock System and the Edible Portions per Purchase Unit System.

Par Stock System

The *Par Stock System* is a common approach that many foodservice operations use to determine the quantity of purchase units needed. The Par Stock system is based on past customer counts and product usage as well as purveyor delivery schedules and order procedures. There are two product levels in a Par Stock system.

The first level is known as the Maximum Par. The *Maximum Par* is the largest quantity of a product to have on hand, based on the storage space available, and the shelf life of the product. Storage space (as discussed in Chapter 10), is often the last thing a restaurateur thinks of when looking for a building in which to operate a restaurant. Busy visualizing the front of the house, and the set up of the equipment in the space identified as the kitchen, the entrepreneur often overlooks storage space. The Maximum Par level cannot exceed the amount of storage space available. Even foodservice operations that have plenty of storage space are at times unable to take advantage of quantity discounts due to the limited shelf life and/or expiration date of certain products. *Shelf life* is defined as the estimated amount or time that a product can be stored without spoilage occurring.

The *Minimum Par* level is the smallest quantity of a product to have on hand based on purveyor lead time. *Lead time* is the time period that begins when the order is placed with the purveyor and ends when the order is received by the foodservice operation. Purchasing Agents must be familiar with their purveyor's lead times to insure minimum par levels, otherwise, the restaurant might run out of the product before the new order can be delivered. If a foodservice operation runs out of a product (86'd), a *Stock Out* occurs. Although a Stock Out is not considered an actual dollar loss, it may result in a loss of sales due to customer dissatisfaction. If a stock out occurs, it is important that the manager handle the situation delicately to insure that the customer returns. The minimum par level should be set high enough to guarantee an uninterrupted supply of products.

Purchasing agents will often record the Maximum Par stock levels on the inventory order sheets used during the purchasing function. Posting the Maximum Par stock level on the order sheet alleviates the time consuming process of determining how much product is needed. The Purchasing Agent can take an inventory of what is on hand, record it on the order sheet, compare it to the Pars stated, and quickly determine how much to purchase. (Figure 8.2) It is strongly recommended that par levels be evaluated, at a minimum, on a seasonal basis as menu items often change as seasons change. Evaluating par stock levels regularly can prevent overstocking and waste.

Edible Portions per Purchase Unit

A second "How Much to Purchase" method is becoming more popular in the computerized foodservice industry. This method is presented by Charles Levinson in the book *Food and Beverage Operations: Cost Control and Systems Management*, and again by John M. Stefanelli in his book *Purchasing: Selection and Procurement for the Hospitality Industry*. This mathematical process of determining the quantity of purchase units needed analyzes each purchase unit to determine how many portions the purchase unit will yield. It would be unlikely that this method would be used to purchase every product. However, the process can be utilized to purchase major ingredients needed in Standard Recipes, special items needed for a catered event or banquet function, or simply for high cost ingredients the Purchasing Agent wishes not to over purchase.

To insure accuracy in the *Edible Portions per Purchase Unit* process, it is important that standard recipes be used, standard portion control be maintained, and specification of food products be developed and adhered to. As with Par Stock, this method depends on customer counts, product usage and delivery schedules, and procedures of purveyors.

The information required to execute this mathematical approach is: the Purchase Unit, the Standard Portion, the Edible Yield %, and the number of customers expected to be served. The *Purchase Unit* refers to the unit stated on the specification sheet used by the food-service operation. The Standard Portion is the size of the portion that is stated on the Standard Recipe. The Standard Portion is normally stated in ounces. As explained in Chapter 7, an Edible Yield % may be determined by performing a yield test. Edible yields are also recommended by purveyors and governmental agencies such as the US Department of Agriculture (Appendix C). The Edible Yield % identifies the amount of the purchased unit which is actually servable. The number of customers would be the forecasted number of people expected to consume the products being served. The number of customers can be determined by utilizing historical customer counts, or expected customers at a special event.

There are three steps to the Edible Portion per Purchase Unit method. Using the *Special Items or Banquet/Catering Approach* to the Edible Portion per Purchase Unit method of "How Much to Buy," we will calculate the quantity of purchase units needed to serve 250 covers. Use the following information:

Item	Purchase Unit	Standard Portion	Edible Yield %
Leg of Lamb	1 lb.	6 oz.	42 %
Green Beans	25 lb.	3 oz.	88 %

Step A: As Purchased Portions per Purchase Unit. The first step is to estimate the number of portions derived from a purchase unit, when the purchase unit is assumed to be 100% usable.

Food Category: SEAFOOD   **Day/Date: Monday, 6/30**

On Hand	PAR	Order	Ingredient
	40 lb.		Sole
	20 lb.		Scrod
	2 dz.		Lobsters (3 dozen Friday)
	10 lb.		60/40 Snow Crab (25 lb. Friday for Sunday)
	10 lb.		Shrimp 16/20
	3 gal.		Bay Scallops
	20 lb.		Tuna Loin

Prepared by:_____

FIGURE 8.2 Order Sheet w/Pars

Formula:

OZ. IN PURCHASE UNIT		÷	STANDARD PORTIONS	=	AS PURCHASED PORTIONS
Leg of Lamb (1 lb.)	16 oz.	÷	6 oz.	=	2.67 per lb.
Green Beans (25 lb.)	400 oz.	÷	3 oz.	=	133.33 per 25 lb.

As illustrated in this example, the As Purchased Portions derived tell us that a pound of Lamb will feed 2.67 people and a case of Green Beans will feed 133.33 people. Although it is rare that every ounce of a purchased product is usable, as most products have some waste, arriving at "As Purchased Portions" is a good first step in understanding how many portions each purchase unit actually yields. Many non-foodservice shoppers use this formula to determine how much to buy for a family dinner. Once the As Purchased Portions have been determined (assuming that the product is 100% edible), it is now time to take into consideration the Edible Yield % of products.

Step B: Edible Portions per Purchase Unit. The formula to determine the actual number of portions derived from a purchase unit is:

Formula:

AS PURCHASED PORTIONS	×	EDIBLE YIELD %	=	EDIBLE PORTIONS
Leg of Lamb 2.67	×	42%	=	1.12per lb.
Green Beans 133.33	×	88%	=	117.33 per 25 lb.

Using the formula above, it becomes clear to us that both the Leg of Lamb and the Green Beans are not 100% edible, and therefore, neither product will yield the number of As Purchased Portions previously calculated. We now know that every purchase unit of Lamb (lb.) will feed 1.12 people and that every case of green beans (25 lb.) will feed 117.33. Even when planning dinner at home for just three people, knowing the yield of each pound of a Leg of Lamb (1.12 in this example), you can easily figure that you would need approximately 3 lb. of lamb to feed your guests.

Step C: Quantity of Purchase Units. Knowing that 250 guests will be served at a banquet, we must now determine the quantity of purchase units needed to feed these 250 customers.

Formula:

# OF COVERS		÷	EDIBLE PORTIONS	=	QUANTITY OF PURCHASE UNITS
Lamb	250	÷	1.12	=	224 lb. (223.21)
Green Beans	250	÷	117.33	=	3-25 lb. cases (2.131)

We now know that the Purchasing Agent will need to order 224 lb. of Lamb and 3-25 lb. cases of Green Beans to feed 250 people. Always round up to the next Purchase Unit to be certain that the foodservice operation has enough product to avoid a stock out, and to provide a padding in case any errors are made in preparation.

This mathematical approach should be used only as a guideline in determining the quantity of purchase units needed. The success of this process is dependent upon maintaining product specifications, proper preparation techniques and portion control techniques. When performed correctly, the Edible Portion per Purchase Unit can be an effective control tool in reducing food cost dollars and waste. The more experienced Purchasing Agent or Executive Chef can easily determine the portions each purchase unit yields by simply performing the third step in the operation. By maintaining stated specifications of products and standard portion control, the number of edible portions achieved from each purchase unit should not change. Once this process is implemented, the only number that needs to be adjusted is the number of customers expected.

In a banquet or catering situation, this method can be utilized effectively to help control food cost and to reduce waste. The number of covers forecasted may include a guaranteed percentage. Foodservice operations with banquet facilities will often plan for a 5% overage, to cover unplanned events such as a tray of food which falls to the floor, or a last minute guest increase. It is always beneficial to say "no problem" rather than to disappoint the host and the guests.

High Cost Product Approach. This mathematical approach can also be utilized in a full-service restaurant setting; however, it is unlikely that it would be the only method used to purchase all products. Foodservice operations purchase hundreds of raw products to produce menu items. Determining each and every ingredient that a customer consumes would be impossible. However, the Edible Portion per Purchase Unit method can be used specifically to control the purchase of high cost regularly used items, such as: meats, seafood, poultry, prepared desserts, and other products.

Example: A dinner menu has entrée offerings of: 2 steak dishes, 3 chicken dishes, 2 scallop dishes, and 3 shrimp dishes. Each of the steak entrées, chicken entrées, scallop entrées, and shrimp entrées offers the same quality and portion size as the other similar entrées within the same menu subclassification. When using the high cost product approach in a full-service restaurant setting it is important to realize that every customer will not have the same menu item (unlike the banquet/catering approach). It is therefore important that we include the Sales Mix of our menu offerings with the other necessary information.

Using the following information and the equations previously introduced, we will use a four step process to determine how many pounds to purchase of the menu items listed, to feed a forecasted weekly customer count of 700 people.

Menu Item	Purchase Unit	Standard Portion	Edible Yield %	Sales Mix %
Steak	1 lb.	12 oz.	85%	20%
Chicken	1 lb.	8 oz.	88%	35%
Scallops	1 lb.	6 oz.	92%	18%
Shrimp	1 lb.	6 oz.	80%	27%

After the Purchase Unit, the Standard Portion, and the Edible Yield % are determined, the sales mix must be examined. The Sales Mix is the percentage that represents the popularity of one item as compared to that of the total items sold within that menu category. For example, the Sales Mix % for steak would be calculated by taking the number of steaks sold, and dividing this number by the total number of entrées sold. This would then tell you what percent of your customers orders steak.

Formula:

NUMBER OF STEAKS SOLD	÷	TOTAL NUMBER OF ENTRÉES SOLD	=	SALES MIX %
Example: 20 steaks sold	÷	100 entrées sold	=	20% Sales Mix

A Sales Mix % is usually used to determine the popularity of a particular menu item within a menu classification comparing it to other items within the same classification; Appetizers with Appetizers, Entrées with Entrées, etc. The information needed to determine a Sales Mix % will be discussed in detail in Chapter 12. When using the mathematical approach for high cost menu items in a full-service restaurant, calculate the As Purchased Portions (Step A), and then the Edible Portions achieved from each purchase unit (Step B).

Step A Formula:

OUNCES IN PURCHASE UNIT		÷	SERVING SIZE	=	AS PURCHASED PORTIONS
Steak	16 oz.	÷	12 oz.	=	1.33 per lb.
Chicken	16 oz.	÷	8 oz.	=	2 per lb.
Scallops	16 oz.	÷	6 oz.	=	2.67 per lb.
Shrimp	16 oz.	÷	6 oz.	=	2.67 per lb.

Step B Formula:

AS PURCHASED PORTIONS		×	EDIBLE YIELD %	=	EDIBLE PORTIONS
Steak	1.33	×	85%	=	1.13 per lb.
Chicken	2	×	88%	=	1.76 per lb.
Scallops	2.67	×	92%	=	2.46 per lb.
Shrimp	2.67	×	80%	=	2.14 per lb.

Once the Edible Portion per Purchase Unit is determined, calculate the customers per menu item (Step C). The number of customers expected to order a particular menu item is based on the Sales Mix %. The customers per menu item number is calculated using the following:

Step C Formula:

FORECASTED COVERS		×	SALES MIX %	=	CUSTOMERS PER MENU ITEM
Steak	700	×	20%	=	140 customers ordering steak
Chicken	700	×	35%	=	245 customers ordering chicken
Scallops	700	×	18%	=	126 customers ordering scallops
Shrimp	700	×	27%	=	189 customers ordering shrimp

The final step (Step D), is used to derive the quantity of purchase units.

Step D Formula:

CUSTOMERS PER MENU ITEM		÷	EDIBLE PORTIONS	=	QUANTITY OF PURCHASE UNITS
Steak	140	÷	1.13	=	124 lb. (123.89 lb.)
Chicken	245	÷	1.76	=	140 lb. (139.20 lb.)
Scallops	126	÷	2.46	=	52 lb. (51.22 lb.)
Shrimp	189	÷	2.14	=	89 lb. (88.32 lb.)

Remember that the amount indicated is but a guideline to purchasing. Although this mathematical process appears very time consuming, it is easily computerized. If the purchase units and specification information remain constant, the Edible Portion number derived from each purchase unit should not change. The only change incurred in both the banquet/catering and full-service restaurant, is the number of customers choosing each menu item. In both the banquet/catering approach and the high cost item approach of the full-service restaurant, the only calculation to be performed on a regular basis is the last step in determining the quantity of purchase units to be procured.

Creating an Approved Purveyor List

Once the business identifies the product or service to be purchased, it must develop specifications that describe the product or service, determine the quantity of purchase units to be purchased, and lastly, order the product from an available and reliable purveyor. *Procurement* is the process in which the chef/manager selects the best purveyor and places an order for products as needed. Locating purveyors who offer products described in the specifications can be a time consuming process, but one that is well worth the effort. It is the role of the Purchasing Agent to identify which purveyors within the locale offer the quality and quantity of products desired, a competitive price, and the delivery time and service needed. Selecting the appropriate purveyors reduces the amount of time needed for procurement.

The decision concerning the selection of purveyors should obviously be performed prior to picking up the phone to place an order. Author John M. Stefanelli, in *Purchasing: Selection and Procurement for the Hospitality Industry*, suggests the following threefold process: take an Initial Survey of possible purveyors; create an Approved Supplier List; and lastly, choose the best purveyor to meet the demand of your business.

The Initial Survey

The first step to the procurement process is to identify the different categories of products and services to be purchased by the foodservice operation. The exact names and purchase units of the products desired should be listed within the appropriate category. When speaking of food costs, the purchase categories would normally consist of: produce, meats, seafood, poultry, dairy, bread, and grocery. When looking at beverage cost, categories might include: beer, wine, alcohol, soft drinks, and bottled water. Within the overhead cost categories, the business may have items such as cleaning supplies, kitchen utensils, linen, paper/plastic, furniture, fixtures, and equipment. There are many different purchasing categories within a restaurant operation.

Once the categories of purchases have been stated, the process of identifying potential purveyors within each category begins. Potential purveyors can be found in the white pages of the phone book, in the yellow pages, and in trade journals. They may also be recommended by trade organizations or competitors. Use your ingenuity to find out which purveyors are available and what they can offer you. Purveyors may be within the restaurant's general vicinity, or across town, city, or state lines. As you identify the potential purveyors, assign each purveyor a purchasing category. Depending upon the size, location, and volume of the foodservice operation, the number of purveyors identified within each purchasing category will vary.

Developing an Approved Purveyor List

After compiling the list of potential purveyors, it is time to identify which ones offer the quality of products and service requirements that fit the foodservice operation. Contact potential purveyors for an appointment to review and evaluate product quality and the availability of service offered. Rather than randomly choosing purveyors, start first by asking other foodservice operations, competitors, the Chamber of Commerce, or even the Better Business Bureau for suggestions. Try to identify and include at least three purveyors from every purchase category on the Approved Purveyor List. Once an Approved Purveyor List has been identified, it is from this list that the foodservice operation will select the purveyor of choice.

Methods of Procurement

Just as the size of the foodservice operation dictates who has the responsibility and the authority to serve as the Purchasing Agent, so will the size of the foodservice operation determine how foodservice operations procure their products from purveyors.

Non-Competitive Procurement

In the small independent operation where the owner is the Manager/Chef and the Purchasing Agent, there may not be enough time left for contacting different purveyors on a daily, or even weekly basis, in order to compete for the best price. This size of business will often use the *non-competitive procurement* method and choose a single purveyor per food category (produce, dairy, meats, grocery, etc.), and will work solely with that purveyor to meet the needs of the foodservice operation. Besides, these foodservice operations usually do not have enough business volume to get the "good deal" offered by quantity discounts. Small businesses will often agree to purchase all products from a single purveyor in a given category, if the purveyor can be fair and reasonable in terms of price and service to the foodservice operation. Medium Independent operations may also utilize this process. It is always a good idea to create the Approved Purveyor List for any size business. At times, a purveyor may not have an item, and the Purchasing Agent may need to purchase it from another source. The original purveyor's prices might also exceed the maximum price per unit selected by the operation. By having the Approved Purveyor List, the chef/manager can occasionally check the prices of other purveyors as well.

One Stop Shopping

Another option for small and medium sized foodservice operation is One Stop Shopping. *One Stop Shopping* is a method of procurement whereby the Purchasing Agent tries to purchase as many products as possible from a single purveyor. When the foodservice operation does not have time to compete for the best price and is also trying to consolidate purchasing efforts, he/she may choose to buy as many products as possible from one purveyor. Purveyors such as Sysco® in the northeast are huge distributors of many purchasing categories. They sell produce, meats, poultry, bread, grocery, dairy, and almost everything else a foodservice operation needs. Advantages of this method of procurement include a need for only one Purchase Order or one phone call, as well as the receiving of one order. Disadvantages to the One Stop Shopping method of procurement include:

1. the availability of an alternative product in case the one normally ordered is unavailable;

2. a limited delivery schedule which may be only once a week;

3. a very large and cumbersome delivery; and

4. a steady growing price increase if the purveyor realizes that he is the only purveyor being used. If choosing the One Stop Shopping method of procurement, be certain that the One Stop Purveyor has alternative products in case the normal product is not available. Also check prices with other purveyors on the Approved Purveyor List on an occasional basis. As a business grows, both in the number of employees and in the sales volume, many more procurement options become available.

Competing for the Best Price

One of the main reasons that time is spent creating an Approved Purveyor List is to enable a foodservice operation to get the best prices. The Purchasing Agent knows that the purveyors listed on the Approved Purveyor List offer comparable product quality, quantity, and service. Price, on the other hand, may vary considerably.

The first step in finding the best price is to develop a *Purveyor Bid Sheet* for all purchase categories and then to list all products needed on the appropriate Purveyor Bid Sheet.

Food Category: SEAFOOD			Day/Date: Mon, 6/30	
Ingredient	**Purchase Unit**	**Purveyor 1**	**Purveyor 2**	**Purveyor 3**
Sole	lb.	$ 6.25	$ 5.95	$ 5.75
Scrod	lb.	$ 3.95	$ 4.50	$ 4.25
Lobsters	ea.	$ 4.95	$ 4.75	$ 6.00
Snow Crab	lb.	$ 7.25	$ 8.50	$ 7.35
Shrimp 16/20	lb.	$ 9.95	$10.25	$ 9.25
Bay Scallops	gal.	$48.89	$38.00	$42.50
Tuna Loin	lb.	$ 6.50	$ 7.25	$ 6.50

Purveyor 1: Boston Fish Company

Purveyor 2: Sidney's Seafood

Purveyor 3: Quality Seafood

FIGURE 8.3 Purveyor Bid Sheet

Next, forward a copy of the specifications of all products listed on the Purveyor Bid Sheet to each purveyor listed on the Approved Supplier List. Once the specifications have been sent to each purveyor on the Approved Supplier List, the Purchasing Agent contacts the purveyor by phone or by computer, to get a price quote for each product listed. He/she then records the price on the Purveyor Bid Sheet. Once the price has been recorded, select the purveyor who offers the best price.

Standing Order

Many products, especially perishable items (bread and dairy), are needed on a regular basis (daily, weekly, etc.). Purveyors will often offer the foodservice operation what is known in the foodservice industry as a Standing Order. *Standing Orders* consist of a prescribed order received on a regular basis. Phone calls need not be made or purchase orders prepared. This process can be utilized within many categories including flowers for dining room tables or side towels for staff. Often the quantity of products and the days of delivery are set (for example, 100 side towels delivered every Monday and Thursday). At other times the Standing Order is based on a Par Stock set by the foodservice operation. This par stock would be similar to the minimum and maximum par stock levels previously explained. The delivery person would know the maximum par stock levels of the items being delivered, would rotate stock, would remove post dated product and "max. out" the pars of the products needed. The Standing Order process can save the Purchasing Agent a lot of order time; However, it is strongly recommended that total control not be given to the delivery person. On the day the Standing Order is to be delivered, be certain to inventory the products on hand, so that when the delivery person presents the invoice, you can be certain it reflects what was actually needed. Don't be taken advantage of.

Cash and Carry

Providing your own delivery service is becoming more popular as large *Cash and Carry* operations expand to all regions of the country. These huge warehouses offer their membership prices competitive with those of wholesale purveyors. The drawback is that the foodservice operation must provide its own transportation of goods, and often its own bags and boxes. When searching for the best price, Cash and Carry is an option for the foodservice operator who has the time to use it. Other Cash and Carry options include going to farmer's markets to pick and choose the freshest produce, or to the docks to purchase the catch of the day. When transporting cash and carry products to be sold to customers, be certain to adhere to proper sanitation principles of handling, time, and temperature.

Contract Buying

In institutional foodservice, where menus are cyclical and customers are a captive market, food is often purchased on a contractual basis. The process of *Contract Buying* is similar to that of competing for the Best Price. Written specifications are forwarded to the purveyors listed on the Approved Purveyor List, and they are asked to place a bid for the contract. The purveyor then returns a written bid offering the requested products at a specific quantity, at a certain cost, and for a designated length of time. When all bids are returned, the Purchasing Agent chooses the bid approved and contracts to purchase the items needed. Contract buying is less frequently used in commercial operations due to customer preferences.

Stockless Purchasing

"When the buyer purchases a large amount of product, but arranges for the supplier to store it and deliver it as needed, the procedure is called *Stockless Purchasing*." (Stefanelli 1992, 192) Many purveyors will offer this service to foodservice operations to encourage large quantity purchases. Stockless purchasing can be used to purchase paper goods such as placemats and napkins that have a printed logo. Businesses that use paper placemats and napkins rarely have enough storage space available to purchase these bulk items in a large quantity. When purchased in smaller numbers, the cost per unit increases. When purchased in large numbers, the cost per unit decreases. It is much more cost effective for a business to purchase 200 cases of cocktail napkins up front than to place 4 separate orders of 50 cases throughout the year. Since it costs the purveyor money to set the printing presses each time an order is placed, a service charge is added to pay for this expense. When purchasing the 200 case order, the presses have only to be set up once. Less service, less charge. Purveyors also offer Stockless Purchasing to foodservice operations due to the environmental conditions of a storage area which may not be conducive to the storage needs of the products purchased. The area may be too damp, too hot, or too cold. Items that are often purchased using Stockless Purchasing include: match books, printed products with a logo, wine needed to fill the requirements of a new wine list, or perhaps a major staple food item such as salsa, a staple food of many Tex-Mex chains. Tex-Mex chains might purchase huge quantities of salsa to get a quantity discount, have them stored in the purveyors warehouse, and then have cases of the product delivered to the foodservice operation as needed.

Foodservice operations may use one or more of these methods of procurement on a regular basis. The size of the business operation and the amount of time the Purchasing Agent has to spend on procuring products will dictate the methods used.

Business Documents in Purchasing

The Specification Sheet, Inventory Sheet, and the Purveyor Bid Sheet are business documents used to assist the Purchasing Agent in documenting the quality standards, the amounts to be purchased, and the prices offered by purveyors in the purchasing function. They all help to control the in-house purchasing process. Once the purchasing decisions have been made, the purchase order is then prepared.

The Purchase Order

The *Purchase Order* is a formal document that informs the selected purveyor of what is ordered, how much is ordered, and the price that has been quoted for items needed by the foodservice operation. (Figure 8.4) The Purchase Order is also an in-house communication tool that inform other departments, such as the Receiving Department and the Kitchen, of what was ordered and from whom. Purchase Orders are normally prepared in triplicate. Copies are provided to the purveyor, the Receiving area, and the business office.

Not all foodservice operations use a formal Purchase Order. The use of this document depends again upon the size and the distribution of purchasing responsibility within a foodservice operation. The larger the restaurant, the country club, or the hotel, the greater the importance of using business cost control documents. The smaller the foodservice operation, the less formal the document. Businesses that choose not to use the formal Purchase Order must still prepare an informal document for management staff and the appropriate departments, listing what was ordered and from whom. In a Small Independent Operation (and often in the Medium Independent Operation), where one person serves as Purchasing Agent as well as Receiving Clerk, only pen and paper are needed to write down the items that have been ordered from each purveyor. No matter what the size of the foodservice operation, a Purchase Order (formal or informal), is an important tool in the cycle of Cost Control that should be utilized.

There are many decisions to be made within the purchasing function. **Who** should make the buying decisions and perform the purchasing function is the first decision. Once the business identifies **Who** will hold the responsibilities of the Purchasing Agent, the **what** to buy, **where** to buy, **how much** to buy, and **when** to buy follow naturally.

ORIGINAL PURCHASE ORDER   NO. 4532-0000

UNIVERSITY INN
One Library Avenue
Collegetown, RI 00001-0001
(401)555-0000

To: Quality Seafood   Ship To: _____

50 Ocean Avenue   _____

Newport, RI 02840   _____

Ship to above unless otherwise noted here

Date 7/1/98	Date Required 7/1/98	Terms n/30	Ship Via	F.O.B.	Requisition #

Quantity		ITEM	Unit Price	Amount
Ordered	Received			
30 lb.		Sole Fillet	$ 5.75 lb	$172.50
15 lb.		Scrod Fillet	$ 4.25 lb.	$ 63.75
1.5 dz.		Lobsters	$ 6.00 ea.	$108.00
10 lb.		Snow Crab	$ 7.35 lb.	$ 73.50
8 lb.		Shrimp 16/20	$ 9.25 lb.	$ 74.00
2 gal.		Bay Scallops	$42.50 gal	$ 85.00
18 lb.		Tuna	$ 6.50 lb.	$117.00

Prepared by _____   Total $693.75

FIGUERE 8.4 Purchase Order

Review Questions

1. Discuss why various people perform the role Purchasing Agent in different size foodservice operations.

2. Research the products available and write specifications for the products below using the guidelines provided in this chapter. A Specification form is provided in Appendix E.

   > Granny Smith Apples
   >
   > Carrots
   >
   > Wheat Bread
   >
   > Coffee
   >
   > Tenderloin
   >
   > Sole Fillet
   >
   > Mint Jelly

3. Explain how a par stock system is developed and what considerations must be thought through before setting par stock levels.

4. Using the information provided, calculate how many purchase units would be needed to prepare a Roasted Turkey dinner serving 300 customers.

Menu Item	Purchase Unit	Portion Size	Edible Yield %
Turkey	1 lb.	6 oz.	40%
Mashed Potatoes	50 lb. bag	4 oz.	81%
Winter Squash	1 lb.	4 oz.	64%
Frozen Green Beans	2.5 lb.	4 oz.	98%
Wine	1.5 liters	6 oz.	98%

5. Using the information provided, calculate the number of **pounds** needed to serve a forecasted weekly customer count of 2,100 covers.

Item	Standard Portion	Edible Yield %	Sales Mix
Steak	10 oz.	75%	32%
Lamb Loin	6 oz.	40%	22%
Baked Ham	6 oz.	65%	28%
Veal Loin	5 oz.	75%	18%

6. Explain the advantages and disadvantages of utilizing the different methods of procurement for each style of independent operation and the multi-unit foodservice operation described in this chapter.

7.   Explain the purpose of a purchase order.

8.   Using the spreadsheet package of your professor's choice, develop a spreadsheet to calculate how many Edible Portions are derived from a Purchase Unit utilizing the Standard Portion and Edible Yield%.

9.   Using the spreadsheet package of your professor's choice, develop a spreadsheet to prepare a purchase order document.

Bibliography

Dittmer, Paul R. and Gerald G. Griffin. *Principles of Food, Beverage, and Labor Cost Controls*. 5th. ed. New York: Van Nostrand Reinhold, 1994.

Keister, Douglas C. *Food and Beverage Control*. Englewood Cliffs, NJ: Prentice-Hall, Inc., 1977

Levinson, Charles. *Food and Beverage Operation*. 2d. ed. Englewood Cliffs, NJ: Prentice-Hall, Inc., 1989.

Sackler, Warren and Samuel R. Trapani. *Foodservice Cost Control Using Lotus 1-2-3*. New York: John Wiley and Sons, Inc., 1995.

Stefanelli, John M. *Purchasing: Selection and Procurement for the Hospitality Industry*. 3d. ed. New York: John Wiley and Sons, Inc., 1992.

Receiving Controls

objectives

Upon completion of this chapter, the student should be able to:

1. implement proper receiving controls within a foodservice operation.
2. follow the flow of goods through the receiving process.
3. prepare the business forms needed to provide the receiving information necessary for proper control of food, beverage, and supplies.
4. demonstrate the use and understand the purpose of the receiving log, receiving report form, and the purchase distribution journal.

key terms

Blind Receiving
Direct Purchase
Food Tag
Invoice
Invoice Receiving
Invoice Stamp

Purchase Distribution Journal
Receiving Clerk
Receiving Log
Receiving Report Form
Storeroom Purchase

Introduction

Receiving is the process in which foodservice operators "check in" the goods delivered to the restaurant to insure that these products meet the quality and quantity standards that have been determined in the purchasing function. During the purchasing function products needed by the foodservice operation were identified, and procured from the supplier offering the best price and service. An order was placed and the delivery made. The receiving process is the foodservice operator's first chance to take control of products and their costs by maximizing the efficiency of their use. The person responsible for the receiving function will be referred to as the *receiving clerk*. The person who serves as the receiving clerk varies depending on the size of the foodservice operation. Normally, only the large foodservice operations that have a formal storeroom process will have a full time receiving clerk. In small and medium operations, this role is often performed by a chef, manager, department head, or trained employee.

Receiving tends to be one of the most ignored aspects of food and beverage cost control. Although every chef and manager realizes the importance of the receiving process, the function is sometimes taken too lightly. Foodservice operators often think a better process of receiving goods "takes too much time." Most foodservice operators, if not all, could better control their costs by simply paying more attention to the receiving controls they currently have in place. Occasionally, it is just a matter of taking more time to check in the goods, while at other times, foodservice operators need a more efficient system altogether. William C. Schwartz, a former accountant for the National Restaurant Association, in his article "Eliminate Poor Receiving Habits," states that "nearly half an operation's variance (difference between actual and ideal food cost), is the result of poor receiving habits. To the average restaurant, this represents a whopping 2% of sales." Mr. Schwartz goes on to say that this 2% of sales would have been additional profit because if it had not been spent to purchase food, it would have resulted in a profit. (Schwartz 1984) Let's put Mr. Schwartz's findings into dollar figures. A foodservice operation brought in $2,000,000 in sales last year. If 2% of that sales figure was spent unnecessarily on the cost of sales, due to improper receiving practices, this business spent $40,000 ($2,000,000 × 2%) more than it needed to by not properly checking in goods. Worse yet, this could have been $40,000 more in profit. The measures that follow will help the foodservice manager to better control food and beverage costs and ultimately to generate increased profits. In this chapter, we will explain in detail how to properly receive goods. We will also examine how goods flow through the receiving process.

Invoice Receiving: The Common Approach

The *invoice* is the bill prepared by the purveyor which accompanies the delivery. It states what was ordered, the quantity, the unit price, the extensions, and total cost. (Figure 9.1) The receiving clerk uses it initially to verify the quantity counts and the weight of the products delivered. The invoice is prepared in duplicate using NCR (No Carbon Required) paper. The invoice is often the only form used to check in products.

Receiving is the foodservice operator's first chance to control products and costs once products have arrived. As mentioned in the Introduction, most foodservice operations could to some degree improve their receiving practices. Receiving Scenario #1: Typically, the products arrive at about 11:45 a.m. The shout of the word "delivery" echoes until it reaches the ears of the chef or manager. Ten minutes and two phone calls later, the chef/manager gets back to check the order. The driver, frantically tapping his foot, gives the invoice to the chef/manager. The chef/manager quickly compares the invoice to the delivery in front of him. He/she signs the invoice, and hurries into the kitchen to help with the lunch rush. The driver leaves. The goods sit in the receiving area (at the back door), until the lunch period is over. Sound familiar?

Invoice Receiving as it was just described, is what is seen at many foodservice operations. This method is not a very effective cost control measure. There was no purchase order, no specifications, no effort to check quality and quantity standards. There are simple measures that can be taken to improve this process and to help to insure that Invoice Receiving is a useful cost control procedure.

Invoice Receiving: A Better Approach

Invoice Receiving can be an effective receiving control method if it is used appropriately. The process should include the use of three purchasing documents (discussed in Chapter 8), as well as several tools and pieces of equipment that can be used to better

		INVOICE		NO. 00246-00	

QUALITY SEAFOOD
50 OCEAN DRIVE
NEWPORT, RI 02840
(401) 555-5555

TO: **UNIVERSITY INN**
ONE LIBRARY AVENUE
COLLEGETOWN, RI 00000

Date: 7/3/98		**Payment Terms:** n/30	**Purchase Order #:** 4532	
Quantity		**ITEM**	**Unit Price**	**Amount**
Ordered	**Received**			
30 lbs.		Sole Fillet	$ 5.75 lb.	$172.50
15 lbs.		Scrod Fillet	$ 4.25 lb.	$ 63.75
1.5 dz.	16	Lobsters	$ 6.00 ea.	$108.00
10 lbs.		Snow Crab	$ 7.35 lb.	$ 73.50
8 lbs.		Shrimp 16/20	$ 9.25 lb.	$ 74.00
2 gals.		Bay Scallops	$42.50 gal.	$ 85.00
18 lbs.		Tuna	$ 6.50 lb.	$117.00
			TOTAL	$693.75

Received by _____

FIGURE 9.1 Invoice

perform the receiving function. Invoice Receiving can be an effective method of receiving goods, particularly when used in conjunction with additional purchase documents, tools, and techniques.

We will revisit the previous scenario, but this time implement the use of the three purchasing forms mentioned, as well as other necessary tools and techniques to insure quantity and quality standards. Receiving Scenario 2: The goods arrive at 10:00 a.m. right smack in the middle of the scheduled receiving hours. The receiving clerk, Tom the Prep Cook, sees the delivery driver open the back door. He stops his "prep" and meets the driver at the receiving door. Tom accepts the invoice from the driver and immediately begins checking in the goods as the first hand truck is emptied. While counting the items, he weighs products to insure that the quantity stated on the invoice is exactly what has been delivered. He checks quality by opening boxes, dumping cases into wire baskets, and checking the temperature of refrigerated and frozen goods with a thermometer. To verify quality, he refers to the Specification for the product that is filed in the specification file box close at hand. Once the delivery has been checked for quality and the stated quantities on the invoice have been confirmed, Tom compares the invoice to the Purchase Order. The Purveyor Bid Sheet is used if any questions concerning price arise. Once all the goods have been checked in, Tom brings the invoice to the chef/manager to sign. Tom hands the invoice back to the driver. The driver leaves, and Tom gets to work putting the goods away.

"Receiving Scenario #2" still utilizes the invoice as the initial document to receive goods, but this time, Tom the Prep Cook utilizes several other receiving techniques to insure product standards. We will now examine Receiving Scenario #2 one step at a time.

Receiving Hours

Established Receiving Hours are an effective tool to insure that when deliveries are made, an employee has the time to properly check in the goods and to put them away immediately. Quality product standards are therefore maintained. Receiving Hours are agreed upon by the purveyor and the foodservice operation. Set Receiving Hours are beneficial not only to the foodservice operator, but also to the purveyor. An agreed upon delivery schedule reduces the time a driver has to wait around, allowing him more deliveries during the day.

Receiving Clerk

Notice that it is not the chef or manager who checks in the goods in Receiving Scenario #2. Chefs and Managers are too busy to devote a lot of time to the receiving function. Receiving demands carefully monitoring products to insure that quality and quantity standards are met. Proper training of another employee may better serve the process.

Invoice

The invoice is the initial document used to receive the goods. It is used to verify that the products delivered are exactly as stated on the invoice prepared by the purveyor. Although a product is listed on the invoice, this does not guarantee that the product has been delivered. The receiving clerk must have a document prepared by the restaurant stating what has been ordered. The Purchasing Documents will be discussed in a moment.

Tools

The scale is the most important tool in the receiving process. Most products are purchased by weight. Even when products are purchased by the case, there are weight range standards that should be met. There is no possible way to insure that a business is receiving the quantity of products purchased by weight, unless the receiving clerk weighs the product. This can be quite difficult to do without good scales. Many foodservice operations do not weigh products, relying totally on the honesty of their purveyors. Although this sounds wonderful, rest assured that the purveyors know exactly which accounts weigh products and which accounts do not. This is not to say that purveyors are intentionally out to get the foodservice operations; but unintentional errors do occur daily in the foodservice industry. Additional product specific equipment, such as the thermometer for refrigerated and frozen goods, is essential to proper "check-in" procedures.

The Specification

The specification is a brief yet detailed description of the product or service being purchased. The specification should be available to the receiving clerk in case a question arises regarding whether or not a product meets a quality or quantity standard.

The Purchase Order

An invoice is a business form prepared by the purveyor, describing the order (units and costs) the foodservice operation has placed. A Purchase Order (whether formal or informal), is a document prepared by the Purchasing Agent that lists exactly what has been ordered. Once the goods have been checked in, the Invoice should be compared item by item with the Purchase Order. Without a Purchase Order, the receiving clerk may unintentionally accept goods that should not be accepted. Failure to use a Purchase Order can contribute to the 2% excessive costs previously mentioned. Once accepted, these products are put away and perhaps never seen again until the monthly inventory. A formal Purchase Order, as described in Chapter 8, lists unit prices of the products ordered. This document can aid the receiving clerk if a price concern arises.

The Purveyor Bid Sheet

Sometimes the foodservice operation uses a piece of paper to record what was purchased and from whom, in lieu of a purchase order. In this case, a Purveyor Bid Sheet can be used to check price information.

Signing the Invoice

Invoices are legal documents. When a foodservice operation opens an account with a purveyor, a signature card is signed by all management staff who have the authority to sign invoices. Once the invoice has been signed, the foodservice operation is legally obligated to pay the total due regardless of any errors. This is why it is extremely important that care be taken to thoroughly check orders.

Putting Goods Away Immediately

To get the maximum shelf life from products, it is important that products not remain out of their proper environment for any longer than absolutely necessary. In fact, many foodservice operations will actually check in refrigerated and frozen goods in their own walk-ins. Another important reason to put goods in their proper place is to insure that the products do not "walk away." Products that are left out in the open or by the back door for long periods of time are often looked at as a temptation for thieves. Alleviate the temptation by putting goods away immediately.

Blind Receiving: The Best Approach

Another method of receiving used in the foodservice industry is known as *Blind Receiving*. This method is said to provide the best control with regards to receiving goods. The method is very similar to Invoice Receiving; except in the Blind Receiving approach, the invoice is not accepted from the driver until after the goods have been checked for quality and quantity. At that time, the receiving clerk prepares a receiving log: a running account of the products actually received as the products are delivered to the foodservice operation.

As the goods are being delivered, the receiving clerk carefully inspects the goods, checking that the products meet the specifications. The receiving clerk weighs products, checks temperatures, counts items, performs proper check in techniques, and then records them on the receiving log.

The preparation of *receiving log* will aid the receiving clerk to more carefully inspect the products delivered. Not having the invoice in hand and not knowing what is supposed to be there, the receiving clerk will take more time to count and weigh products, and to check their quality. Once the receiving log is complete, the invoice is then accepted from the driver and compared to the receiving log, making adjustments as needed. After the receiving log has been compared to the invoice, the invoice is then compared to the purchase order, again insuring that the products stated on the invoice had been ordered by the foodservice operation.

Both the Invoice Receiving technique and the Blind Receiving approach can be effective receiving techniques, if the receiving clerk is properly trained and the foodservice operation allows ample time for the process.

Requests for Credit and Pick-Ups

Credit Memos

There are times when a product is identified as not meeting the quality standards of the foodservice operation, or perhaps, has never been ordered. When these unwanted products appear, the receiving clerk can request a credit memo from the purveyor's driver. A credit memo is a business form that adjusts the total of the invoice, by indicating on the memo which items have been rejected and returned to the purveyor. The credit memo is prepared by the driver, usually in copy, and is attached to each copy of the invoice indicating the change to the invoice. (Figure 9.2)

Pick Up Memos

At times, products that are not needed by the foodservice operation get by both the receiving clerk and the management staff. Perhaps a case of twenty-four 10 oz. bottles of sparkling water was delivered rather than a case of twenty-four 10 oz. bottles of non-sparkling water. If the foodservice operation rarely gets a request for bottled sparkling water, the foodservice manager would call the purveyor to request a pick up. A Pick Up memo would be prepared by the purveyor to "pick-up" the product from the foodservice operation. When the driver brings the next order, he will also bring the Pick Up memo to pick up the unwanted case. The Pick Up memo would be signed by the foodservice manager when the driver takes it so that the foodservice operation's account can be adjusted appropriately.

		Request for Credit Memo		

QUALITY SEAFOOD　　　　　　　　　　　**Date: 7/03/98**
50 OCEAN AVENUE
NEWPORT, RI 00000　　　　　　　　　　**Invoice: 00246-00**

QTY	UNIT	ITEM	UNIT PRICE	TOTAL
2	ea.	Lobsters	$6.00 ea.	$12.00
			TOTAL:	$12.00

Driver's Signature _____

Approved by _____

FIGURE 9.2 Request for Credit Memo

The Flow of Costs

Once the goods have been received, the invoice signed, and the goods put away, the bookkeeping function begins to track the flow of costs through the foodservice operation. This process begins at the receiving area where the invoice is stamped with a bookkeeping tool known as the Invoice Stamp. (Figure 9.3) The *Invoice Stamp* is an inked rubber stamp that consolidates all the invoice information into a given area, usually on the back of the invoice. The Invoice Stamp can be unique to every business and is specially ordered by the foodservice manager to include the information that the foodservice operation is interested in tracking.

The Invoice Stamp normally identifies the date the goods were received, and the individual who checked in the goods. You may remember from the receiving process that the person who signs the invoice is not necessarily the person who checked in the goods. By knowing who checked in the goods and who put them away, we can confirm whether or not the product was actually delivered. Information concerning unit prices, extensions, and invoice totals are initialed to confirm accuracy. The checking of this information readies the invoice for payment and allows the bookkeeper to post the invoice to the current Accounts Payable file. When the invoice comes due, the manager will pull the actual invoice from the current Accounts payable file, and will initial the area Approved for Payment. The bookkeeper will prepare the check, record the invoice number on the check, and transfer the date paid and the check number to the check number area on the Invoice Stamp. The recording of the invoice number on the check informs the purveyor of the actual invoice being paid. The check number is recorded on the invoice to show which check was used to pay the invoice and to support proof of payment. Most purveyors will send a monthly Statement of Accounts to verify all transactions that have taken place between the purveyor and the foodservice operation. This statement helps both businesses to keep accurate records.

A

Recieved by: Rick	Date: 7/03/98
Unit Prices: OK	Extensions: Lob = $96.00
Totals: $681.75	CM: $12.00–Lobster

Approved for Payment: _____

Check #: _____ Date: _____

Purchase Distribution Journal

Acct. # Seafood	$ 681.75
Acct. # _____	$ _____
Acct. # _____	$ _____
Acct. # _____	$ _____

B

Recieved by : Rick	Date: 7/03/98
Unit Prices: OK	Extensions: Lob = $96.00
Totals: $681.75	CM: $12.00–Lobsters

Approved for Payment: _____

Check #: _____ Payment Date: _____

Receiving Report Form

Directs : $681.75

Stores: _____

FIGURE 9.3 Invoice Stamps

Other information that may be included within the invoice stamp may be used to help track where the products go after leaving the receiving area. Two effective tracking methods will now be discussed. First, used with Invoice Stamp A, the Purchase Distribution Journal (commonly used by foodservice operations to track how much is being spent in the different areas of costs), and secondly, used with Invoice Stamp B, the Receiving Report Form (normally used by the foodservice operations which have a formal storeroom process to track the movement of goods).

The Purchase Distribution Journal

The *Purchase Distribution Journal* (Figure 9.4) assists the chef/manager to identify how much money is being spent in the different areas of cost. Foodservice operations may track not only food costs, but also the different types of food categories: produce, meats, seafood, poultry, dairy, breads, etc. Beverage Costs may be broken into liquor, wines, draught beer, bottled beer, soda, etc. Overhead Costs may include paper/plastic supplies, linen, kitchen utensils, glassware, silverware, non-essentials, cleaning supplies, etc. Numbers are often used to classify these different types of purchases on the foodservice

Purchase Distribution Journal   **Category: Food**   **Month/Year: July '98**

Date	Invoice #	Meats	Seafood	Poultry	Produce	Grocery	Dairy	Bakery	Other	Total Invoice
7/01	127645	$987.75		$198.56						$1,186.31
7/02	0635				$645.50					$ 645.50
7/03	00246-00		$681.75							$ 681.75
7/03	11135						$145.60			$ 145.60
7/03	246778-12					$998.34		$56.95		$1,055.29

FIGURE 9.4 Purchase Distribution Journal

operation's "Chart of Accounts." The chart of accounts is a numbering system that assigns a number to each of the different types of purchases. This system assists foodservice operations to classify costs accurately and consistently. A sample chart of accounts can be found in Appendix D. This chart of accounts has been developed by the accounting firm of Laventhol and Horwath and has been adopted and recommended by the National Restaurant Association. As the goods are received, the receiving clerk will identify the account the purchase should be posted to, so that the bookkeeper can post the information to the Purchase Distribution Journal. Implementing a chart of accounts system, and tracking how much money is being spent in each of the different cost categories, can help management to identify the big picture of cost control.

Depending upon the number of purchase categories, the Purchase Distribution Journal might be broken down into several journals. One journal might identify food purchases, another beverage purchases, and yet a third for purchases in the Overhead Cost category. The Purchase Distribution Journal is normally prepared on a monthly basis. At the end of the month, a cost analysis can be prepared by totaling each of the purchasing categories and determining the percent of sales that each represents. In addition to knowing what percent of food sales is spent to purchase food products, a business can also identify the percent each category represents of total sales.

Receiving Scenario #3: It is March 6, and the foodservice operation has just received word from the accountant that the February food cost % reached an all time high of 38 %, six percentage points above what the operation considers to be normal. The foodservice manager is furious. How could the food cost % rise by 6%? If the foodservice operation has a Purchase Distribution Journal, the foodservice operator can easily identify the category of purchases that were higher than normal last month. Without the Purchase Distribution Journal the over expenditures might never be identified. Even though it is too late to control February's food cost, the foodservice manager who has the Purchase Distribution Journal as an information tool can now implement an additional control procedure to examine the excessive cost category.

The Receiving Report Form

A *Receiving Report Form* (Figure 9.5) is a tool used to track the movement of goods by classifying them into tracks/types. From the receiving area products move into one of two areas, storage or production. A *Direct Purchase*, is a purchase which when delivered goes directly into the production area. A Direct Purchase is assigned to the cost of sales when received. A *Storeroom Purchase*, is a purchase which when delivered is taken to the storeroom to be stored until needed. The Storeroom Purchase is assigned to the cost of sales when requisitioned. The Receiving Report form helps the chef/manager to identify where the goods are so that the goods can be more efficiently controlled.

There are often products classified as storeroom purchases that do not have a clearly designated purchase unit. Examples include an "As Purchased" meat product, or an undressed fish. It is important that the cost as well as the quantity of the product be identified before putting it into the storeroom. Before this product is transferred to the storeroom, a food tag should be filled out and attached so that the storeroom clerk can accurately assign it to food cost when the product is requisitioned. The use of a *food tag* is also helpful in the process of taking a monthly physical inventory. This will be discussed in Chapter 10, "Storage and Inventory Controls." (Figure 9.6).

Both the Purchase Distribution Journal and the Receiving Report Form can help the business to identify costs and product movement throughout the foodservice operation. Once the month is complete, new forms are started and the process of tracking product and costs continues.

Receiving Report Form

Month: July '98

Page: 1

Date	Invoice #	Purveyor	Description	Food	Beverage	Other	$ Directs	$ Stores	General Info
7/01	127645	TJ	Meats/Poultry	$1,186.31	$	$	$	$1,186.31	
7/02	0635	CFV	Produce	$ 645.50			$645.50		
7/03	00246-00	OS	Seafood	$ 681.75			$681.75		
7/03	11135	KD	Dairy	$ 145.50			$145.50		
7/03	246778-12	STC	Grocery/Bakery	$1,055.29			$ 56.95	$ 998.34	

FIGURE 9.5 Receiving Report Form

```
┌─────────────────────────────────────────────────┐
│  # 12435              Date Received _____  │
│                                                   │
│  Item _____  │
│                                                   │
│  Weight _____  │
│                                                   │
│  Unit Cost _____  │
│                                                   │
│  Total Cost _____  │
│                                                   │
│  Purveyor _____  │
│                                                   │
│  Date Issued _____  │
│                                                   │
├─────────────────────────────────────────────────┤
│  # 12435              Date Received _____  │
│                                                   │
│  Item _____  │
│                                                   │
│  Weight _____  │
│                                                   │
│  Unit Cost _____  │
│                                                   │
│  Total Cost _____  │
│                                                   │
│  Date Issued _____  │
│                                                   │
└─────────────────────────────────────────────────┘
```

FIGURE 9.6 Food Tag

Review Questions

1. Compare and contrast "Invoice Receiving" and "Blind Receiving." Why is Invoice Receiving more commonly used, if Blind Receiving is said to have better control?

2. How can a foodservice operation improve its receiving techniques?

3. How can you implement a Blind Receiving technique that would be effective and efficient within your foodservice operation?

4. Prepare a chart of accounts for a foodservice operation of your choice.

5. What is the difference between a "Direct Purchase" and a "Storeroom Purchase"? When is each assigned to daily food cost?

6. Using the computer program of your professor's choice, create a receiving report form that best meets the needs of your foodservice operation.

Bibliography

Dittmer, Paul R. and Gerald G. Griffin. *Principles of Food, Beverage, and Labor Cost Controls,* 5th ed. New York: Van Nostrand Reinhold, 1994.

Keister, Douglas C. *Food and Beverage Control.* Englewood Cliffs, NJ: Prentice-Hall, Inc., 1977.

Laventhol and Horwarth. *Uniform System of Accounts for Restaurants,* 6th ed. Washington, D.C.: The National Restaurant Association, 1990.

Schwartz, William C. "Eliminate Poor Receiving Habits." *Nation's Restaurants News,* April 9, 1984.

Stefanelli, John M., *Purchasing: Selection and Procurement for the Hospitality Industry,* 3d. ed. New York: John Wiley and Sons, Inc., 1992.

Storage and Inventory Controls

objectives

Upon completion of this chapter, the student should be able to:

1. develop standards with regards to proper storage controls.
2. perform and cost a physical inventory.
3. calculate the Cost of Sales.
4. maintain a perpetual inventory
5. implement efficient and cost effective issuing controls.

key terms

Bin Card
Cost of Beverage Sold Formula
Cost of Food Sold Formula
FIFO
Inventory Turnover

Perpetual Inventory
Physical Inventory
Requisition
Transfer Memo

Introduction

Once products have been received, the products that did not go directly into production are moved to the storage area to be stored until needed. The purpose of maintaining proper storage control is to prevent spoilage and the theft of goods, by both employees and non-employees. The control procedures of storage facilities are similar within all foodservice operations, but will differ in implementation depending upon the size of the foodservice operation. Normally, the larger foodservice operation will employ a full time storage clerk who is responsible for maintaining storage controls and for issuing products to production when needed. The smaller foodservice operation will usually not have a formal storeroom process with a full time storage clerk. Instead it will have to develop standard operating procedures regarding the movement of products in and out of the storeroom. Regardless of the size of the foodservice operation and the person in charge of storage controls, many of the same standard storage control procedures must be implemented. The person who is responsible for storage controls will be referred to as the storage clerk.

Establishing Effective Storage Controls

There are several areas of concern that need to be addressed when designing proper storage facilities and when implementing effective storage controls. Each area of concern will be discussed individually and in detail with special attention to efficiently and effectively maintaining storage control.

The Size of the Storage Area

The size of the storage area always tends to be smaller than what is desired by the foodservice operator. When a foodservice operator first looks at a facility, it is common for him/her to think only of the food and beverage items that will be stored there. Glassware, serviceware, paper supplies, cleaning supplies, extra furniture, fixtures and equipment, office supplies, paper work from past years, etc., must also be stored. Be certain to carefully consider the amount of storage space needed for the various types of storage. It is recommended by the Research Department of the National Restaurant Association that the space needed for all storage be approximately 5 square feet per seat in the dining room.

Location

Ideally, the storage facility should be located somewhere between the receiving and production area in order to ease the flow of goods through the foodservice operation. This may be easy to plan when building a new building, but unfortunately, in an existing building, you will have to work as best you can from wherever the storage space is located. Inconveniently located storage space not only makes daily operations more tedious but may increase the risk of theft and pilferage.

Theft and Pilferage

Theft usually refers to the unauthorized removal of goods by a non-employee. Non-employees can be customers and/or delivery personnel. Pilferage is employee theft. Pilferage is a real issue with regards to security and cost control within the foodservice industry. Employees are often caught removing products from the restaurant for their own personal use. Although employees may inadvertently take a piece of silverware or a side towel home in their apron, these items rarely see their way back to the restaurant. The restaurant must incur an additional cost to replace these items.

There must be storage controls in place to prevent both theft and pilferage. In a formal storage facility there is usually a storage clerk in the storeroom during operational hours to control products entering and leaving the storeroom. In facilities that do not have a formal storeroom and thus do not employ a storage clerk, the most common method utilized for storage control is a simple lock and key. It makes good sense to have storage facilities locked at all times and to allow people to enter the storeroom only when accompanied by authorized personnel. This procedure can be a real headache for the kitchen, bar, or dining room that is unprepared for production. Proper planning of production needs (Chapter 11), helps to relieve the burden. Another security control that is now seen more regularly in the foodservice industry is the use of the camera. Hidden or not, a camera can identify any improper activity.

Storage Conditions

To maintain quality products and to insure maximum shelf life of the product, products must be stored at recommended temperatures and must be consumed prior to the end of the product's shelf-life. The shelf life of a product is the recommended amount of time the product will maintain its quality for use in production. It is also important that products be stored well out of the Temperature Danger Zone (41°F to 135°F) so that foodborne illness does not result. All perishable and non-perishable products have a recommended shelf life and recommended storage temperatures to maximize the useful life of the product, and to prevent food borne illness. Storage temperature guidelines recommended by the Educational Foundation of the National Restaurant Association follow.

Obviously, knowing the proper storage temperature is important, but temperatures do not check themselves. Temperatures of refrigeration equipment must be checked routinely, at least 3 times daily. Inspections at opening time, after lunch, and before closing are necessary to guarantee that the equipment is maintaining its proper temperatures. This responsibility should be part of a kitchen employee's job description.

Storage Scenario #1: It is 10:00 p.m. and all but a few dinners have been prepared and served. The head line cook, Keith, informs the Manager On Duty (M.O.D.) that the temperature gauge in the main walk-in is running at about 45°F. The manager calls the Refrigeration Repair Service and leaves a message with the answering service. It's almost midnight and most of the kitchen employees are in the final stages of completing their job responsibilities. All are almost ready to clock out. No call has been received from the refrigeration company and there is no decline on the temperature gauge in the walk-in. The M.O.D. decides to empty the walk-in and to assist Keith and the kitchen staff to find other space (reach-ins, bar coolers, keg coolers), to store the goods until the walk-in can be repaired. At 1:00 a.m., the refrigeration repair service calls to see if they can be of assistance. The M.O.D. asks them to arrive at 7.00 a.m. the next morning to repair the walk-in.

In Storage Scenario #1, Keith performs his job responsibly. He knows what the temperature of the walk-in should be, he checks it a number of times and watches to be certain that the rise in temperature is not due to the regular opening and closing of the door of the walk-in. Once he realizes that there is a problem, he informs the manager.

Temperature Danger Zone:		41°F	to	135°F
Refrigeration Recommended Temperatures:	Meat and Poultry	32°F	to	40°F
	Fish	30°F	to	34°F
	Shellfish	35°F	to	45°F
	Eggs	38°F	to	40°F
	Dairy	38°F	to	40°F
	Fruits and Vegetables	41°F	to	45°F
Freezer Storage:		−10°F	to	0°F
Dry Storage		50°F	ideal	

The Educational Foundation of the National Restaurant Association, *Applied Foodservice Sanitation*, 4th ed., 1992.

FIGURE 10.1 Temperatures

Storage Scenario #1 continues. . . . Less than a week later, the temperature in the walk-in is again running high. It's Keith's night off. A different manager is on duty and the high temperature goes unnoticed. The next morning the opening manager is performing the opening inspection and identifies that the walk-in temperature reads 53°F. Thousands of dollars are lost. Food that has been in the Temperature Danger Zone for too long a period of time has spoiled and cannot be safely used.

Storage Equipment

Storage Equipment refers to shelving units, proper storage containers, and moving equipment that makes the storage process easier and more efficient. It is recommended that perishable items be stored on slotted shelving units so that air may circulate among the products stored in refrigeration and freezer units. It is also recommended that non-perishable, canned, bottled, and dry goods be stored on solid shelving. However, many foodservice operations find that slotted shelving is less expensive than solid shelving and often use it for all products.

Storage Scenario #2: The bar manager receives a delivery of non-perishable food items (cases of canned juices, cocktail onions, Worcestershire sauce, cocktail olives and a gallon of maraschino cherries), needed to produce and garnish beverages. The bartender who checks in the goods promptly transfers the products to the storage area to put them away. Everything in the dry storage area is placed in an orderly fashion on slotted shelving units, each consisting of five slotted shelves. The bartender opens a case of four 1 gallon glass jars of maraschino cherries to properly put them away on the next to the top shelf of the shelving unit. As the bartender rotates the stock of maraschino cherries already on hand, one of the glass gallon jars crashes into another, cracking and spilling its contents not only on the shelf on which it was stored, but now is dripping all the way down to the floor. What a mess!

Even though solid shelving is more expensive, it can help to save a great deal of time, energy, effort, and frustration. Foodservice operators who purchase slotted shelving units often use sheet pans to line the slotted shelves to prevent catastrophes such as the one in Storage Scenario #2. In the long run, solid shelving units are much more durable, sturdy, and practical.

Proper storage containers are also important. It is recommended that products not be stored in the container in which they have been purchased, unless the product has been purchased in its usable container (such as a 1/2 gallon of orange juice or a 14 oz. bottle of ketchup). The true intent of the statement is that products should be stored in air tight, pest protected containers, to protect against contamination and food borne illness. Cardboard cases and thick, heavy paper bags do not provide protection from insects and rodents. In fact, roaches think of cardboard cases as condominiums and often travel to and from different establishments in the cardboard itself, rather than in the product. It is strongly recommended that all food products, perishable or not, be removed from paper and cardboard containers and transferred to airtight containers.

Cleanliness

In addition to storing products in proper storage containers, it is extremely important that the storage areas be kept clean so as not to attract rodents and insects. Storage areas must be broom swept daily and a regular pest control schedule should be implemented. Whether you see insects or not, routine pest control maintenance is extremely important. Once you see a bug or two, chances are that you have thousands in cracks, walls, and equipment. Storage Scenario #3: Richard has been recently hired as the Executive Chef of a brand new hotel in the southern region of the U.S., where the weather is warm and insects are plentiful. The brand new hotel does not yet pose a pest problem, but Chef Richard schedules an appointment with the Head of Maintenance to discuss hiring a company to perform routine maintenance pest control for the new restaurant. Chef Richard knows the importance of routine maintenance whether or not a pest problem exists. The Head of Maintenance does not see the necessity of spending the money if there is no current problem. Chef Richard insists. The Head of Maintenance denies the request. They spend almost two months debating the issue of Pest Control maintenance, and still the Head of Maintenance refuses to hire a service. Chef Richard goes to the General Manager of the Hotel to state his case. The General Manager hears his case, and tells Chef Richard that he will inform him of his decision by the end of the week.

Thursday night, as Chef Richard is performing the closing inspection of the kitchen, he sees a black mark on the hot water pipe running down the wall to the sink. He moves closer to get a better look. He finds about fifteen roaches gathered together absorbing the heat from the hot water pipe. Now there is a real problem. If he can see fifteen, there have to be more; but just how many more? Chef Richard continues to check all the warm areas in the kitchen looking for roaches. He finds them in the cappuccino machine, the motor of the cold water cooler, and the baskets in which the bread is served. They are everywhere. Chef Richard is frustrated that the foodservice operation went so quickly from being pest free to totally infested, since this could have been prevented.

Routine pest control maintenance is important everywhere. The frequency of routine service may vary from region to region depending on the weather. Routine pest control maintenance (prior to a problem), is a sound measure, not only to control cost due to contamination of products, but also to insure that the business is not ruined by unwanted pests.

Storage Scenario #3 continues . . . The decision of the hotel's General Manager is to override that of the Head of Maintenance and to allow Chef Richard to hire a Pest Control Service. Chef Richard now informs the General Manager of the desperate need for the service and tells him of all the areas where he has now located roaches. Chef Richard calls several Pest Maintenance Control services to discuss the process of getting rid of the pest problem.

Pests such as roaches, ants, rats, and mice are a real problem. It is far easier to prevent a pest problem than to correct a pest problem. The best Pest Control services will tell you that one chemical will not end your problem. At the first service, the fogging and spraying will kill the roaches which have currently invaded your property. But as these roaches meet their death they deliver their egg sacks. Another chemical must be used to kill these eggs which have already built an immunity to the first chemical used. Each egg sack is estimated to house anywhere from nine to twenty-five new roaches. The roach problem continues.

Setting Up the Storage Areas

"Every item has a space, and every item in its space" is the best way to describe setting up storage areas. All products in dry storage, walk-ins, and freezers should have a designated location, and these products should not be found anywhere but in that assigned location. There is nothing more frustrating to a chef than not finding a product where it should be. The assumption is that the product must have been used up when it is not found in its proper location. The chef orders more. As the chef is putting away the new delivery, he finds four cases of the product that he was just looking for in a location other than where it should have been. If this is a perishable product, chances are the foodservice operation will not be able to use and sell all of the product before it spoils. If this is a non-perishable product, they will probably be able to use the product, but they will have tied up money in inventory that could have been used somewhere else. In either case, good storage and cost controls were not in place.

Well organized storage facilities will often use shelving labels to identify product location. Others will have floor plans and shelving plans tacked to the wall or to the shelving units themselves, indicating the product location, so that products can be easily found. Identifying a specific location for all products allows inventory sheets to be prepared in advance and in storage order, reducing the amount of time needed for the monthly physical inventory.

FIFO (First In, First Out)

First In, First Out is the method of stock rotation that should be used to insure that products are used up before their shelf life expires. FIFO makes dollars and cents (and sense). If a product is purchased first, it should be used first. If this is common sense, why is it often a headache for most foodservice operators to get their employees to rotate stock properly? Stock rotation is a tedious, time consuming process due to the set up of most storerooms. Storage areas must be "employee friendly" if a manager expects an employee to rotate stock properly and efficiently.

There are two things foodservice operators can do to make rotating stock "employee friendly" and to encourage proper stock rotation. The first is to date products that do not already have expiration dates on them. The second is to organize the facility so that the actual process of stock rotation is easier for the employees to perform. Figure 10.2 illustrates two methods of Storage Facility Set Up, one which does not encourage proper stock rotation and another which does encourage proper stock rotation.

Poorly set up storage areas (as seen in Figure 10.2A) are those that have shelves that line the wall, making it very difficult to rotate stock. When the new stock needs to be put away, employees must pull the older product off the shelf to put the new product to the back. Then, they must place the older product back on the shelves in front of the new. This process is very tedious and time consuming. Storage Set Up, as in Figure 10.2A, tempts the employee to cheat in the process of proper stock rotation. A more efficient storage set up (Figure 10.2B) is provided by free standing shelves where products can be removed from one side and stocked from the other side. This set up provides an easier and less time consuming task for the employee.

Establishing Standard Inventory Controls

Foodservice operations often use two types of inventories. The first is the physical inventory, which is an actual count of all food and beverage products on hand. The second is the perpetual inventory, which tracks food and beverage products on paper, rather than physically. Both inventories are valid methods in establishing inventory controls.

Physical Inventory

Once a month, usually the first morning of the month prior to any production, chefs and managers, often accompanied by a controller, will count all the food and beverage items in all storage and production areas. This process is known as a Physical Inventory. A *Physical Inventory* is an actual count of all products on hand that will be used to produce sales. The two people taking the inventory will go from storage area to storage area counting and recording the products on hand. Although a physical inventory can be taken by one person, two people normally perform the inventory; one counts, while the

A

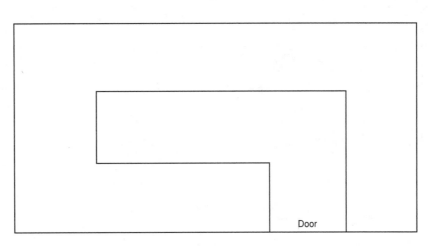

B

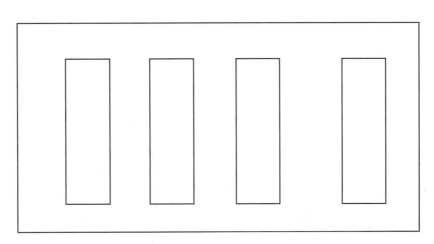

FIGURE 10.2 Storeroom Set Up

other records the quantity on the inventory sheets. The presence of two people makes the process more efficient. The controller is a representative from the accounting office who oversees the counts and records the quantities on the inventory sheets.

Inventory sheets should be prepared prior to taking the physical inventory (Figure 10.3). The preparation of these forms ahead of time increases efficiency and reduces the time it takes to perform the inventory. Inventory sheets should list the items by the location of the item rather than alphabetically. Taking a physical inventory location by location, rack by rack, shelf by shelf, insures that nothing will be missed in the count. Although alphabetical preparation of inventory sheets appears organized, using them is totally unrealistic and creates chaos.

A physical inventory is taken once a month so that it can be used to calculate the monthly Cost and Cost % of Sales. The physical inventory closes the books on the previous month, and opens the books for the current month. Most chef/managers look at a physical inventory as a check-up process. An explanation of how most foodservice managers place a dollar value on the physical inventory and how this figure is used to determine the monthly Cost of Sales follows.

INVENTORY SHEET   **Page:**

Category: Beverage/Beer   **Location:**

Qty	Unit	Item	Cost	Unit	Extension
		Coors, 12 oz.	$13.59	cs-24	
		Coors Lite, 12 oz.	$13.80	cs-24	
		Budweiser, 12 oz.	$13.45	cs-24	
		Miller High Life, 12 oz.	$13.25	cs-24	
		Heineken, 12 oz.	$21.20	cs-24	
		Becks, 12 oz.	$20.80	cs-24	

Prepared by: _____   Page Total |
_____   Total |

FIGURE 10.3 Inventory Sheet

Costing and Extending the Physical Inventory

Once the physical inventory has been counted and recorded on the inventory sheets, the inventory must be extended and totaled so it may be used to determine the monthly Cost of Sales. Due to the constant inventory turnover of food and beverage products, and the seasonal differences in prices, the most common method used to cost the physical inventory is the Latest Purchase Price method. This method is recommended by Laventhol and Harworth in their book prepared for the National Restaurant Association, *Uniform System of Accounts for Restaurants* (1990). The foodservice manager identifies the last price paid for each item from the invoices and then records them in the Unit Column of the Inventory Sheets. Knowing both the quantity and unit costs of the items (multiply quantity × unit costs), the foodservice manager can carefully extend and total the inventory. The Latest Purchase Price method is usually used for inventory values. When inventory needs to be replaced, the last price paid for a product is usually used as it is often still its market price. Although other methods of inventory costing may be chosen, research shows that the Latest Purchase Price is the most popular and the easiest to use. Computerized inventory spreadsheet programs are also available for foodservice operators. Only the quantity and price need to be posted to the spreadsheet, and then the computer quickly and accurately extends and totals the inventory. Once the total food inventory and the total beverage inventory have been determined, the Cost of Food Sold and the Cost of Beverages Sold can be reached.

Determining the Cost of Sales

The formulas to determine the *Cost of Food Sold* and the *Cost of Beverages Sold* are basically the same. Both are illustrated in Figure 10.4.

If we are calculating the Cost of Sales for the month of February, the opening inventory would be the total of the monthly physical inventory taken on February 1, and the closing inventory would be the total of the monthly physical inventory taken on March 1. When it's time to calculate the Cost of Sales for the month of March, the March 1 inventory becomes the opening inventory, and the total of the monthly physical inventory taken on April 1 is March's closing inventory, and so on. The cost of the monthly physical inventory needs to be calculated so that the Cost of Sales can be determined to prepare the monthly Income Statement.

Cost of Food Sold Formula

	Opening Food Inventory
+	Food Purchases
=	Total Food Available for Sale

	Total Food Available for Sale
−	Closing Food Inventory
=	Cost of Food Sold

Cost of Beverage Sold Formula

	Opening Beverage Inventory
+	Beverage Purchases
=	Total Beverages Available for Sale

	Total Beverages Available for Sale
−	Closing Beverage Inventory
=	Cost of Beverages Sold

FIGURE 10.4 Cost of Sales Formulas

Perpetual Inventory

A *perpetual inventory* is a bookkeeping inventory that keeps a daily running balance of the quantity and costs of products on hand. It is very difficult to keep a perpetual inventory for the food items needed to run a foodservice operation as there are thousands of ingredients to track. The Perpetual Inventory is still, however, an effective tool to control beverage inventory.

Many foodservice operations still control their beverage inventory using a perpetual inventory tool known as the *bin card*. The Beverage Bin Card (Figure 10.5) is used in conjunction with a Par Stock system at the Bar. The Bin Card is normally stored close to where the beverages are stored. It can be used to identify where the beverages should be stored. Every item has a place, and every item in its place. As beverage products are delivered and put into storage, the inventory on the Bin Card is increased. As beverages are requisitioned for use, the perpetual inventory is reduced and noted on the Bin Card. At any point in time, the manager can go to the liquor storage and compare the bookkeeping perpetual inventory to the actual physical inventory of the product on hand. If the information on these two documents is not the same, an error has occurred.

Stock #: 5200-0114

Product Name: **Mountain Sparkling Water**   **Unit: case/24-10 oz. bottles**

Date		Storage In		Storage Out		Balance on Hand	
Month	Day	Units	Costs	Units	Costs	1 cs.	$ 12
4	01	15 cs.	$180			16 cs.	$192
4	04			4 cs.	$48	12 cs.	$144
4	08			6 cs.	$72	6 cs.	$ 72
4	13			4 cs.	$48	2 cs.	$ 24
4	15	14 cs.	$168			16 cs.	$192

FIGURE 10.5 Bin Card

Inventory Turnover

Inventory Turnover refers to the number of times an inventory replaces itself on an annual basis. The inventory turnover rate is calculated separately for food and beverage products. To calculate the Food Inventory Turnover rate, we use the following formula:

Formula:

| ANNUAL COST OF | ÷ | AVG. MONTHLY | = | FOOD INVENTORY |
| FOOD SOLD | | FOOD INVENTORY | | TURNOVER |

A Beverage Inventory Turnover rate is calculated using the same formula but includes the Annual Cost of Beverages Sold and Average Beverage Inventory. The average inventory refers to the average monthly inventory for each product (total the twelve monthly inventories and divide the total by twelve). The Food Inventory Turnover Rate may average approximately 30 times per year (2–3 times per month). The Beverage Inventory Turnover Rate may average approximately 10 times per year (a little less than about once per month). These turnover rates are just averages. A good Food or Beverage Inventory rate for your business may be a little higher or lower than these depending upon the amount of storage space available. The Inventory Turnover Rate is often used as an evaluation tool. Determining an Inventory Turnover Rate which is much higher than normal might indicate that the foodservice manager is spending too much time and energy purchasing and receiving goods. When the results are lower than normal, this could indicate that the foodservice operation is storing too much product and tying up money in inventory that could be used elsewhere.

The Flow of Goods Continues

When the goods are received they are identified as a Direct Purchase or a Storeroom Purchase. The direct purchases go directly into production and the storeroom purchases are taken to the storeroom to be stored until needed for production. The Receiving Report Form (discussed in Chapter 9), identifies those products that enter the storeroom. If a foodservice operation does not employ a Receiving Report Form, these items can be identified on the invoice.

Issuing Food Products

A *Requisition* is a business form that lists and describes all items removed from the storeroom. A requisition is a request to remove the products from storage so that they may be used for production (Figure 10.6). The amounts requisitioned will normally depend on production forecasts (Chapter 11). The requisition is prepared by the chef/manager and filled by the storage clerk. Once the requisition has been filled, the products are sent to the department that requested the products.

In foodservice operations where there are no formal storerooms, and where food requisitions are not utilized, a pad of paper is often used to record what is needed from the storeroom. Once the items are listed, the chef/manager will okay the products to be issued and will escort the employee to the storeroom to fill the requisition. When there is no formal storeroom process, it is extremely important that the storeroom facilities always be locked and that only authorized personnel have access to the keys.

Storeroom Requisition				Location: Beach Bar	
Quantity	**Unit**	**Iss**	**Item**	**Unit Cost**	**Total**
2	cs.		Coors	$13.59/cs-24	$27.18
3	cs.		Coors Lite	$13.80/cs-24	$41.40
2	cs.		Budweiser	$13.45/cs-24	$26.90
2	cs.		Miller High Life	$13.25/cs-24	$26.50
1	cs.		Heineken	$21.20/cs-24	$21.20
1	cs.		Becks	$20.80/cs-24	$20.80
2	cs.		Mountain Sparkling Water	$12.00/cs-24	$24.00
3	qt.		Rose's Lime Juice	$35.59/cs-24	$ 8.91
				Total:	$196.89

Requisitioned by _____

Filled by _____

FIGURE 10.6 Storage Requisition

Issuing Beverage Products

Although beverage products are often issued using a beverage requisition, greater controls of alcoholic beverages need to be maintained. Employees are more likely to pilfer a bottle of liquor or wine than a food item. To insure that only the beverage products that are needed at the bar are requisitioned, beverage operations should develop a beverage par stock system at every location where alcohol is sold. A beverage par stock system is similar to the par stock system previously discussed in Chapter 8, but the system is now used as a control of in-process inventory rather than as an aid to purchasing. In fact, in-process inventory can be looked at as par stock in production areas.

To help control in-process inventories, it is common practice that when bottles are emptied they are not immediately disposed of. Instead, they are stored until the end of the shift when the closing bartender will count and record the bottles emptied on a Break Sheet. A Break Sheet does not illustrate how many bottles were literally broken, but instead, how many and what kinds of beverages were consumed and emptied. The Break Sheet will also identify bottles that may have been removed legally from the restaurant to be sent elsewhere (such as a guest room). The Break Sheet is used for all liquor and bottled wine. The Break Sheet can help a full service foodservice operation to identify which beverage products are most popular as well as to analyze the par stock system at the bar. The Break Sheet is then used to prepare a Beverage Requisition which lists the beverage items to be sent to the bar location. If the Par Stock at the bar is properly maintained, and the Break sheet properly prepared, the Par Stock at the bar should be

		Food and Beverage Transfer		

Day/Date: Tuesday, April 5

From Department: Bar   **To Department: Kitchen**

Quantity	Unit	Item	Unit Cost	Total
1	qt.	Lime Juice	$39.59/cs-12	$3.30
1/4	cs.	Mountain Sparkling Water	$12.00/cs-24	$3.00
				$6.30

Authorized by: _____

FIGURE 10.7 *Food and Beverage Transfer*

filled to the maximum par stock level when the Beverage Requisition is filled. If not, a "hole"occurs (a product is not at the maximum par level), indicating that pilferage may have occurred. It is a good cost control practice to implement a Break Sheet as a tool to control cost. The Break Sheet can be a formal document or simply a pad of paper that is used to record bottles "broken" on a on-going, daily basis.

Transferring Products

Often, food and beverage products are transferred from one department to another. For instance, the kitchen may have requisitioned a case of oranges to prepare orange wedges to be used as garnishes for dinner plates. The Bar may need six oranges to prepare slices of oranges to be used to garnish a variety of beverages. Rather than preparing a requisition for just six oranges, the Bar may request them from the kitchen. To do this, a Food and Beverage Transfer document (Figure 10.7) must be filled out by the person doing the transferring. A Food and Beverage *Transfer memo* identifies products that were once charged to one department, and assigns their cost to the department to which they are transferred.

The kitchen and bar often share and trade products that are needed by both departments. Just as oranges are needed by the bar and kitchen, so might creme de menthe be needed by both. This sharing and transferring of products should be tracked so that each department is charged appropriately for the products used to produce sales. Whether food or beverage, products must be assigned to the appropriate category of costs.

In a smaller business, where few formal documents are utilized, managers will forego the Food and Beverage Transfer memo, and simply classify products as food costs or beverage costs. When transferring six oranges from the kitchen to the bar, in the small or medium size foodservice operation, a Food and Beverage Transfer memo may not be used. Instead, the total cost of oranges might be assigned to food cost because the kitchen uses most of the oranges. To "wash out" the excess food cost, all limes may be assigned to beverage cost, because the kitchen may use a few limes while the bar uses most of them.

The use of Storage and Issuing documents is based on the size of the foodservice operation. The larger the business the more formal the business documents used. Whether small, medium, or large, foodservice operations need to implement the most cost effective systems possible.

Review Questions

1. Develop a flow chart illustrating the movement of food products from the receiving area to the production area. Which business forms would be needed to properly control the flow of food and to control their costs?

2. Develop a flow chart illustrating the movement of beverage products from the receiving area to the production area. Which business forms would be needed to properly control the flow of beverages and to control their costs?

3. Using the inventory sheet found in Appendix F, post the following information. Extend and total the inventory for items found in the beer cooler located at the Beach Bar of a small hotel.

Bottled Beer

Coors 12 oz.	45 bottles	$13.59/cs-24
Coors Lite 12 oz.	32 bottles	$13.80/cs-24
Budweiser 12 oz.	15 bottles	$13.45/cs-24
Miller High Life 12 oz.	22 bottles	$13.25/cs-24
Heineken 12 oz.	14 bottles	$21.20/cs-24
Becks 12 oz.	16 bottles	$20.80/cs-24

4. Using the information below, calculate the Cost of Food Sold and the Cost of Food Sold % for the months of April, May, and June.

Food Inventory *opening/closing*		Food Sales	Food Purchases
April 1	$12,450	April $255,600	April $82,325
May 1	$11,620	May $221,800	May $75,250
June 1	$12,740	June $283,200	June $92,760
July 1	$11,420	July $303,250	July $90,800

5. Using the following information, calculate the Cost of Beverages Sold and the Cost of Beverages Sold % for the months of July, August, and September.

Beverage Inventory		Beverage Sales		Beverage Purchases	
July 1	$5,500	July	$130,500	July	$23,500
August 1	$6,200	August	$142,250	August	$25,350
September 1	$5,400	September	$135,230	September	$24,400
October 1	$6,100	October	$129,200	October	$23,870

6. Using the spread sheet of your professor's choice, develop an inventory spread sheet that a foodservice manager might use to total inventory.

Bibliography

Dittmer, Paul R. and Gerald G. Griffin. *Principles of Food, Beverage, and Labor Cost Controls.* 5th ed. New York: Van Nostrand Reinhold, 1994.

The Educational Foundation of the National Restaurant Association, *Applied Foodservice Sanitation,* 4th ed. 1992.

Keister, Douglas C. *Food and Beverage Control.* Englewood Cliffs, NJ: Prentice-Hall, Inc., 1977.

Laventhol and Horwarth. *Uniform System of Accounts for Restaurants.* 6th ed. Washington D.C.: National Restaurant Association, 1990.

National Restaurant Association, *Conducting a Feasibility Study for a New Restaurant, A Do It Yourself Handbook,* 1983.

Stefanelli, John M. *Purchasing: Selection and Procurement for the Hospitality Industry,* 3d ed. New York: John Wiley and Sons, Inc., 1992.

Daily Production Control and Analysis

objectives

Upon completion of this chapter, the student should be able to:

1. utilize proper methods of portion control to maintain consistency and to control the costs of both food and beverage items.
2. plan food production using past sales history to forecast production.
3. prepare and use a Production Forecast Report.
4. reconcile production reports with sales reports.
5. calculate Daily Food and Beverage Cost Reports to determine daily cost percents.

key terms

Daily Beverage Cost %
Daily Food Cost %
In House Promotion
In Process Inventories
Preparation
Presentation
Production

Production Forecast Report
Standard Portion
Standard Presentation
Standard Recipe
Standard Yield
Steward Sales

Introduction

As we continue through the cost control cycle we now arrive at the production stage. *Production* is the step at which food and beverage products and production areas are readied for service to the customer. Production includes *preparation* and *presentation*. During the preparation phase, food and beverage items are "prepped" as are the production areas. The presentation phase encompasses the transfer of food from the production areas to where the customer is served. Cost control measures must be implemented in both phases in order to attain the goals of production. The goals of production can be viewed as consistency, customer satisfaction, and cost control. Control areas will be identified and control procedures explained to show how goals of production are met.

Once the control measures have been explained, we will analyze daily production and sales activities. Production Analysis is the process in which the chef/manager determines how well costs were controlled through the production process by determining Daily Cost percents. In this chapter we will discuss control and analysis techniques needed in production control.

Food Production Controls

Food cost control standards must be adhered to in order to maintain a consistent product and to reach the goal of profit desired by the foodservice operation. The following areas must be carefully examined and developed to insure profitability.

Standard Recipe

Preparation begins with the development of a standard recipe. A *Standard Recipe* is a written formula that requires the same quantity of ingredients, quality of ingredients, and method of preparation each time the recipe is prepared. A Standard Recipe helps the foodservice operation to provide a consistent product at a controlled cost. A Standard Recipe should be prepared for all food items served. In the preparation stage of production, the chef/manager must set the criteria by which the standard recipe is to be prepared. Production standards rely on the proper purchasing, receiving, and storage processes to insure quality. The chef/manager must also develop standard procedures if preparation and train staff members to prepare the product correctly so that a consistent product is achieved.

When a Standard Recipe is prepared using the same quantity and quality of ingredients and the same method of preparation, the Standard Recipe will consistently deliver the same Standard Yield. A *Standard Yield* is the quantity of servable food product attained from a Standard Recipe. A Standard Yield can be stated in the total quantity of food product (3 gallons of clam chowder), or in the number of portions attained (40 servings). In order to guarantee the standard yield of a recipe, a Standard Portion must be determined. A *Standard Portion* is the quantity of food that is consistently served to each customer. Portion control measures must be stated on the standard recipes and equipment must be used to insure that standard portion control is maintained. When developing standard recipes for menu items, it is important not only to think about the quality and quantity of ingredients needed to prepare the recipes, but also to identify the means by which standard portion control can be maintained.

Standard Portion Control

Standard Portion Control can be maintained by weight, volume, count, and the size of the container in which a product is served. Standard Portion control is not only important in maintaining a consistent quantity served to the customer, but is also necessary in insuring the expected profit on every portion of product sold. When developing a Standard Recipe, time should be spent in determining the tools and equipment needed to maintain Standard Portion control.

Weight

When the Standard Portion is stated by weight, the scale is the tool needed to maintain portion control. When a product is advertised at a specified weight, it is generally understood that the weight stated is a pre-cooked weight. This information is acquired when weighing products during the preparation phase or when purchasing products in their pre-prepared edible portion form. Weighing products in the production phase places an unnecessary burden on production staff and slows production time. Weighing and portioning products into individual bags or separating them with parchment paper prior to the cooking process not only controls standard portion size but also increases speed and accuracy in the production phase.

Volume

Standard Portion control of volume measures is evaluated by ladle, scoop, and spoon measurements, or by the size of the container in which the product is served. Volume Standard Portion control usually takes place at the end of the production phase. For example, standard portion control can be implemented by serving a 2 oz. ladle of hollandaise sauce over Eggs Benedict or a Number 8 Scoop of ice cream with a slice of apple pie.

Count

Menu items are often portioned by the count. It may be four shrimp for a Shrimp Cocktail, twelve Chicken Wings, or eight Mozzarella Sticks to an order. To maintain standard counts for portion control, orders should be portioned and separated prior to the cooking of products whenever possible. This will insure accuracy and speed up production time.

Size of Container

Standard Portion control of volume measurement can be maintained by the size of container in which the product is served. If Standard Portion Control is being maintained through the size of the container, employees must be trained on how to fill a container appropriately to provide consistency and cost control. If it is left up to the employees, some may very well over portion on a regular basis, and this will eventually affect food cost. Six ounces of soup served in a coffee cup may very well end up as seven to eight ounces. It is important for both consistency and cost control that proper Standard Portion control be implemented. The appropriate equipment must be available to employees so that control may be achieved.

Standard Presentation

To maintain a consistent and cost efficient menu item, it is important to have a standard presentation. *Standard Presentation* refers to the way a product is consistently arranged on a plate in a set pattern each time it is served. Standard Presentation is especially important in banquet settings as well as at a table where customers have ordered the same menu item. Customers want to be sure that the plate that is set in front of them is exactly the same in quantity and appearance as the plate set in front of their dining companion. A Standard Presentation should be developed for all menu items. Some foodservice chains train their employees by using pictures and diagrams showing how the menu item should look. These pictures and diagrams are posted in the kitchen for daily use. Standard Presentation is important in serving a consistent product.

Beverage Production Controls

As discussed within the Storage and Issuing Control Chapter, beverage control is normally confirmed using a Break Sheet. A Break Sheet can be a formal pre-prepared document or simply a piece of paper listing all bottles used up (emptied) during a shift. The use of the Break Sheet system helps to maintain par stock at the bar and informs the next day's bartender of the liquors, beers, and wines to be stocked. The Break Sheet process is the beginning of the preparation stage of production control. It is a helpful way to confirm that all the products needed for production are on hand.

Standard Recipes

Just as food menu items need standard recipes to maintain a consistent product and to control costs, so do beverage items need a standard recipe. Many of the more traditional and popular drinks have standard recipes that are documented and published in bartending books. Foodservice operations sometimes have their own variations to these traditional and popular drinks and should develop standard recipes of their own. A Beverage standard Recipe states the ingredients of the beverage, the exact measurement of the ingredients, the garnish to be used, and the size and type of glass in which the product is served. Standard recipes are used to maintain a consistent product, to encourage customer satisfaction, and to control beverage costs. Standard Recipes are the basis of all cost controls.

Standard Portion Control

Obviously, all beverages are served in glassware, so the first step in effective standard portion control is to be certain that the beverage is served in the correct size glass as stated on the standard recipe. The size and style of glass should be identified on the standard recipe and used each time the beverage is prepared. Another concern of effective beverage standard portion control is the amount of alcohol used to make each drink. A jigger is a portion control tool used to control the quantity of alcohol used in a drink. As effective as the jigger is in consistency and cost control, the use of a jigger often slows the process of drink making and sometimes gets a negative response from the customer. Many foodservice operations have implemented the use of the "free pour" which is based on a three count of liquor poured directly into the glass. Unfortunately, the "free pour" is not as effective a cost control measure as is the use of a jigger. It takes a great deal of practice and professionalism for a bartender to become proficient at measuring by "free pour." With increased alcohol awareness as well as liquor liability, use of the jigger is not only better for cost control but is also a tool to help insure that the customer is not being over served.

Standard Presentation

A standard garnish should be determined for all beverages. The garnish is the fruit or vegetable product that accompanies the beverage. Secondly, the standard size and type of glass should be used each and every time the beverage is prepared. "Regular customers" usually know the standard size and type of glass used for the beverage they order. They expect a consistent presentation. Each of these simple yet important standards will help a foodservice operation to meet production goals.

As discussed within Food Production Controls and Beverage Production Controls, these standards must be determined long before the Production process takes place. These basic standards help to provide consistency, customer satisfaction, and cost control.

Forecasting Production

Products that arrive to the production area are requisitioned from the storeroom. They arrive directly from the receiving area, or are transferred from one department to another. In Chapter 10, we discussed how products are removed from the storage areas through the use of a requisition, and how products transferred from one department to another are accounted for. Chapter 9 showed how direct purchases found their way to the production area. But how did the chef/manager determine the amount of product needed?

The Production Forecast Report

Once the standard recipe and portion control measures have been developed, the process of production can begin. The Production phase as described in the introduction begins when the menu items are actually produced. Before the production process occurs, the chef/manager must determine the need for production and must prepare a Production Forecast Report. The *Production Forecast Report* is a document used in the preparation stage of production to help the chef/manager make an educated guess as to the number of customers expected during a given meal period, the menu item that those customers will order, and the quantity of each item to prepare for production. This forecast is determined by using the past sales history of customers served and menu items sold. (Figure 11.1).

The number of customers previously served can be tracked using several different procedures, including guest checks, hostess seating control sheets and register readings. Once tracked, the number of customers served on a given day often starts to show a consistent pattern. For instance, every weekday night the foodservice operation serves approximately 120 dinners while on Friday and Saturday nights, the number of customers served climbs to 180. The number of customers projected should also take into consideration the number of reservations made, any holidays, and special events or activities which might take place near the location of the restaurant. Work experience in a business over a period of time will usually help chef/managers in predicting accurate guest numbers as well. Once forecasted, the number of customers expected should be posted to the production forecast report.

In Chapter 12, we will explain how individual menu items sold are tracked and counted. Once counted, the number of individual menu items is compared to the number of total items sold within the same menu category, and a popularity percentage is determined. This popularity percentage is known as a Sales Mix. A Sales Mix percentage illustrates how popular a menu item is as compared to other menu items within the same menu category. The Sales Mix can be used to help forecast which menu items customers are most likely to choose.

Sales Mixes fall into regular patterns as do customers counts. The more familiar a chef/manager becomes with customer preference, the better he/she will be at forecasting the production needs of the foodservice operation. The Sales Mix percent of the items can be posted to the Forecast Production Sheet to help determine the number of portions of each menu item to be prepared.

Once the Sales Mix is posted to the Production Forecast Report, the number of customers forecasted (covers) is multiplied by the Sales Mix % of each menu item. The result of this process is the number of portions to be prepped to meet production needs or Forecasted Preparation.

Formula:

COVERS	$\times$	SALES MIX %	=	FORECASTED PREPARATION
Baked Stuffed Sole: 200	$\times$	20%	=	40 portions

The forecasted preparation should be adjusted by the chef/manager if there are any special events or excessive reservations for a particular evening, and the adjustment should be posted to the Added Preparation Column. The reason for the additional preparation of menu items should be stated on the productions sheet. The Added Preparation Column should be added to the Forecasted Preparation to attain the Total Forecast Column.

Once the Total Forecast has been determined, an inventory of unused product from the previous meal should be taken and recorded in the On Hand Column. The difference between the Total Forecast Column and the Number On Hand Column gives the number of portions that need to be prepped for the upcoming meal period.

Forecasted Covers: 200

Menu Item	Sales Mix %	Forecasted Preparation	Added Prep	Total Forecast	Product On Hand	Needed Prep	Total Avail	Amt LO Time RO	Errors	Kitchen Sold
Baked Stuffed Sole	20%	40	-0-	40	2	38	40	2	1	37
Broiled Scrod	22%	44	-0-	44	6	38	44	4	1	39
Lobster	12%	24	10	34	-0-	34	34	2	-0-	32
Shrimp Scampi	15%	30	-0-	30	-0-	30	30	9:30 PM	-0-	30
Baked Scallops	18%	36	-0-	36	4	32	36	8	-0-	28
Grilled Tuna Steak	13%	26	-0-	26	5	21	26	8:30 PM	-0-	26
Totals	**100%**	**200**	**10**	**210**	**17**	**193**	**210**	**16**	**2**	**192**

Additional Prep: Special Reservation for 10 ordering Baked Stuffed Lobsters

Reason for Error: Foodserver ordered Scrod should have been Sole.

FIGURE 11.1 Production Forecast Report

Formula:

TOTAL FORECAST	–	PRODUCT ON HAND	=	NEEDED PREPARATION
Baked Stuffed Sole: 40 portions	–	2	=	38 portions

The On Hand Column should then be added to the Needed Preparation Column and the total of both posted in the Total Available for Production Column. The Total Available for Production Column should be compared to an actual count of product available for sale prior to the meal's production phase. Once the dining period is complete, another inventory of product is taken and the amount left over, or the time at which the product runs out, is recorded in the appropriate column. The amount left over will be used as the amount "on hand" for the next meal's production needs. If an item runs out, rather than recording a zero, the time is recorded to help the chef/manager in preparing future forecasts. If a zero were recorded rather than the time, it would not be known if the kitchen regularly exhausted the supply of product at 7:30 p.m., or at 9:45 p.m, just before the kitchen closed. The time at which the product runs out is a useful tool to maintain the Sales Mix. An accurate sales mix is an effective forecasting tool.

Errors that are made during the production phase must be accounted for. The number and kind of production error should be posted to the Error column on the Production Forecast Report, thus tracking all food items used during production. The difference between the Total Available for Production and the Amount Left Over/Time Ran Out Column (including errors made during production), determines the number of menu items the Kitchen Sold.

Production and Sales Reconciliation

Often daily production results will be compared to daily sales results to insure that all menu items leaving the kitchen are indeed accounted for through sales. Some foodservice operations compare all menu items produced to menu items sold while others perform the reconciliation for only high food cost menu items such as seafood and beef products. A close watch is kept to insure that all products leaving the production areas are charged for. With increased cash register computerization and the use of Price Look Ups (PLUs), the sales information needed to perform the reconciliation can be quickly attained through a cash register reading. The reading can then be compared to the Production Forecast Report for accuracy before day's end. If there is a discrepancy, it is the chef/manager's responsibility to discover the reason. An overdone entrée that was returned and not recorded on the error card or an appetizer that was ordered but never charged for on the guest check might be reasons for the discrepancy.

Completing the Production Forecast Report can help the chef/manager to determine what must be requisitioned from the storage areas as well as what needs to be purchased daily to meet production needs. It also assists the kitchen in identifying the number of products available for sale prior to and after the production process, so as to better control food costs. The Production and Sales Reconciliation confirms that items that have left the production area have been sold and paid for. Standard Procedures to support the reconciliation will be discussed in "Standard Ordering Procedures" (Figure 11.2).

In-Process Inventories

Many foodservice operations use an in-process inventory par stock system instead of customer counts or a sales mix and Production Forecast Reports, to insure that the foodservice operation is prepared to meet production needs. This is particularly true in beverage production controls. *In-process inventory* is the amount of product available in production areas. Foodservice operations implementing the in-process inventory system

Day/Date: Saturday, 4/07

Menu Item	Recorded Sales	Error Card	Total Account	Kitchen Sold	Dif	Reason
Baked Stuffed Sole	36	-0-	36	37	1	Error not recorded
Broiled Scrod	38	1	39	39	-0-	
Lobster	32	-0-	32	32	-0-	
Shrimp Scampi	30	-0-	30	30	-0-	
Baked Scallops	28	-0-	28	28	-0-	
Grilled Tuna Steak	26	-0-	26	26	-0-	
Total	**190**	**1**	**191**	**192**	**1**	

FIGURE 11.2 Production/Sales Reconciliation

have a maximum par for production each day. Rather than utilizing a Production Forecast Report, they implement an In-Process Inventory Preparation Sheet. The In-Process Inventory "Prep Sheet" is also based on the sales history of the products themselves. The business develops a standard quantity (maximum par) to be available daily to meet production needs. The preparation staff is informed of this par and preps the number of menu items as stated on the Prep Sheet. This method can be as effective as the Production Forecast Report, but procedures must still be implemented to track the number of each menu item sold. It is also important when using the In-Process Inventory Par Stock System that additional preparation of menu items need to be noted, so that the par stock level of that menu item might be changed to meet business needs. The in-process inventory par levels should be evaluated on a regular basis.

The Flow of Goods

Once standards have been developed and production has been planned for, the actual preparation begins and continues to the presentation stage. Goods must first be ordered from production areas.

Standard Ordering Procedures

It should be standard policy at all foodservice operations that nothing be prepared or removed from the kitchen or the bar unless accounted for by a soft copy guest check. The soft copy guest check, or dupe, serves as payment for the products purchased from the kitchen. It represents cash. The dupe is what the foodserver uses to place orders with the kitchen and bar. The soft copy is a permission slip used to order and to remove food and beverage products requested by customers from the production areas. The soft guest check can be the top copy of a hand prepared guest check or may be a computerized tape of the items ordered through a computerized cash register system. The dupe or soft guest check process is a standard operating procedure that guarantees that the menu item has been properly recorded as a sale. On occasion, a request is made for a product without using a prepared soft guest check. A request of this type can lead to improper cost control as the sale was never recorded and the money never collected for the products consumed by the customer. The use of standard ordering procedures is important to both production and sales control.

Standard Pick Up Procedures

Once the order has been placed using a soft copy guest check, a standard procedure must be implemented to inform the foodserver of when the order is ready for service. This can be done effectively through timing, lights, or foodserver pagers. Often it is the foodserver's responsibility to know the preparation times for all menu items. Once the order is placed, the foodserver promptly returns to the kitchen to pick up the order within the designated time period. This procedure can work well for the well trained kitchen and foodservice staff. The lighting system often seen in dining rooms or near the kitchen door can also be an effective technique used to inform the foodserver that an order is ready. The use of these lights is more common in casual businesses than in fine dining facilities. The most recent development used to inform the foodserver that an order is ready is the pager (a vibrating buzzer attached to the foodserver's apron). When the order is ready, the expediter informs the foodserver by sending an electronic pulse that "buzzes" the foodserver. Although this method is less obvious to the customer, it often takes the foodserver time to get accustomed to it.

Once the products have been delivered and consumed by the customer, the foodserver prepares the guest check. The guest check is then paid by the customer and the sales transaction is complete. This discussion of the flow of products and cash will continue in the Sales Control section of Chapter 12.

Determining Daily Cost %

When speaking of Food Cost % and Beverage Cost %, the chef/manager usually refers to the percent listed on the preceding month's Income Statement. Unfortunately, the Food Cost % and Beverage Cost % of which he/she speaks is historical data, and the chef/manager can do nothing at that point to improve those figures. It is important to know what the daily food cost % and the daily beverage cost % are in order to control costs on a daily basis. If cost %s are identified on a daily basis, chef/managers can identify and correct the cost problem long before the end of the month.

Month/Year: April'98

Day	Date	Daily Purchases	Daily Sales	Daily Cost %	To-Date Purchases	To-Date Sales	To-Date Cost %
M	4/01	$457.50	$1,354.75	33.7 %	$ 457.50	$ 1,354.75	33.7%
T	4/02	$398.68	$1,115.98	35.7 %	$ 856.18	$ 2,470.73	34.7%.
W	4/03	$444.21	$1,408.52	31.5 %	$1,300.39	$ 3,879.25	33.5%
T	4/04	$495.32	$1,688.21	29.3 %	$1,795.71	$ 5,567.46	32.3%
F	4/05	$703.25	$2,035.87	34.5 %	$2,498.96	$ 7,603.33	32.9%
S	4/06	$254.35	$2,450.79	10.4 %	$2,753.31	$10,054.12	27.4%
S	4/07	$101.26	$1,985.67	5.1 %	$2,854.57	$12,039.79	23.7%
M	4/08	$463.42	$1,375.65	33.7 %	$3,317.99	$13,415.44	24.7%
T	4/09						
W	4/10						

FIGURE 11.3 Daily Food Cost % Form—Simple Approach

WebCOM™

$$457.50 + 398.68 = 856.18$$

$$1354.75 + 1115.98 = 2470.73$$

Foodservice operations determine their *daily food cost %* and *daily beverage cost %* using the information that has been tracked through the cycle of cost control. The more information tracked through the cycle, the more accurate the daily food cost and daily beverage cost percent are. Daily Cost Percent Reports are prepared for a one month time period. Once the month has ended, a new Daily Cost Percent report is started. The following procedures may be used to determine daily food and beverage cost percents.

Determining Daily Cost %—A Simple Approach

The Simple Approach in determining a working daily cost percent is normally used by small foodservice operations that do not take the time to implement the business forms needed to track the movement of products and their costs through the cycle of cost control. As discussed in the purchasing Chapter, the small foodservice operation uses few business forms and tracks limited amounts of information. The Daily Food Cost and Daily Beverage Cost Percents of small operations will only provide a general trend of the cost Percent. The only information needed to calculate the Daily Cost % using the Simple Approach is the information stated on the purveyor's invoice and the register reading that records daily sales. The total of a day's food invoices is posted to the Daily Purchases Column and the total of the day's food sales is posted to the Daily Sales Column.

Once the daily purchase and daily sales figures have been posted to the Daily Food Cost report, the Daily Food Cost percent is calculated.

Formula:

DAILY PURCHASES	÷	DAILY SALES	=	DAILY COST %
Day 1 Example: $457.50	÷	$1,354.75	=	33.7%

Because a business purchases a product on a given day, it does not mean that the product is used to produce sales on that day. A purchase does not become a cost until it is used in production. The Daily Cost Percent as calculated in the Simple Approach is not really a Food Cost Percent but rather a number that represents the percentage of Daily Purchases reflected in Daily Sales. Food Cost can never be higher than total purchases. The To-Date Food Cost Percent offers a more accurate picture of the Daily Food Cost Percent. To derive a To-Date Food Cost Percent, we must first calculate the To-Date Purchases by totaling all the daily purchases made and posting them to the To-Date Purchase Column. The To-Date Sales Column must then be calculated by totaling all the Daily Sales figures during the month. Once the To-Date Purchases and To-Date Sales have been calculated, the To-Date Food Cost Percent is calculated as follows:

Formula:

TO-DATE PURCHASES	÷	TO-DATE SALES	=	TO-DATE COST %
Day 2 Example: $856.18	÷	$2,470.73	=	34.7%

Because there are high purchase days and low sales days, and low purchase days and high sales days, it takes approximately seven to ten days for the Cost Percent achieved to illustrate a cost trend. This process is very simple as it relates to the amount of information needed to prepare this form, but it also lacks the accuracy that most foodservice operations desire when calculating Daily Cost Percents. For the small foodservice operation, this method is the only one that can be used due to the lack of tracking procedures for food and beverage items. The Simple Approach is better than nothing at all.

Figure 11.3 shows food purchases and food sales, and calculates food cost percents. The Purchases divided by Sales formula discussed above can also be utilized to derive the Daily Beverage Cost Percent and the To-Date Beverage Cost Percent. The process of tracking the invoices received from the purveyor and recording the daily sales are the same. The only difference would be in the results of the Daily Beverage Cost Percent. Foodservice operations are more likely to receive Beverage Purchases one or two days per week rather than every day as Food Purchases are made. This provides even less accuracy in the Daily Beverage Cost Percent figures.

Determining a Daily Cost %—An Accurate Approach

As the size and sales volume of foodservice operations increase, more business forms are implemented as tools to track the movement and costs of food and beverage products. Within the medium and large operations, the method chosen to determine the daily food cost percent and the daily beverage cost percent relies on the use of these business forms. Calculating an accurate daily food cost percent will be explained using a procedure that has a large number of business forms. The greater the amount of information provided the more accurate the working food cost percent. Knowing how to get the most accurate account of the daily cost percents will assist the foodservice operator to develop his/her own daily cost percent reports to meet the needs of the operation.

Daily Food Cost %—An Accurate Method

In Figure 11.4 the column headings illustrate the movement of food items needed to derive an accurate working Daily Food Cost Percent.

There are three steps to the Accurate Approach in determining the Daily Food Cost Percent.

Step 1: Determining the Cost of Food Used. The Cost of Food Used is the total cost of food for a day regardless of what it is used for. To calculate the Cost of Food Used, the chef/manager must gather all the information concerning products sent to the kitchen to meet production needs. The following formula shows how to calculate the Cost of Food Used.

Step 1 Formula:

REQUISITIONS	+	DIRECT PURCHASES	+	TRANSFERS TO KITCHEN	=	COST OF FOOD USED
Day 1 Example: $356.25	+	$101.50	+	$15.32	=	$473.07

Requisitions are the business forms that list and describe all items removed from the storeroom. Direct Purchases are those products which when delivered go directly into the production area. Transfers to the Kitchen are those products transferred from other departments to be used in food production. Depending upon the set up of the foodservice operation, transfers to the Kitchen may have separate columns for different types of transfers. Transfers from the Bar to the Kitchen identify liquor, beer, and wine needed for food production. Transfers from the Bakeshop include bread, rolls, and desserts. The Cost of Food Used informs the chef/manager of the amount of food sent to the kitchen during the day, but does not identify the quantity of these items actually used to produce sales. A food purchase does not become a food cost until it is used to produce food sales. The next step is to determine the Cost of Food Sold.

Month/Year: April '98

Day	Date	Reqs	Direct Purch	Trans To Kitchen	Cost Food Used	Trans from Kitchen	Emp Meals	IHP	Daily Cost of Food Sold	Daily Sales	Daily Food Cost %	To-Date Cost of Food Sold	To-Date Food Sales	To-Date Food Cost %
M	4/01	$356.25	$101.50	$15.32	$473.07	$25.60	$125.00	$21.63	$300.84	$ 945.63	31.8%	$ 300.84	$ 945.63	31.8%
T	4/02	$298.70	$112.73	$22.40	$433.93	$15.40	$110.50	$15.62	$292.41	$ 920.54	31.8%	$ 593.25	$ 1,866.17	31.8%
W	4/03	$350.93	$125.52	$12.75	$489.20	$30.56	$109.75	$ 9.72	$339.17	$ 1,211.42	28.0%	$ 932.42	$ 3,077.59	30.3%
T	4/04	$401.72	$150.34	$18.25	$570.31	$22.68	$112.25	$18.32	$417.06	$ 1,269.36	32.9%	$1,349.48	$ 4,346.95	31.0%
F	4/05	$425.85	$225.49	$16.75	$668.09	$25.68	$121.14	$25.00	$496.27	$ 1,535.78	32.3%	$1,845.75	$ 5,882.73	31.4%
S	4/06	$529.32	$105.75	$17.42	$652.49	$27.40	$126.80	$25.50	$472.79	$ 1,702.41	27.8%	$2,318.54	$ 7,585.14	30.6%
S	4/07	$515.44	$ 52.76	$12.85	$581.05	$22.53	$124.62	$22.40	$411.50	$ 1,645.20	25.0%	$2,730.04	$ 9,230.34	29.6%
M	4/08	$342.50	$108.52	$14.75	$465.77	$18.50	$108.76	$ 8.50	$330.01	$ 965.32	34.2%	$3,060.05	$10,195.66	30.0%
T	4/09													
W	4/10													

FIGURE 11.4 Daily Food Cost Percent Chart: An Accurate Approach

Step 2: Determining the Cost of Food Sold. The Cost of Food Sold (or Food Cost), refers to the amount of money spent to purchase the food items used to produce daily food sales. To determine the Cost of Food Sold, we must subtract all food items that were not used to produce food sales from the Cost of Food Used.

Step 2 Formula:

COST OF FOOD USED	−	(TRANSFERS FROM THE KITCHEN, EMPLOYEE MEALS, AND IN HOUSE PROMOTION EXPENSE)	=	DAILY COST OF FOOD SOLD
Day One Example: $473.07	−	(25.60 + 125.00 + 21.63)	=	$300.84

Transfers from the Kitchen

Although the Transfers from the Kitchen include transfers to all and any department, this column most often represents food products that are sent to Bar Production areas to be used as garnishes. Even though the garnishes are food, they are not used to produce food sales and should therefore be classified as beverage costs rather than food costs. Many Daily Food Cost forms used in larger hotels have separate "Transfers From" columns to identify the individual departments to which food is transferred, such as Room Service, Mini Bar, and To Go Items.

Other Transfers from the Kitchen might include steward sales and signing privileges of management staff. *Steward Sales* are those purchases that employees are allowed to make from the purveyors through the restaurant. The purchase of a Thanksgiving Day Turkey might be allowed as a steward sale. The product is purchased and included on the invoice of the foodservice operation but is paid for by the employee. This cost needs to be deducted from the Cost of Food Used.

Signing privileges of management staff when they dine within the foodservice establishment should also be subtracted from the Cost of Food Used. Management staff often have the benefit of dining at no cost. It does however cost the business to serve the food even if a food sale has not occurred. A benefit has been provided an employee, and the value of the meal should be assigned to labor cost. What is important to remember when determining the daily Cost of Food Sold, is that only the products used to produce food sales are included in the Cost of Food Sold figure.

Employee Meals

Many foodservice operations provide employees their meals. Employers may provide meals at no cost, at a partial cost, or at a full cost to employees. Regardless of the option offered, a meal value must be assigned to each meal provided.

When a meal is provided at no cost to the employee, the meal value is assigned to Labor Cost. The cost of the food used to prepare the meal is subtracted from the Cost of Food Used, which in turn is reflected in a reduction in the daily food cost. A meal provided at a cost to both the employer and employee is assigned to Employee Meals (the portion paid by the employer), and to food cost (the portion paid by the employee).

In House Promotions

In House Promotions are internal advertising expenses for food items that are given away to loyal customers. Chef/managers will often provide an appetizer "with compliments from the chef," to thank customers for their patronage. The cost of the food used to produce the

In House Promotion does not result in a food sale and is therefore not included in the Cost of Food Sold. Another example of an In House Promotion is food items prepared and sent to the bar to be used to promote beverage sales. Since these hors d'oeuvres are complimentary to the customer, they do not produce food sales. These hors d'oeuvres are also not used to produce a beverage product so they cannot be classified as a beverage cost. These products are promotional. They are used to get the customers to stay a little longer and to spend more money. Although a cost of doing business, it is neither a food nor beverage cost, but rather an internal advertising expense.

Step 3: Determining the Daily Food Cost %. The formula listed below allows the foodservice manager to account for all products used to produce food sales. The process used in determining the Daily Food Cost percent is similar to that used in the Simple Approach to Determining a Daily Food Cost %. Simply replace the Daily Purchases (in the simple approach) by the Daily Cost of Food Sold figure.

Step 3 Formula A:

DAILY COST OF FOOD SOLD $\div$ DAILY SALES $=$ DAILY FOOD COST %

Day 1 Example: $300.84 $\div$ $945.63 $=$ 31.8%

As accurate as the Daily Food Cost Percent is, it does not take into consideration the In-Process Inventories. In-Process Inventories are those products that are sent to the kitchen via requisitions, direct purchases, or transfers but which are not used in their entirety. Instead, they are left over products not used to produce daily food sales. It is for this reason that the To-Date Cost of Food Sold, the To-Date Sales, and the To-Date Food Cost % should still be utilized. Even though the Daily Food Cost % is fairly accurate, the To-Date Food Cost % will be more and more accurate as the month progresses and in process inventories are used up. If a chef requisitions a fifty pound bag of flour, chances are very good that the entire fifty pounds are not used to produce sales on a single day. The fifty pounds may be used over a one week period. The To-Date % Column accounts for in-process inventories. The formula to calculate the To-Date Food Cost % in the Accurate Approach is as follows:.

Step 3 Formula B:

TO-DATE COST OF FOOD SOLD $\div$ TO-DATE SALES $=$ TO-DATE FOOD COST %

Day 2 Example: $593.25 $\div$ $1,866.17 $=$ 31.8%

The Accurate Approach can be adjusted to meet the needs of any foodservice operation and is easily transferred to a computerized spreadsheet program to alleviate some of the time consuming mathematical procedures. Calculating a Daily Food Cost % is a useful tool in helping the chef/manager to identify how the foodservice operation is performing long before the month's end.

Calculating the Daily Beverage Cost %— An Accurate Approach

To determine the Daily Beverage Cost %, a foodservice operation may choose the Simple Approach previously explained, or may desire a more accurate determination of the working Daily Beverage Cost %. The following is an explanation of an Accurate Approach that will better identify the foodservice operation's beverage costs on a daily basis. (Figure 11.5).

The Daily Beverage Cost % is calculated daily but is kept for a one month time period. As in the accurate approach to determine the Daily Food Cost %, there are three steps in determining a fairly accurate Daily Beverage Cost %. The following items must be considered in calculating an Accurate Daily Beverage Cost Percent.

Month/Year: April '98

Day	Date	Issues	Trans To Bar	Additions	Cost of Bev. Used	Trans From Bar	IHP	Sign Priv	Subtrac- tions	Daily Cost of Bev. Sold	Daily Bev. Sales	Daily Bev. Cost %	To-Date Cost of Bev. Sold	To-Date Bev. Sales	To-Date Bev. Cost %
M	4/01	$112.50	$ 5.68	-0-	$118.18	$ 4.50	$15.00	$12.50	-0-	$ 86.18	$425.50	20.3%	$ 86.18	$ 425.50	20.3%
T	4/02	$ 82.75	$ 6.50	-0-	$ 89.25	$ 3.75	$ 9.75	$ 8.00	-0-	$ 67.75	$376.75	18.0%	$153.93	$ 802.25	19.2%
W	4/03	$ 76.50	$ 4.75	-0-	$ 81.25	$ 5.25	$ 8.25	$ 6.50	-0-	$ 61.25	$342.35	17.9%	$215.18	$1,144.60	18.9%
T	4/04	$120.95	$10.50	-0-	$131.45	$ 6.50	$10.50	-0-	-0-	$114.45	$431.20	26.5%	$329.63	$1,575.80	20.9%
F	4/05	$121.40	$12.25	-0-	$133.65	$ 7.25	$18.50	$12.75	-0-	$ 95.15	$462.75	20.6%	$424.78	$2,038.55	20.8%
S	4/06	$125.60	$15.50	-0-	$141.10	$12.25	$21.50	$15.50	-0-	$ 91.85	$498.12	18.4%	$516.63	$2,536.67	20.4%.
S	4/07	$108.35	$ 4.75	-0-	$113.10	$ 8.50	$ 8.75	$ 3.50	-0-	$ 92.35	$486.72	19.0%	$608.98	$3,023.39	20.1%
M	4/08	$ 98.72	$ 5.25	-0-	$103.97	$ 6.25	$ 5.50	-0-	-0-	$ 92.22	$434.70	21.2%	$701.20	$3,458.09	20.3%
T	4/09														
W	4/10														

FIGURE 11.5 Daily Beverage Cost %: An Accurate Approach

Webcom™

Step 1: Determining the Cost of Beverages Used. The first step is to identify all the areas from which alcohol is sent to the Beverage Production Area.

Formula:

ISSUES	+	TRANSFERS	+	ADDITIONS	=	COST OF BEVERAGES USED
Day 1 Example: $112.50	+	$5.68	+	-0-	=	$118.18

Issues

These can be issues recorded on requisitions from liquor storage, wine storage, bottled beer storage, keg beer storage, as well as any issues from food storage areas that would be used to produce the beverages being prepared. Food Issues from storage can include mixes such as juices, sodas, milk, and cream products. They may also include items such as containers of non-perishable garnish products such as maraschino cherries, olives, cocktail onions, frozen strawberries, whipped cream, cinnamon sticks, and any other product used to prepare a beverage item.

Transfers to the Bar

Transfers to the Bar most often reflect food items that have been transferred from the kitchen to the bar to produce the beverage being sold. As explained in the storage control chapter, rather than preparing a Food Requisition for six oranges, the bar will often transfer the six oranges from the kitchen and transfer the cost using a Transfer Memo.

Additions

Foodservice operations utilize an Addition Column for items that are neither issues nor transfers but which need to be included in the Cost of Beverages Used. Items might include fresh strawberries purchased from a farmers' market to be used as a garnish, or a direct purchase sent immediately to the beverage production area when delivered. All products sent to Beverage Production must be accounted for and included in the Cost of Beverages Used.

Step 2: Cost of Beverages Sold. To derive the Cost of Beverages Sold we must reduce the Cost of Beverages Used by subtracting any beverage products that are sent to beverage production and are not used to produce a beverage sale.

Formula:

COST OF BEVERAGES USED	−	(TRANSFERS FROM THE BAR, IN HOUSE PROMOTIONS, SIGNING PRIVILEGES, AND SUBTRACTIONS)	=	COST OF BEVERAGES SOLD
$118.18	−	($450 + $15.00 + $12.50)	=	$86.18

Transfers from the Bar

These items can be noted as Transfers From the Bar to other departments. This column most often represents alcoholic beverage items that are used in cooking.

In House Promotions

The In House Promotions column identifies the beverage items that are given away "with compliments of the manager." The product given away should not be included in the Cost of Beverage Sales because it is not used to produce a Beverage Sale. Instead, the cost should be documented as an internal advertising expense.

Signing Privileges

Often management staff will have the privilege of signing to purchase a beverage at no cost, thus a beverage sale is not incurred and the cost must not be included in the Cost of Beverage Sold. The signing privilege is looked at as an employee benefit and should be accounted for as a labor cost.

Subtractions

This column is used to record any other costs that should not be included as a Cost of Beverage Sold. Some foodservice operations include errors within this column. In reality the error should be included in the Cost of Beverage Sold. A production error will increase beverage cost.

Step 3: Calculating the Daily Beverage Cost %. Step 3 should be performed using the same procedure as identified in Step 3 of Determining the Daily Food Cost percent. "Daily Beverage Cost %" is calculated as follows:

Formula:

DAILY COST OF BEVERAGES SOLD	÷	DAILY BEVERAGE SALES	=	DAILY BEVERAGE COST %
Day 1 Example: $86.18	÷	$425.50	=	20.3%

A running total of the Cost of Beverages Sold is posted to the To-Date Cost of Beverages Sold column. The total Beverage Sales are then posted to the To-Date Beverage Sales column. Lastly, the To-Date Cost of Beverages Sold is divided by the To-Date Beverage Sales to determine a To-Date Beverage Cost %.

Formula:

TO-DATE COST OF BEVERAGES SOLD	÷	TO-DATE BEVERAGE SALES	=	TO-DATE BEVERAGE COST %
Day 2 Example: $153.93	÷	$802.25	=	19.2%

As the month progresses, the in-process inventories are again accounted for in the To-Date Beverage Cost Percent. This formula can be used by managers to calculate a fairly accurate working Beverage Cost % on a daily basis. Often foodservice operations will track not only total Beverage Sales but individual totals for liquor sales, wine sales, beer sales, and non-alcoholic beverage sales. These foodservice operations will usually develop a Daily Beverage Cost Percent form for each type of beverage product served.

Knowing the working daily food cost and beverage cost percents can be a useful tool in assisting chef/managers to control cost and to identify product usage. Implementing such a tool can prevent an outrageous surprise of high costs at the end of the month.

Review Questions

1. Using the three recipes given in Chapter 8, question #4, identify the portion control tools needed to prepare, produce, and present each menu item.

2. Using the following information and the Daily Cost–Simple Approach Sheet in Appendix F, calculate the Daily Cost % and To-Date Cost %.

Date	Day	Today's Purchases	Today's Sales
Aug. 1	W	$ 567.25	$ 2,182.75
Aug. 2	T	$ 637.80	$ 2,485.08
Aug. 3	F	$ 878.92	$ 3,345.20
Aug. 4	S	$ 250.65	$ 3,255.10
Aug. 5	S	$ 98.72	$ 2,867.35
Aug. 6	M	$ 589.60	$ 2,320.56

3. Given the following numbers and the information provided on the Accurate Approach Food Cost form in Appendix F, calculate the Daily Food Cost % and To-Date Food Cost %.

Date/Day	Reqs.	Direct Purchase	Transfers to Kitchen	Transfers from Kitchen	Emp. Meals	IHP Food	Daily Sales
Aug. 1 W	$356.50	$325.00	$18.50	$25.90	$72.50	$35.60	$2,096.30
Aug. 2 T	$256.65	$109.86	$36.00	$12.50	$65.50	$28.25	$1,360.45
Aug. 3 F	$312.26	$ 98.94	$27.50	$23.00	$88.75	$18.50	$1,150.89

4. Using the following information and the Daily Beverage Cost % form in Appendix F, calculate the Daily Beverage Cost % and To-Date Beverage Cost %.

Date/Day	Issues	Transfers to Bar	Additions	Transfers from Bar	IHP	Signing Privilege	Subtract	Beverage Sales
Aug. 1 W	$156.25	$10.75	$ 3.50	$10.25	$25.85	-0-	$ 7.50	$ 846.00
Aug. 2 T	$258.65	$29.75	$ 15.00	$15.35	$35.75	$25.75	-0-	$1,380.53
Aug. 3 F	$305.42	$42.00	-0-	$22.00	$45.00	$12.50	-0-	$1,786.12

5. Using the spreadsheet program of your professor's choice, develop a spreadsheet to determine Daily Food Cost % and the To-Date Food Cost % for a medium sized foodservice operation.

6. Using the spreadsheet program of your professor's choice, develop a spreadsheet to determine Daily Beverage Cost % and To-Date Beverage Cost %.

Bibliography

Dittmer, Paul R. and Gerald G. Griffin. *Principles of Food, Beverage, and Labor Cost Controls*. 5th ed. New York: Van Nostrand Reinhold, 1994.

Keister, Douglas C. *Food and Beverage Control*. Englewood Cliffs, NJ: Prentice-Hall, Inc., 1977.

Sackler, Warren and Samuel R. Trapani. *Foodservice Cost Control Using Lotus 1-2-3*. New York: John Wiley and Sons, Inc., 1995.

Sales Controls and Analysis

objectives

Upon completion of this chapter, the student should be able to:

1. implement proper guest check controls to meet business needs.
2. follow the flow of sales from the guest check to the income statement.
3. calculate Sales Mix from sales history reports.
4. calculate the Break-Even Point of Sales.
5. complete a Menu Engineering worksheet.

key terms

Actual Sales	*Menu Engineering*
Average Sale per Cover	*Potential Sales*
Break-even	*Sales*
Contribution to Sales	*Sales Journal*
Cover	*Sales Mix*
Guest Check Audit	*Turnover Rate*
Guest Check Issuance	

Introduction

Foodservice *sales* are usually thought of as the total dollar amount spent by customers to purchase products (food and beverage) and services when dining in a foodservice establishment. Tracking the dollar value of products and services sold to customers is only part of the procedure of sales control. To be successful, businesses must also be aware of the number of customers they serve and of the items they sell those customers.

"Sales Control" is a system set up to maintain the flow of sales money brought in through products and services sold to customers. It is a tracking system used to identify the number of people served during a given meal period, and a tool used to determine how well menu items are selling. Information gathered through this system is then used to prepare a sales analysis that identifies and analyzes current sales and is also used to forecast future sales.

It is important to refer to the cycle of cost control to realize that sales affect the amount of product to purchase, the amount of product to produce, and the number of employees to schedule. Sales have an effect on every step of the cost control cycle. As sales tracking systems are discussed, we will learn how this information can be used to help control the costs of operating a business.

The Flow of Sales

Where does "Sales" begin? *Potential Sales* begin when a manager creates a menu, since the menu is a merchandising tool used to promote sales. Potential Sales can be forecasted by setting the selling prices of menu items to be sold (Chapter 7). However, to keep track of Actual Sales, we will begin when the customer places an order with the foodserver. Picture this: A party of four enters the establishment and is greeted by the Maître D´ (host/hostess). The Maître D´ escorts the foursome to their table and presents them with menus. The foodserver approaches the table, welcomes the customers, and introduces himself/herself. The foodserver asks if the patrons would like to start with something refreshing to drink. The customers request a liter bottle of sparkling water. The foodserver records the order on a guest check. Voilà! The process of recording actual sales has begun. From this point on the order is recorded in the cash register. The actual process of putting the order into a cash register and placing the order depends upon the type of cash register/control system the restaurant uses. The basic flow of recorded sales is as follows:

Guest Check $\longrightarrow$ Cash Register $\longrightarrow$ Sales Journal $\longrightarrow$ Income Statement

All restaurants, regardless of the control system they use, will follow this model in tracking sales. Each of these areas of sales control will be discussed in sequence.

Guest Check Control

As more foodservice operations become computerized, fewer hand prepared guest checks are seen. Computerization of guest check and sales controls alleviates much of the tedious summation of day to day sales activities that was at one time compiled from the hand prepared guest checks. The guest check itself is now controlled by the cash register. A guest check is issued within a computerized system when the server opens a check for the table being served. If a guest check has been started within the system and has not been recorded as paid at the completion of the meal period, the cash register records the name or the number of the server responsible for that check.

Hand Prepared Guest Checks

Even though foodservice operations are using computerized cash register systems more frequently, we will examine the steps needed to assure sales control of Hand Prepared Guest Checks. It is usually the small business that cannot yet afford a computerized cash register system, or the very old business that has not yet changed with the times, that is still using hand prepared guest checks. Hand prepared guest checks are purchased from paper supply companies and are usually produced using NCR paper (No Carbon Required), that has a soft paper top sheet (the dupe), and a light cardboard customer copy. The foodsever takes the order from the customer and records it on the original form which simultaneously transfers on to the hard bottom copy. The soft form is then removed and taken to the kitchen to place the order. The hard copy is kept by the foodserver to be tallied and presented to the customer when the dining experience is complete.

When a foodservice operation uses hand prepared guest checks, extra steps must be taken to insure proper control. Having the foodservice operation's logo printed on the check is a good control measure. Although more costly, it helps to keep track of guest checks and deters outside checks from finding their way into your restaurant.

Foodservice operators must develop a standard procedure to control guest checks, in order to insure that all are returned either paid for or unused. The foodservice operator must also develop a procedure to review guest checks and to guarantee that they have been used appropriately by sales personnel (the correct price charged, all items are charged for, etc.).

Issuing Guest Checks

It is important when using hand prepared guest checks that the checks have machine imprinted sequential numbers on them. The machine imprinted sequential numbering system helps foodservice managers to account for the guest checks used by the food-server. Guest checks should be issued and used in numerical sequence. The numbers of the guest checks issued to each foodserver should be recorded per shift on a *Guest Check Issuance Sheet* (Figure 12.1). A Foodserver Check Out Sheet should accompany the issued guest checks so that the foodserver is aware of the sequence of guest checks assigned to him/her (Figure 12.2). It is important that the foodserver inspect the guest checks received to be certain that the numbers on the check issued correspond to the numbers that have been recorded as issued. This inspection should occur prior to the start of the shift. During the shift, the foodservers must be certain to use the guest checks in sequential order. At the end of the shift, it is the foodservers responsibility to record all checks that were used and to return all unused checks. The check numbers are also recorded in the space provided on the Foodserver Check Out Sheet. By knowing what checks were issued, what checks were used, and what checks were returned unused, managers/chefs can be certain that no foodserver or bartender is walking away with a check that is unaccounted for.

The foodserver check out sheet may also include other sales control information that is invaluable to the operation. It may include information concerning the number of covers, or the sale of certain food and beverage items that the restaurant wants to monitor. Keeping track of the number of desserts sold, the number of sirloins, or even the number of cups of coffee and tea, is often regarded as useful information. If the foodservice operation had a computerized cash register system, this information would be provided automatically by taking a register reading. When a foodservice operation is not computerized, management must implement other measures such as the food-server check out sheet, to gather the important sales control information.

University Inn   **Date: March 3, 1998**

Server	Checks Issued	#Issued	Return Unused	#Unused	#Used	Total	Notes
#24	02345–02359	15	02354–02359	6	9	15	-0-
#35	03768–03782	15	03780–03782	3	12	15	-0-
#36	03821–03835	15	none	0	15	15	-0-
#39	02522–02541	20	02539–02541	3	17	20	-0-

FIGURE 12.1 Guest Check Issuance Sheet

```
┌─────────────────────────────────────────────────────────────────────┐
│                   FOODSERVER CHECK OUT SHEET                          │
│  Server:  Susan #24                              Date 3/3/98          │
│                                                  B      L      D      │
│                                                                       │
│  Checks Issued:        02345–02359                                    │
│                        _____ # 15                     │
│  Checks Unused:        02354–2359                                     │
│                        _____ # 6                      │
│  Number of Steaks Sold:                                               │
│  NY Sirloin        _____                                      │
│  Filet             _____                                      │
│  London Broil      _____                                      │
│  Number of Desserts Sold    _____                            │
│  Number of Coffee/Tea Sold  _____                            │
│  Notes to Bookkeeper:                                                 │
└─────────────────────────────────────────────────────────────────────┘
```

FIGURE 12.2 Foodserver Check Out Sheet

Guest Check Audit

Another Hand Prepared guest check control is the *Guest Check Audit* (Figure 12.3). Depending upon the size of the foodservice operation, this process may be used daily for all service personnel, or performed randomly, by selecting a few service personnel to audit. The purpose of the Guest Check Audit is to guarantee that the guest checks have been used correctly. Management compares prices on guest checks with the prices on the menu looking for any discrepancies (undercharges, overcharges). Soft and hard copies of each foodserver's used guest checks are also examined to see if everything ordered has been charged for (remember that no food or beverage item should leave the production area unless it has been documented on a dupe). It is also important that the soft copy of hand-prepared checks not be returned to the foodserver. A dishonest employee might be tempted to substitute similar guest checks and pocket the money. It is obvious that guest check control prior to computerized Point of Sales cash register system was very time consuming. Even though most foodservices are now utilizing computerized systems, those that are not using a computer system must implement safeguards to insure proper sales controls.

Cash Register Procedures

Most, if not all, foodservice operations utilize cash registers. Whether computerized or not, a cash register has two purposes: 1) to record a sales transactions, and 2) to store payments received for sales transactions. The only difference in cash registers is the amount of information that they are able to record.

Date	Server	Checks Unused	Checks Used	Checks Missing	Errors Hard/Soft	Error Pricing	Error Tax	Error Compute	Uninitialed Crossouts	Total Under Over Charge	Explanation
3/3	#24	6	15	-0-	-0-	$ .50	-0-	-0-	-0-	$ .50	
3/3	#35	3	12	-0-	-0-	-0-	-0-	$1.00	-0-	($1.00)	
3/3	#36	0	14	1	-0-	-0-	-0-	-0-	-0-	-0-	
3/3	#39	3	17	-0-	1	-0-	-0-	-0-	-0-	($3.50)	didn't charge

FIGURE 12.3 Guest Check Audit

Recording Sales Transactions

Sales, as previously defined, is the total dollar amount brought in through the sale of products and services sold to customers. Cash Registers have the capacity to keep track of different types of sales. The two major classifications of sales for a foodservice operation are Food Sales and Beverage Sales. "Food Sales" is defined as the total dollar amount of money brought in through the sale of food items. "Beverage Sales" refers to the total dollar amount of money brought in through the sale of beverage items. These are the two primary classifications that all foodservice operations track. Restaurants may also have additional sales categories that are placed under the heading of "Other Income." "To Go Food Sales," "Merchandise Sales," "Catering Sales,"and "Gift Certificate Sales" are usually listed here. Hotel operations might include sales categories relating to each of the foodservice operations within the hotel (fine-dining, casual, beach bar), as well as Room Service Sales and Banquet Sales. Beyond the clarification of sales into categories, foodservice operations track food and beverage sales by meal period, to determine exactly how much each meal period contributes to the overall daily sales (Figure 12.4). The number of categories and meal period sales a business chooses to track depends on the depth of analysis it desires. Separating sales into categories can also provide information that can be used to develop and monitor marketing efforts.

Sales taxes (state and/or local) often accompany sales. The foodservice operation is responsible for collecting and recording sales taxes separate from sales. Sales taxes are posted to a separate liability account until paid as required.

Computerized Cash Registers can also record sales information other than the sales dollar amount. They can track customers and their menu selections. Computerized cash register systems will record the number of people served as the guest check is opened, and list menu selections that are tracked utilizing a PLU (Price Look Up) numerical code. In the PLU system every item is assigned a numerical code. The cash register tallies the number of each item sold when the register reading is taken.

In a foodservice operation that utilizes hand prepared guest checks, this information can be attained by thoroughly preparing the information area of the guest check.

Food Sales

	$ Sales	%
By Meal Period		
Breakfast	$ 400	4.4%
Lunch	$2,100	22.9%
Dinner	$4,200	45.7%
TOTAL DINING ROOM	$6,700	73 %
BANQUETS	$2,500	27.0%
TAKE-OUT	$ 0	0.0%
OUTSIDE CATERING	$ 0	0.0%
TOTAL FOOD SALES	$9,200	100.0%

FIGURE 12.4 Sales by Category

UNIVERSITY INN   **Date: March 3, 1998**

Weather: Dry, Cool Evening   **Meal: Dinner**

Hostess: **Page: 2**

Name of Party	Description	#Party	Time In	Smoke/Non	Est.Wait	Time Seat	Table	Server #
Johansen	Red Tie	4	6:05	NS	-0-	6:05	A-2	#24
Smith	Cute Child	6	6:10	NS	-0-	6:10	B-14	#35
Schwenk	Dark Hair	2	6:10	NS	-0-	6:10	A-1	#24
Diana	All Women	3	6:10	S	20	6:25	C-22	#36
Tom	Nice Coat	2	6:15	NS	25	6:40	B-15	#35
Marra	Chef	4	6:30	NS	30			
Flynn	Blue Dress	2	6:35	NS	30			

FIGURE 12.5 Seating Control Sheet

A Foodserver Check Out Sheet (Figure 12.2), or a Seating Control Sheet (Figure 12.5), can be used to track the number of customers served, while a Menu Scatter Sheet (Figure 12.6) can be utilized to record the selections each customer makes.

The computerized cash register system has greatly reduced the amount of time and energy needed to gather sales information. Gathering sales control information tallied from hand prepared guest checks is very time consuming, but necessary, in order to analyze current sales activity and to project future sales.

A Place Holder for Payments

The second purpose of a cash register is to hold the payments for the sales transactions that have taken place. As guest checks are paid for, payment (cash, credit card vouchers, checks, gift certificates) is collected and kept in the cash register until Cash Out. Cash Out is a process performed by the cashier to prove that the amount of sales recorded is equal to the total of payment received. It is up to the foodservice operation to decide which methods of payment will be accepted. It is often thought that the more extensive the methods of payment, the larger the customer base. Businesses that accept cash only may restrict their market share, since many people elect not to carry cash. However, the foodservice operator must realize that credit card transactions may involve a service charge.

Regardless which forms of payment are accepted, the business must develop standard procedures concerning payment. Circling credit card expiration dates to insure that the credit card is current; requiring a signature on the guest checks as well as on the credit card voucher; and asking for a valid picture ID when accepting checks are all sound practices. Customers sometimes think that these controls are ridiculous; however, most appreciate this special care when their credit card or checks are lost or stolen.

There are times when money received as payment must be removed from the cash drawer. Paid Out Receipts are pieces of paper that are placed in the cash drawer to document any money taken out of the cash register during the sales period. The Paid Out Receipt is used to account for money removed to pay credit card tips, to replace lost coins in a juke box, to purchase stamps, COD invoices, etc. Paid Out Receipts are just as important as cash. The Paid Out Receipt represents cash that was once part of the original bank or a proceed from sales transaction. If a Paid Out Receipt is lost, the cash drawer will be short money.

Menu Scatter Sheet: University Inn

Week Ending: March 8, 1998

Menu Items	App	Sal	Ent	Des	Monday	Tuesday	Wednesday	Thursday	Friday	Saturday	Sunday	Total
Wings	X				18	12	20	22	28	33	16	149
Mozzarella	X				16	8	15	18	15	27	16	115
Egg Rolls	X				8	10	11	13	15	12	8	77
Caesar Salad		X			12	8	8	15	18	22	18	101

FIGURE 12.6 Menu Scatter Sheet

Cash Register Reading

Once the sales activity is complete, it is time to take a Cash Register Reading. A Cash Register Reading is an actual print out of sales. The original register reading consisted of a simple paper tape listing daily activity. Computerized cash register readings now offer a full spreadsheet of information. Although routinely used to tally total daily sales activity, businesses often take a register reading for every meal period, and then total the sales activity to get a daily sales figure. The daily sales figures in each category are then posted to the Daily Sales Journal. All cash registers have the capability to provide a food sales total, a beverage sales total, and a tally of sales tax. Most computerized cash register systems will also print out a total of each item sold (sales mix), a summary of how the items contributed to total sales, and a description of the methods of payment used.

Sales Journal

The *Sales Journal* (Figure 12.7) is a compilation of daily sales records. The totals of each sales category are posted daily and are totaled at the end of each month. This journal is often used to track the type of payments that have been received in payment of those sales. The sales totals of each category in the Sales Journal are then used to prepare the monthly income statement. Many computer programs automatically transfer sales totals to a Sales Journal once the daily register reading has been taken.

The Annual Sales Journal

The Annual Sales Journal is made up of the monthly sales totals of each of the Sales Categories. The total of the Annual Sales Journal is used in preparing the Annual Income Statement (Chapter 6).

Once the foodservice operator has gathered all the sales information and prepared the sales journals, this information can be used to compare the daily, weekly, or monthly total of sales in each category. This can be done to show increases and decreases of sales activities in the categories of sales that the foodservice manager chooses to track. The analysis can help a business to identify increases in sales that may have resulted from additional marketing, and to forecast for the upcoming season.

Tracking Customers and Their Choices

With a computerized cash register, many of the procedures described can be completed by performing a register reading. Once all the sales information has been gathered, it is important to use it to analyze how well the foodservice operation is doing. We will want to know the number of customers who visit the establishment, the amount of money they are spending, the menu items they select, and the profit derived.

Covers

A *cover* can be defined as the number of people served by the restaurant during a given meal period. It is good practice to keep track of how many people the business normally serves at breakfast, lunch, and dinner. It can help the chef to better plan production and the manager to accurately schedule personnel for those meals. Methods have already been discussed concerning how to track the number of covers.

Sales Journal   **Month: March 1998**

| | Type of Sale | | | | | | Method of Payment | | | | | | |
Day	Food Sales	Beverage Sales	Other Sales	Total Sales	Sales Tax	Charge Tips	Total Collected	Cash	Checks	MC/V	AMX	O-CC	Other	Total Payments
1	$1,535.25	$ 850.75	-0-	$2,386.00	$167.02	$160.00	$2,713.02	$ 799.22	$263.00	$802.65	$642.25	$130.90	$75.00	$2,713.02
2	$1,624.05	$1,230.40	$25.00	$2,879.45	$201.56	$205.50	$3,286.51	$1,063.42	$195.75	$995.89	$856.45	$ 85.00	$90.00	$3,286.51
3														
4														

FIGURE 12.7 Sales Journal

Turnover Rate

Turnover rate refers to the average number of times guests have occupied all the seats in the dining room during a given meal period. The formula for calculating the turnover rate is

Formula:

COVERS SERVED ÷ NUMBER OF SEATS = TURNOVER RATE

Example: 250 ÷ 100 = 2.5

If a restaurant serves 250 people and has 100 seats in its dining room, the turnover rate is 2.5 or 250%. The average turnover rate depends upon the type of restaurant operation. A fine dining, classical restaurant may only have an average turnover of 1.5, while a fast paced family pub might have an average turnover of 4.0. The turnover rate is normally calculated using only the number of customers served in the dining room(s) (it does not include bar, lounge, or take out food traffic).

Average Sales per Cover

A sound estimate of what each customer is expected to spend is a welcomed forecasting tool for the foodservice manager. The *Average Sales per Cover* is the average amount spent by each person entering the restaurant. This term is also referred to as Guest Check Average. The formula for determining the Average Sales per Cover is:

Formula:

TOTAL SALES ÷ # COVERS SERVED = AVERAGE SALES PER COVER

Example: $4,200 ÷ 250 = $16.80

If a restaurant brings in $4,200 in sales, serving 250 covers, the Average Sale per Cover is $16.80. The Average Sales per Cover formula is often used to help forecast how much money a foodservice operation may bring in. If a restaurant has an Average Sale per Cover of $16.80 and knows it normally serves 400 customers on Saturday night, then the foodservice manager can forecast the expected sales and budget.

Formula:

AVERAGE SALE PER COVER × FORECASTED COVERS = FORECASTED SALES

Example: $16.80 × 400 covers = $ 6,720

An Average Sales per Cover is usually prepared for the whole restaurant, as well as for each of the sales persons (foodserver, bartender). If a foodserver is responsible for $600 in sales and has served 35 customers, the Individual Average Sale per Cover would be calculated as follows:

Formula:

INDIVIDUAL ÷ INDIVIDUAL # COVERS = INDIVIDUAL AVERAGE
TOTAL SALES   SERVED   SALE/COVER

Example: $600 ÷ 35 = $17.14

The Individual Average Sales per Cover is often used by foodservice operators to identify their best salespeople. The greater the individual sales, the larger the profit the business makes. Restaurants often reward their best salespeople with good shifts and good sections.

Where does a manager get the information to determine the Average Sales per Cover? Total sales can be attained from the Register Reading or the Daily Sales Journal. The Number of Covers can be taken from a tally of the guest checks, the Hostess Seating Control Sheet, or from the number of customers entered into the cash register system. The Hostess Seating Control Sheet usually offers the most accurate customer count, as foodservers may intentionally or unintentionally misrepresent the number of customers served to make themselves look better as sales persons. If a foursome is seated in a section and two people order appetizers, and the other two people order entrées, the foodserver might only record two covers. This misrepresentation would skew both the overall Average Sales per Cover, and the Individual Average Sales per Cover as well. The Cover and Average Sales per Cover amounts are important in predicting future sales totals. This is where the Sales Mix comes into play.

Sales Mix

The *sales mix* (often referred to as the Popularity Index), represents the percent of customers who order each menu item. The sales mix percentage is normally calculated per food category. Appetizers are compared to other appetizers sold, entrées to other entrées, desserts to desserts. To calculate a sales mix, take the number of each item sold and divide it by the total items sold in each category.

Formula:

	NUMBER OF EACH ENTRÉE SOLD	÷	TOTAL ENTRÉES SOLD	=	SALES MIX
Entrée: Stuffed Shrimp	60	÷	250	=	24.0%
Steak au Poivre	44	÷	250	=	17.6%
Grilled Chicken	66	÷	250	=	26.4%
Fillet of Sole	80	÷	250	=	32.0%
Total Entrées	250			=	100.0%

Just as the Average Sales per Cover can help forecast the potential sales, the sales mix can help to determine how many customers will order each menu item. Foodservice operators who calculate sales mix percentages on a routine basis will see patterns concerning the items ordered and the time periods during which they are requested. The Sales Mix should be kept on a daily basis as percentages change daily. A 17.6% sales mix for Steak au poivre on a Tuesday night might increase to 30% on a Saturday night.

Knowing the specific sales mix percentages of your menu items can help in forecasting production during a given meal period. The following examples use the sales mix percentages for the entrées previously determined to forecast production needs.

Production Forecast

Entrées	Expected Covers	×	Sales Mix %	=	Amount to Prep
Stuffed Shrimp	220	×	24%(.24)	=	53 (52.8)
Steak au Poivre	220	×	17.6%(.176)	=	39(38.7)
Grilled Chicken	220	×	26.4%(.264)	=	58
Fillet of Sole	220	×	32%(.32)	=	70
Total Preparation					220

If foodservice operators can accurately forecast the menu items that need to be produced, they can more accurately predict what needs to be purchased to produce those items.

Contribution to Sales %

The *Contribution to Sales* is a percentage that represents each menu item's contribution to total sales. Rather than just comparing menu items with other menu items within a particular category, Contribution to Sales % looks at the entire menu and the sale of each and every menu item. The Sales Mix % compares the number of each item sold while the Contribution to Sales % analyzes the dollar value that each menu item contributes to sales. All food items are compared to Total Food Sales and all beverage items are compared to Total Beverage Sales. The formula to calculate the Contribution to Sales percent is:

Formula:

$ OF EACH MENU ITEM SOLD   ÷   TOTAL SALES   =   CONTRIBUTION TO SALES %

Sales Analysis

There are many different ways of performing Menu and Sales Analysis, some are simple and others more complex. Two types of analysis will be discussed. The first, Break-Even Analysis, is a procedure used to determine the amount of sales needed before realizing a profit. "Menu Engineering," developed and presented by Michael L. Kasavana and Donald I. Smith in their book *Menu Engineering—A Practical Guide to Menu Analysis*, is a unique and fun way to analyze menu items by classifying the menu items as Stars, Plowhorses, Puzzles, and Dogs.

The Break-Even Point of Sales

Break-Even is the point at which the sales dollar brought in is equal to the costs expended to produce those sales. Formula: Labor Cost $ + Overhead Cost $ + Cost of Sales $ = Break-Even Sales $. There is no profit at the Break-Even point of sales. The Break-Even point of sales may be used as a tool to assist foodservice operators in deciding which days of the week or times of the year to stay open or close.

Calculating the Break-Even Point of Sales

The Break-Even Point of Sales can be determined annually, quarterly, monthly, weekly or on a daily basis. Most foodservice operations operate (pay labor and purchase goods), on a weekly cycle. A weekly Break-Even point allows the foodservice operation to use the sales dollar determined and analyze whether a profit has been made. A Weekly evaluation allows time to implement control measures which might be needed. When Calculating the Break-Even Point of Sales, both Labor Costs and Overhead Costs are classified as fixed costs. Fixed costs are those which are not expected to increase or decrease as sales fluctuate.

A Labor Cost dollar can be determined by compiling payroll journals, payroll taxes, and benefits paid from the weekly payroll ledger. A weekly Overhead Cost can be determined by knowing the annual overhead cost and dividing that figure by 52 (weeks). The cost of sales is a variable cost. A variable cost is a cost that fluctuates in direct relation to the increase and decrease of sales: as sales goes up, the variable cost increases; as sales goes down, the variable cost decreases. Because actual sales are not yet known, the foodservice operator will use the Cost of Sales %. Even though variable costs rise and fall as sales do, the variable cost % should remain fairly constant if proper standards of control are implemented.

Setting Up the Formula

The formula to solve for the Break-Even Point of Sales is:

Formula:

$$[(\text{LABOR COST \$} + \text{OVERHEAD COST \$}) \div (100 - \text{COST OF SALES \%})] = \text{BREAK-EVEN SALES}$$

A simple way to solve for the Break-Even Point of Sales is to utilize a tool that is similar to the Simplified Profit and Loss Statement. Remember: Cost of Sales (Food and Beverage) is a variable cost. Labor Cost and Overhead Cost within the Break-Even Formula are fixed costs.

Break-Even Sales	$ _____	_____ %
Variable Cost	$ _____	_____ % Variable Cost %
Fixed Cost	$ _____	_____ % Fixed Cost %

Application of the Formula

Let's use the following information to solve for the Break-Even Point of Sales. The University Inn has an estimated Weekly Labor Cost of $3,200 and an estimated weekly Overhead Cost of $2,600. The restaurant normally maintains a 35% Cost of Sales. What is the Break-Even Point of Sales?

Post the given information to the appropriate blank on the Break-Even Chart. Fixed Costs (Labor Cost and Overhead Cost), total $5,800. Cost of Sales % is the Variable Cost %.

Break-Even Sales	$ _____	_____ %
Variable Cost	$ _____	__35__ % Variable Cost %
Fixed Cost	$ __5,800__	_____ % Fixed Cost %

Since Sales is always 100% and our variable cost % here is 35%, our fixed cost can be determined as 65% (100%–35%).

Break-Even Sales	$ _____	__100__ %
Variable Cost	$ _____	__35__ % Variable Cost %
Fixed Cost	$ __5,800__	__65__ % Fixed Cost %

Solve for the Break-Even Point of Sales. If the fixed cost is $5,800 and this is 65% of the Break-Even Point of Sales, we can calculated the Break-Even Point of Sales by dividing the Fixed Cost by the Fixed Cost %.

Formula:

FIXED COST ÷ FIXED COST % = BREAK-EVEN POINT OF SALES

$5,800 ÷ 65% (.65) = $8,923

The Break-Even Point of Sales is calculated as $8,923. The foodservice operator now knows how much he/she needs to make in sales per week to cover operating expenses. If the foodservice operator knows the business needs to bring $8,923 in sales to Break-Even Sales and wants to maintain a 35% Cost of Sales, what would the Cost of Sales budget be?

Break-Even Sales	$ _____8,923_____	_____100 %_____
Variable Cost	$ _____	_____35 % Variable Cost %
Fixed Cost	$ _____5,800_____	_____65 % Fixed Cost %

The formula to determine the Cost of Sales at Break-Even is:

Formula:

BREAK-EVEN POINT OF SALES × VARIABLE COST % = VARIABLE COST $ AT BREAK-EVEN

$8,923. × 35% = $3,123.

The Variable Cost $ at Break-Even Point lets the foodservice operator know how much money is available to purchase the food and beverage items needed to produce sales while remaining within budgetary guidelines. This information is useful when trying to control food and beverage costs. The Break-Even Point can be used to determine estimated weekly profit. This is what is known as Break-Even Analysis.

Break-Even Analysis

The Break-Even Point of Sales can be compared to actual weekly sales and can be used to determine whether or not a profit has been made. Using the information from the previous example, we know that the University Inn needs to bring in $8,923. per week to Break-Even. Let us say that the foodservice operation brings in $10,500 worth of actual sales in a given week. Let us say that the foodservice operation brings in $10,500 worth of actual sales in a given week. What is the University Inn's profit?

The first step in the Break-Even Analysis is to determine the difference between the Actual Sales and the Break-Even Sales. The difference will be called Additional Sales.

Formula:

ACTUAL SALES − BREAK-EVEN POINT OF SALES = ADDITIONAL SALES

$10,500 − $8,923 = $1,577

The University Inn has sales of $1,577 more than the dollar amount needed to Break-Even (Additional Sales). As we already know, this figure does not represent clear profit, since a sales increase requires a variable cost increase. If sales rise by $1,577, how much was spent to purchase the goods that were sold?

Formula:

ADDITIONAL SALES × COST OF SALES% = ADDITIONAL VARIABLE COST

$1,577 × 35%(.35) = $552

If the University Inn spent an additional $552 to purchase the goods sold, and the Labor Cost and Overhead Cost are fixed,the University Inn realized a profit of $1,025.

Formula:

$$\text{ADDITIONAL SALES} - \text{ADDITIONAL VARIABLE COST} = \text{PROFIT}$$
$$\$1,577 \qquad - \qquad \$552 \qquad = \$1,025$$

The University Inn can expect an approximate profit of $1,000 for the week.

Thus far, the Break-Even Point of Sales has been referred to as a specific dollar amount needed to cover expenses. The Break-Even Point of Sales may also be based on the average sale per cover. Based on the information already given for the University Inn example, let us add that our average sale per cover is $16.80. The formula to determine the number of covers needed to be served to Break-Even follows:

Formula:

$$[\text{FIXED COSTS \$} \div (\text{AVERAGE SALE} \times \text{FIXED COST \%})] = \text{BREAK-EVEN}$$
$$\text{PER COVER} \qquad\qquad\qquad \text{COVERS}$$
$$[\$5,800 \quad \div \quad (\$16.80 \quad \times \quad 65\%)] \quad = \text{532 Covers}$$

Knowing the number of customers needed to Break-Even can also help the foodservice operator to realize when profit making begins. If the foodservice operation normally brings in 150 customers per day, we take the 532 Break-Even customer figure and divide it by the 150 customers per day to arrive at an approximate four day period for the business to Break-Even. Knowing the foodservice operation's Break-Even Point of Sales, and the number of customers to be served to reach the Break-Even point, is useful information for the foodservice operator. A business that has historical sales and cost information, simply has to plug the numbers into the formula. For a new business, forecasted costs must be used rather than actual data. The more attention to detail in tracking the sales and cost information needed, the more reliable the Break-Even point.

Menu Engineering

The process of Menu Engineering was developed by Michael L. Kasavana and Donald I. Smith in *Menu Engineering: A Practical Guide to Menu Analysis*. *Menu Engineering* analyzes the popularity and contribution margin of each menu item, and classifies the items as "Stars," "Plowhorses," "Puzzles,"and "Dogs." The following definitions will help you to understand the **Menu Engineering Process**.

Stars	High popularity, high contribution margin items
Plowhorses	High popularity, low contribution margin items
Puzzles	Low popularity, high contribution margin items
Dogs	Low popularity, low contribution margin items

The popularity of a menu item can be determined by tracking the number of each item sold. To determine the contribution margin of each menu item the foodservice operator must know the selling price and food cost of each item.

In order to be able to perform the Menu Engineering process, the foodservice manager must have the following information available regarding the items in the analysis: the number of each menu item sold, the selling price of each menu item, and the food cost of each menu item. Menu Engineering is explained below (Figure 12.8). Each column is labeled by letter and thoroughly explained column by column.

Column A

Column A is prepared by simply listing the menu items of the sales category being analyzed. Menu Engineering is intended to be used to analyze menu items within the same menu classification.

Column B

Column B states the number of times each item within the category has been sold during a stated time period. The total of Column B represents the total number of items sold within the category being analyzed.

Column C

Column C asks for the Sales Mix %. The formula to solve for this is:

Formula:

NUMBER OF EACH ITEM	÷	TOTAL ITEMS SOLD	=	SALES MIX %
Chicken Wings: 143	÷	971	=	14.7%

The percentages in this column should add up to 100%.

Column D

Post each Menu Item's Selling Price to Column D.

Column E

Post each Menu Item's Food Cost to Column E. Please note that the Menu Item's Food Cost must include all food cost included in serving the customer. As discussed in Chapter 7, a Standard Portion Cost of a menu item is often a Standard Plate cost. The food cost may include garnishes, bread and rolls, and accompaniment to the entrée ordered.

Column F

The Contribution Margin is calculated by subtracting the Menu Items Food Cost from the Menu Items Selling Price. The Contribution Margin informs the business of how much each menu item contributes to other costs and profit (Col. D − Col. E = Col. F).

Formula:

MENU SELLING PRICE	−	FOOD COST	=	CONTRIBUTION MARGIN
Chicken Wings: $6.50	−	$1.95	=	$4.55

Food Category: Appetizers **Time Period: March 1998**

	A	B	C	D	E	F	G	H	I	J	K	L	M
	Menu Items	No. Sold	Sales Mix %	Selling Price	Food Cost	Cont. Margin	Total Sales	Total Food Cost	Total CM	CM%	Sales Mix Category	Cont. Margin Category	Menu Classification
Wings		143	14.7%	$6.50	$1.95	$4.55	$ 929.50	$278.85	$650.65	15.9%	High	High	Star
Mozzarella		103	10.6%	$4.95	$1.60	$3.35	$ 509.85	$164.80	$345.05	8.4%	High	Low	Plowhorse
Egg Roll		69	7.1%	$5.50	$1.40	$4.10	$ 379.50	$ 96.60	$282.90	6.9%	Low	Low	Dog
Calamari		171	17.6%	$6.95	$1.80	$5.15	$1188.45	$307.80	$880.65	21.5%	High	High	Star
Stuffies		200	20.6%	$4.25	$.85	$3.40	$ 850.00	$170.00	$680.00	16.6%	High	Low	Plowhorse
Shrimp		57	5.9%	$7.50	$3.40	$4.10	$ 427.50	$193.80	$233.70	5.7%	Low	Low	Dog
Nachos		171	17.6%	$5.95	$1.50	$4.45	$1017.45	$256.50	$760.95	18.5%	High	High	Star
Quesadilla		57	5.9%	$5.95	$1.20	$4.75	$ 339.15	$ 68.40	$270.75	6.6%	Low	High	Puzzle
Totals		971	100%				$5,641.40	$1,536.75	$4,104.65				

Desired Sales Mix %: 8.75% Average Contribution Margin: $4.23 Potential Food Cost %: 27.2%

FIGURE 12.8 Menu Engineering

WebCOM™

Column G

Total Sales is calculated by multiplying the number of each menu item sold by the menu item's selling price (Col. B × Col. D = Col. G).

Formula:

TOTAL NUMBER SOLD × MENU SELLING PRICE = TOTAL SALES

Chicken Wings: 143   × $6.50   = $929.50

Column H

The Total Food Cost is calculated by multiplying the number of each menu item sold by the menu item's food cost (Col. B × Col. E = Col. H).

Formula:

TOTAL NUMBER SOLD × FOOD COST = TOTAL FOOD COST

Chicken Wings: 143   × $1.95   = $278.85

Column I

The Total Contribution Margin (CM) is calculated by multiplying the number of each menu item sold by the menu item's contribution margin (Col. B × Col. F = Col. I).

Formula:

TOTAL NUMBER SOLD × CONTRIBUTION MARGIN = TOTAL CONTRIBUTION MARGIN

Chicken Wings: 143   × $4.55   = $650.65

The amount solved for in Column I can be confirmed by subtracting the Total Food Cost from the Total Sales for each menu item.

Column J

The Contribution Margin % illustrates the percentage of the total contribution margin represented by each menu item. To solve for the Contribution Margin %, divide each menu item's Total Contribution Margin by the Total of Column I.

Formula:

INDIVIDUAL TOTAL CM ÷ TOTAL CM = CONTRIBUTION MARGIN %

Chicken Wings: $650.65   ÷ $4,104.65   =   15.9%

Column K

Column K is the Sales Mix Category. Menu items listed here fall into a high or a low category based on popularity. The formula used to determine whether a menu item is high or low has two steps:

Step One: 100% ÷ Number of Menu Items = Expected Sales Mix %

Step One Example: 100% ÷ 8 Menu Items   = 12.5% Expected Sales Mix

If all menu items analyzed are selling at the same rate, each menu item will have the same Sales Mix %. In Figure 12.8, we are analyzing eight appetizers. If the foodservice manager expects to sell appetizers at the same rate, a Sales Mix % of 12.5 % is expected for each menu item. If you are analyzing ten items, each menu item has 10% Expected Sales Mix (100% ÷ 10 menu items = 10%). If you are analyzing fifteen items, each menu item has a 6.67 % Expected Sales Mix (100% ÷ 15 menu items = 6.67%). And so on. The first step in assigning a category a high or low designation is to solve for the Expected Sales Mix percent.

Step Two:	Expected Sales Mix	×	70%	=	Desired Sales Mix %
Step Two Example:	12.5%	×	70%	=	8.75%

The Desired Sales Mix % is a standard that foodservice operators have set to help to identify whether or not a menu item is popular and carries its own weight. The 70% "hurdle rate" is a unique guide developed to identify whether or not a menu item maintains the popularity standard as developed by Kasavana and Smith. If the Sales Mix % of a menu item is less than the Desired Sales Mix %, then the menu item is considered LOW in the Sales Mix Category (Column K). If the Sales Mix % of a menu item is equal to or greater than the Desired Sales Mix %, then the menu item is considered HIGH in the Sales Mix Category (Column K).

Column L

Column L is where the Contribution Margin Category is assigned. The first step is to determine the Average Contribution Margin by taking the Total Contribution Margin (Column I), and dividing it by the total number of menu items sold (Column B). Using the example in Figure 12.8, the Average Contribution Margin would be as follows:

Example: Total Contribution ÷ Total Menu Items = Average Contribution
        Margin   Margin

      $4,104.65   ÷   971   = $4.23

If the Contribution Margin of each menu item (Column F) is lower than the Average Contribution Margin ($4.23), the menu item is considered LOW. If the Contribution Margin of each menu item is higher than the Average Contribution Margin ($4.23), the menu item is considered HIGH.

Column M

The Menu Item Classification column qualifies each menu item into the four classifications already mentioned: "Stars," "Plowhorses," "Puzzles," and "Dogs."

Sales Mix %	Contribution Margin	Classification
High	High	Star
High	Low	Plowhorse
Low	High	Puzzle
Low	Low	Dog

Other valuable pieces of information such as the Potential Food Cost % can be obtained from the Menu Engineering worksheet. The Potential Food Cost % is calculated by taking the total of Column H (Food Cost), and dividing it by Column G (Food Sales). This provides the chef/manager with an estimated food cost percent for the menu category he/she is analyzing. The following shows how the Potential Food Cost % is calculated in Figure 12.8.

Formula:

TOTAL FOOD COST	÷	TOTAL FOOD SALES	=	POTENTIAL FOOD COST %
$1,536.75	÷	$5,641.40	=	27.2%

Decision Making Based on Menu Classification

Once the classification of the menu item has been identified, pricing, content, design, and positioning decisions should be made. Here are some recommendations to be considered when making decisions concerning each of these categories.

Stars

Stars are high in both popularity and contribution margin. This is to say that the menu items that are classified as stars are not only selling well but are contributing considerably to the profit of the business. Many times, the star is the restaurants "signature item." When examining the menu items classified as stars, note the following:

1. pay attention to locating them in a highly visible area of the menu

2. raise their prices slightly so that the contribution margin will increase without affecting the item's popularity, or . . .

3. just leave them alone. If they're stars, they are already a hit.

Plowhorses

Plowhorses are high in popularity but low in contribution margin. A Plowhorse still contributes to the overall profits of a business, but does not singularly contribute much. The popularity of the item allows the operation to sell a lot of these items, although the dollar contribution per item is limited. Plowhorses should be kept on the menu, but the foodserver wants to do what he/she can to increase the contribution margin by selling additional items to the customer. When evaluating Plowhorses, consider:

1. increasing the price. Be careful! Your first instinct may be very well to increase the price of the product, but customers are often sensitive to price increases. It may be possible to increase the price, but only enough to cover increased food costs that affect the menu item.

2. not reducing quality or quantity standards of the Plowhorse menu item. Instead, change the items that accompany the plowhorse menu items to lower cost products, reducing the overall food cost of the menu item.

3. relocating the menu item to allow for the more popular and higher contribution margin menu items to be in the profile areas.

Puzzles

Puzzles are items that contribute well individually to the contribution margin but are not very popular. Decision guidelines for puzzles include:

1.   relocating the menu item to a high profile area on the menu or including it in a high merchandising campaign. Sometimes just renaming the puzzle may be enough to market the item.

2.   removing the menu item. If the puzzle is very low in popularity, labor intensive, or made up of highly perishable product, remove it. At times the puzzle is kept on the menu to keep the "regular" customer happy.

3.   decreasing the menu item's selling price. Maybe the only reason that the menu item is a puzzle and not a star is because it is overpriced.

Dogs

A Dog is a menu item that is unpopular and does not contribute to the profit of the business. The following recommendations should be considered for the Dog:

1.   remove the item from the menu; especially if the dog has no ingredients similar to those of other menu items.

2.   raise the Dog's price so that the item has the potential of becoming a puzzle. This may seem puzzling as, "who would pay for a higher priced dog?"

3.   keep the dog on the menu, because their sales are often accompanied by other profitable sales.

Menu Engineering is an analysis tool used to help identify how well menu items are selling. Menu Engineering helps a foodservice operator to identify a menu item's popularity and its contribution to the profits of the business. Sales Control and Analysis are important in the cycle of cost control. It is within this step that recommendations are made for menu improvements.

Review Questions

1.   Describe three ways to track covers. Which method has the most control? Explain why.

2.   Calculate the Turnover Rates for the following and identify the type of foodservice operation (Classical, Family, Fast Food) that would typically have each of these Turnover Rates.

	Covers Served	Dining Room Seats
a.	100	100
b.	50	25
c.	360	80
d.	250	50
e.	300	55

3. Calculate the Average Sale per Cover using the information provided. What type of foodservice operation would typically have a similar Average Sale per Cover?

	Total Sales	Covers
a.	$3,500	200
b.	$1,250	45
c.	$7,800	325
d.	$1,340	180
e.	$1,440	300

4. Calculate the Sales Mix % for the following Desserts:

	Menu item	Number Sold
a.	Chocolate Heaven	15
b.	Chocolate Chip Pie	22
c.	Deep Dish Apple Pie	8
d.	Mile High Lemon Meringue Pie	18
e.	Strawberry Ladyfinger Torte	12

5. Using the Sales Mix % results from question 4, forecast the number of each dessert needed for Saturday night's forecasted 160 covers.

6. The following are sales totals from each menu category on a menu. Determine the Contribution to Sales % for each category.

a.	Appetizers	$ 550.75
b.	Soups	$ 375.00
c.	Salads	$ 325.25
d.	Entrées	$1,578.50
e.	Desserts	$ 675.25

7. Using the following information, calculate the weekly Break-Even Point of Sales and the Cost of Sales $ at the Break-Even Point.

	Labor Cost	Overhead Cost	Cost of Sales %
a.	$ 3,200	$2,800	38%
b.	$ 1,600	$1,500	40%
c.	$ 6,800	$4,400	32%
d.	$12,200	$9,500	35%

8. Using the Break-Even Point of Sales calculated in question 7 and the Final Sales figures below, calculate Additional Sales, Additional Cost of Sales $, and Estimated Profit.

	Final Sales
a.	$12,000
b.	$ 6,000
c.	$18,500
d.	$36,550

9. Using the information given below, determine the number of covers needed to reach the Break-Even Point of Sales.

	Labor Cost	Overhead Cost	Cost of Sales %	Average Sale per Cover
a.	$ 2,500	$ 1,800	35%	$15.50
b.	$ 4,300	$ 3,900	28%	$32.00
c.	$ 5,500	$ 3,850	34%	$13.75
d.	$ 7,500	$ 6,000	30%	$40.00
e.	$12,300	$11,200	32%	$25.00

10A. Post the following information to the Menu Engineering worksheet in Appendix F, and solve by identifying each menu item as a Star, Plowhorse, Puzzle, or Dog.

Menu Item	Number Sold	Menu Price	Food Cost
Steak Oscar	32	$19.50	$7.40
Veal Marsala	24	$14.95	$6.05
Basked Stuffed Sole	42	$16.95	$4.75
Broiled Salmon	38	$15.50	$4.50
Rosemary Chicken	18	$14.25	$3.75

10B. Based on your findings, what recommendations would you make concerning each menu item?

11. Using the spreadsheet program of your professor's choice, develop a Menu Engineering Spread Sheet.

Bibliography

Dittmer, Paul R. and Gerald G. Griffin. *Principles of Food, Beverage, and Labor Cost Controls*, 5th ed. New York, NY: Van Nostrand Reinhold, 1994.

Drysdale, John A. *Profitable Menu Planning*. Englewood Cliffs, NJ: Prentice Hall Career & Technology Prentice Hall Inc., 1994.

Kasavana, Michael L, and Donald I. Smith. *Menu Engineering: A Practical Guide to Menu Analysis*. Okemos, Michigan: Hospitality Publications, Inc., 1990.

Keister, Douglas C. *Food and Beverage Control*. Englewood Cliffs, NJ: Prentice-Hall, Inc., 1997.

Kotschevar, Lendal H. and Marcel R. Escoffier. *Management by Menu*, 3d. ed. The Educational Foundation of the National Restaurant Association, 1994.

Laventhol and Horwarth. *Uniform System of Accounts for Restaurants*. 6th ed. Washington, D.C.: National Restaurant Association, 1990.

Essential Operating Expenses

Labor Cost Control

objectives

Upon completion of this chapter, the student should be able to:

1. explain the three components of labor cost: wages, salary and benefits.
2. prepare a work schedule utilizing the three methods of irregular, swing and split.
3. calculate the departmental labor cost.
4. utilize the requirements of the Fair Labor Standards Act.
5. explain the law concerning TIP declaration.
6. calculate taxable income, determine withholdings for Federal Income Tax, Social Security, Medicare, and determine net pay.
7. calculate the employer's total labor cost.

key terms

Benefits	*Job Analysis*
Departmental Labor Cost	*Job Description*
Direct Income	*Job Specification*
Directly Tipped Employee	*Meal Credit*
Employee Meals	*Non-Exempt Employee*
Exempt Employee	*Organizational Chart*
FICA	*Salary*
FSLA	*Split Scheduling*
FUTA	*Swing Scheduling*
Federal Income Tax	*Tip Credit*
I-9	*W-2*
IRCA	*W-4*
Indirectly Tipped Employee	*Wage*
Irregular Scheduling	

Introduction

Labor Cost can be defined as the total amount spent to pay employees wages, salaries and benefits. A wage is an hourly rate of pay. Salary is a fixed amount of income based on the job performed rather than the amount of time it takes to perform the job. Benefits are all the contributions the employer makes on behalf of the employee. Employees are often unaware that a foodservice operation's labor costs include more than wages and salaries. All businesses provide benefits that are required under federal law. In addition, some employers offer additional benefits that are completely voluntary. The labor cost of a foodservice operation includes all benefits offered to employees whether voluntary or not. Labor Cost percent is that percent of sales that is spent to pay wages, salaries, and benefits. Often, it can be as high, if not higher, than the Cost of Sales %. Labor Cost % can range from 15–40%, depending upon the type of foodservice operation.

Knowing what is involved in the foodservice operation's labor cost dollar is important; however, it is just the first step to labor cost control. Labor Cost Control is controlling the dollars the foodservice operation is spending in labor costs without jeopardizing the quality of product and service. The true purpose of labor cost control is not to try to reduce labor cost dollars but rather to get the most of every labor cost dollar spent.

It is important that foodservice managers and foodservice employees know the labor laws. Both the employer and the employee benefit by knowing that employees are being paid correctly and within the law. Foodservice operations must pay their employees properly and fairly. If not, consequences can be devastating.

Labor Cost: What Is It?

As previously defined, labor cost is the cost of paying employees wages, salaries, and benefits. We will now examine these three areas to conclude what a chef/manager might do to get the most out of a labor cost dollar.

Wages

A *wage* is a pay rate that is based on an hourly time period. The employee receives an hourly wage for each hour he/she works. Gross pay is normally calculated by multiplying the total hours worked by the hourly rate. There are standards that must be met by employers when paying employees wages. The Fair Labor Standards Act (*FLSA*), written in 1938, implemented the first Federal Minimum Wage and also determined a fair work week of 40 hours. The Federal Minimum Wage is the least amount an employer may pay an employee for one hour of work. As of September 1997, the Federal Minimum Wage is $5.15 per hour. Employers must pay their employees at least $5.15 per hour for every hour worked under the fair work week of 40 hours. This is true in every state within the United States of America with the exception of those states where the State Minimum Wage is higher than the Federal Minimum Wage. If a state has a higher State Minimum Wage than the Federal Minimum Wage the employer must abide by the state law.

There are two exceptions to the Federal Minimum Wage law as stated within the FLSA. There are special rules for hiring full time students under the age of eighteen that include a reduced minimum wage and restricted hours during which they are allowed to work. The current federal law concerning the full-time student wage rate states that individuals under the age of eighteen may not be paid less than 85% of the current minimum wage. Most states also have special guidelines for employees under eighteen.

The second exception to the FLSA concerns those employees who customarily receive gratuities (TIPS: *to insure prompt service*), as part of their income. An employee who customarily receives gratuities, directly or indirectly, must claim the money received through TIPS as part of their gross earnings. A directly tipped employee is an employee who receives gratuities directly from the customer. An indirectly tipped employee is an employee who usually receives a portion of the gratuities earned by directly tipped employees. If an employee normally receives at least $30.00 per month in gratuities, the employer is allowed to take a TIP credit per hour to pay the tipped employee. The federal *TIP credit* is 50% of the Federal Minimum Wage. Again, some states have implemented their own TIP credit policy. If the state's tip credit policy is more beneficial to the employee, it supersedes the Federal regulation. Tips earned by employees must be declared as income. Federal guidelines concerning TIP declaration will be discussed later in this chapter.

In addition to the Federal Minimum Wage, the Fair Labor Standards Act has also declared a fair work week of 40 hours. The implementation of the 40 hour work week also defined overtime laws. Federal law as it relates to overtime pay, is 1.5 times the hourly rate of pay for all hours over forty per week. Some states, and even some companies, have their own overtime rules such as time and a half for every hour after eight hours per day. If a state or company has its own overtime rules and procedures, the employer must again use the overtime policy which is most beneficial to the employee.

Employees who normally receive wages for work performed are considered *non-exempt employees*. They are not exempt from federal and state wage and hour laws as described in the Fair Labor Standards Act.

Salary

A *salary* is a fixed amount of income based on the job performed rather than the amount of time needed to perform the job. In order to be legally paid a salary within the foodservice industry and to be exempt from the provisions of the FLSA, certain requirements must be fulfilled. First, the employee's primary duty is to work in a management capacity at least 60% of the time he/she is working. Secondly, the employee must have at least two or more full time employees directly responsible to him/her. Thirdly, the employee must earn at least $250.00 per week. There are additional federal guidelines that must be met if the employee earns less that $250.00 per week. It is interesting to note that employers often neglect this law and may find themselves and the foodservice operation in a situation of paying back wages and fines.

Can a line cook be (legally) paid a salary? Yes, if the position fills the three requirements listed. Does the line cook work solely behind the line? Or does he/she perform other management functions at least 60% of the time? Does the line cook have full responsibility over at least two full time employees? And lastly, does the line cook earn at least $250.00 per week? In order to be legally paid a salary within the foodservice industry, all supervisory requirements must be met.

Wage earners often find themselves offered a salary for "a job well done." They look to this as a reward for being a true member of the team. They accept a weekly salary of $450 (which sounds pretty appealing), for a forty hour work week. In reality, the forty hour work week is actually 55 to 60 hours per week, and when earning a salary, no overtime is paid. Some employers knowingly try to take advantage of employees in this way. Others do it unknowingly through their ignorance (lack of knowledge) of the law. The Department of Labor was created to provide assistance to both the employer and the employee. There is a Federal Department of Labor, and Departments of Labor in many states as well. These bureaus exist to insure that employees are paid fairly and correctly.

Employees who normally receive a salary for work performed are considered *exempt employees*. They are exempt from federal and state wage and hour laws as described in the Fair Labor Standards Act.

Benefits and Federal Taxes

Labor Cost *Benefits* can be defined as benefits provided an employee at no cost to the employee. Benefits might include health insurance, paid vacations, sick days, *employee meals*, uniforms, holiday pay, and bonuses, all of which are strictly voluntary on the part of the employer. Federally mandated benefits, usually thought of as employer labor taxes, are benefits that employers must contribute to, and provide for their employees at no cost to the employee. Workman's Compensation is an insurance paid by the employer to protect the employee who might be injured on the job. Rates of Workman's Compensation vary according to the safety record of the foodservice establishment. In addition to workman's compensation, there are two other federal labor laws that affect labor cost.

FICA, Federal Insurance Contribution Act, is a payroll tax that is contributed to by both the employee and the employer. The Federal Insurance Contribution Act includes two types of benefits: Social Security, which is a retirement supplement for workers who have contributed, and Medicare, which is health care for those who are of retirement age. FICA taxes are based on both the employee's income and TIPS earned. Currently employers must withhold 6.2% of an employee's earnings up to a taxable wage base of $80,400 annually for Social Security purposes. A taxable wage base is the annual amount of income that is subject to social security taxes. Employers must also withhold 1.45% of all income and tips earned by employees annually for Medicare. There is no taxable wage base for Medicare withholdings. Medicare withholdings are based on all income earned annually.

At this point a question may arise: "If this money is coming out of my paycheck, then why is it part of the employer's labor cost dollar?" Every penny withheld from the employee's pay must be matched by the employer. Employees currently contribute a total of 7.65% of their income to FICA and employers also contribute 7.65%, in addition to the wages and salaries paid the employee.

FUTA, Federal Unemployment Tax Act, is solely an employer contribution. Employers will contribute 6.2% of an employee's first $7,000 of annual income and tips to unemployment in 1998. Although a tax, this contribution is a benefit for the worker who is laid off due to a lack of work caused by a seasonal demand, or by the reorganization of a company's work force. Many states also have their own unemployment programs. Due to a high labor turnover in the foodservice industry, FUTA can be a very costly benefit to foodservice employers. Labor turnover rate refers to the number of times a staff is replaced annually. For example, if a restaurant normally employs 60 people, but throughout the year has had 150 employees who have filled those 60 positions, the labor turnover rate would be 2.5.

Formula:

TOTAL # EMPLOYEES ÷ # NEEDED EMPLOYEES = LABOR TURNOVER RATE

Example:　　150　　　　÷　　　　60　　　　=　　　　2.5 (250%)

The National Restaurant Association estimates the average labor turnover rate for the foodservice industry at 300%. This percentage is much higher than that of other types of businesses. Why is the labor turnover rate so high in the foodservice industry? The answer to this can be debated for hours. Reasons often reflect answers such as: the foodservice industry attracts employees who are only working until they "win the lottery" or get a "real job" acting or teaching. Some say it's because so many employers do not implement a good training program and employees get "fed up"not knowing their job, so they leave to find another. Employers respond by asking why they should spend money training these employees when they are just going to leave anyway. The debate is endless.

So, how does a high labor turnover rate affect the FUTA contributions of an employer? At the beginning of every year, as well as each time a new employee is hired, foodservice employers must contribute 6.2% of the employee's gross income to FUTA and continue to contribute the 6.2% throughout the year until the employee has earned $7,000. FUTA is not withheld from an employee's pay but is paid by the employer in addition to the employee's gross income. A foodservice operation with a low turnover rate might well finish contributing it's annual FUTA contributions by mid-year as most of its workers will have earned $7,000 by then. A foodservice operation with a high turnover rate might be paying FUTA contributions throughout the year since every employee who leaves must be replaced. FUTA taxes paid for the new employee begin a new and are paid until the new employee earns $7,000 or until the end of the year, whichever comes first.

As seen in the example provided, an employer's labor cost dollar does not just include the wages and salaries that are paid the employee. Many other expenses are also incurred. Study the following example to see how FICA and FUTA taxes affect the total labor cost. It's the second week in February and the University Inn's wages and salaries for the weekly payroll total $4,000. In addition to that $4,000, the employer must also pay an additional 6.2% to Social Security, 1.45% to Medicare, and 6.2% to FUTA. How much in additional labor costs would have to be expended for these three contributions?

Wages and Salaries			Payroll Taxes		Employer Contribution		
$4,000	×	6.2%	Social Security	=	$248		
	×	1.45%	Medicare	=	58		
	×	6.2%	FUTA	=	248		
Weekly Total:	$ 4,000			+	$ 554	=	$ 4,554
Half Year Total:	$104,000			+	$14,404	=	$118,404
Yearly Total:	$208,000			+	$28,808	=	$236,808

By including the three contributions listed above, the employer is paying an additional 13.85% (or in this case an additional $554 per week, almost $30,000 per year) over and beyond the wages and salaries paid to the employees. If an employer also makes voluntary contributions to health and dental plans, bonuses, vacations, sick days, holiday pay, employee parties, uniforms, etc., the employers labor cost is quite sizable when added to wages and salaries paid.

There are many voluntary benefits that may be provided to the employee at the expense of the employer that are increasingly becoming available to foodservice employees. The federal government has guidelines on how these benefits should be provided. The most common voluntary benefit, and the only voluntary benefit to be discussed within this chapter, is the employee meal. As stated in previous chapters, employee meals should not be included in food cost but rather in labor cost. There are several options for employers concerning offering employee meals. The federal government allows employers to reduce the cash wages paid an employee in an amount equal to the actual cost of the meal to the foodservice operation. Many states also have provisions for meal credits. It is recommended that the foodservice operation contact the Department of Labor within its state for information.

Employers have the option to provide meals to employees at a cost, at no cost, or at a discount. Employee meals may be provided through employee dining services. A single offering may be prepared each day, or a menu item might be selected. Meals provided the employee at no charge should not be considered as part of the employee's gross income, if the meals are furnished on premises and for the convenience of the employer. The employer does not pay FICA or FUTA taxes on the value of these meals provided.

To calculate the value of the employee meals, the employer must simply assign a fair food cost value to the food provided. This value is then transferred from food cost to labor cost. Often the employer will offer the employee a discounted meal price (such as 50% off the menu selling price). The money paid by the employee remains as a food cost because it is producing a sale. Food provided an employee at no cost is assigned to labor cost. Another method used by the employer allows each employee a set dollar amount for the purchase of meals. An employee might be allowed to order anything desired under a $7.00 sales price. The value of the food cost would be based on the working food cost, and that value would be assigned to labor cost. Any time an employee orders an item which costs more than $7.00, he/she is responsible to pay the difference.

As previously stated, there is a federal law that allows employers to deduct a *meal credit* from the employee's wages and salaries. If an employer provides employees meals on a regular basis, he/she may charge a reasonable amount for these meals. A reasonable fee might be $0.25 per hour from each employee, charged whether or not the employee chooses to dine.

Remember that only tip credits and meal credits can be deducted from employees who are paid a minimum wage. Federal law states that shortages and breakages may only be deducted from employees who earn more than minimum wage. Many states have implemented laws that disallow such deductions. Both Federal and State laws and regulations should be examined prior to paying wages, salaries, mandatory taxes, voluntary benefits, etc.

Hiring the Right Employee

Before any hiring takes place, it is important that the foodservice operator know exactly what and who he/she is looking for. The first thing that needs to be done is to chart out the structure of the foodservice operation using an organizational chart. An *organizational chart* identifies the different levels of authority and responsibility within the foodservice operation. It is important that employees know and understand the chain of command. Figure 13.1 illustrates the organization chart of a medium sized foodservice operation.

The Organizational Chart divides the foodservice operation into departments. Foodservice operations often analyze their weekly payroll based on the percent each department represents of the total labor cost. This percentage is known as the Departmental Labor Cost percent. The number of departments within a foodservice operation depends upon the number of employees and the size of the foodservice operation. The *Departmental Labor Cost* identifies the amount of money spent within each department and the percent of total labor cost each department represents. If at the end of a week, the labor cost is determined to be higher than usual, the departmental labor cost % can help to identify which department spent more than usual. Once the organizational chart has been identified, the following three step process is strongly recommended to aid foodservice operators to hire and train efficient and effective personnel.

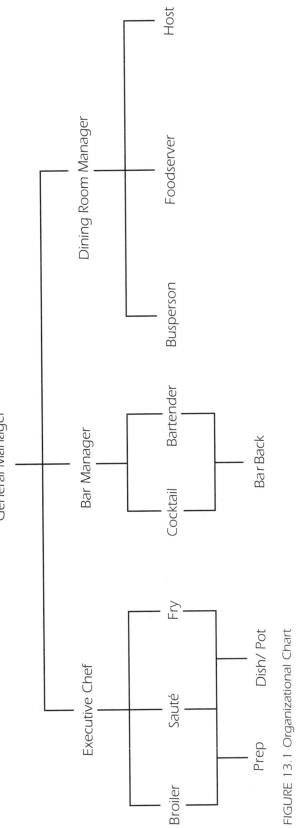

FIGURE 13.1 Organizational Chart

Job Analysis

A *Job Analysis* is the first step in understanding a job. It is the actual process of observing a job being performed, interviewing current employees performing the job, and perhaps performing a job in order to really understand it. The job analysis should be done prior to preparing a job description so that the chef/manager might have a solid understanding of the job in order to prepare an effective job description.

Job Description

A *Job Description* is a detailed list of all duties and responsibilities to be performed to complete a given job. Job descriptions are needed for every job within the foodservice operation. Access to documented job descriptions allows employees to easily refer to them to make sure their opening, actual shift, and closing duties are properly performed. Job Descriptions are a great training tool and can also be used by seasoned employees.

Job Specification

Once the employer knows what needs to be done to complete a job, the employer must also identify what skills and personality traits are needed to properly perform that job. A *Job Specification* is a list of skills and personality traits necessary for a job. During the interviewing process, the chef/manager can refer to the job specification and develop questions to insure that the individual being interviewed possesses the skills needed. A job specification usually identifies three types of skills: technical skills, interpersonal skills, and comprehensive skills.

Technical skills are those that refer to job knowledge (knowing how to perform a job). For example, if the chef/manager were developing a job specification for a broiler cook, some of the technical skills needed would include how to identify meat products and how to filet fish. A knowledge of proper temperatures of cooked meats would also be needed.

Interpersonal skills refer to those human relation skills that are necessary to perform the job. In the example of the Broiler Cook, who will also serve as expediter, good communication skills (the ability to give directions and orders), organizational skills, and time management skills are necessary. The skills individuals need to perform a job should be well explained prior to hiring. It is much easier for a chef/manager to train someone who has a knowledge of what is expected of him/her.

The third skill needed becomes more important as the individual climbs up the ranks on the organizational chart. The Comprehensive skill is an overall understanding of how each job relates to every other function within the foodservice operation.

Once the job has been analyzed and described, and the skills needed have been identified, it is recommended that the chef/manager develop interview questions to keep on file. When a position becomes available, the chef/manager can easily pull the questions from the interview file. Using an established set of questions for all interviews allows for a more equitable evaluation of potential employees.

The New Hire

Once an individual has been hired by the chef/manager, he/she must fill out two federal forms, the I-9 and the W-4, prior to performing any work function (Figure 13.2 and 13.3). It is the law that employers keep these forms on file for each and every employee employed by the foodservice operation. Severe penalties may be imposed if the employer fails to comply.

Immigration Reform Control Act *(IRCA)*

All employees hired after November 9, 1986, must fill out an I-9 form to prove employment eligibility within the United States of America. Employers must retain these forms so they may be available for inspection by officers of the Immigration and Naturalization Service and the Department of Labor. The *I-9* form documents the identity and employment eligibility of the employee. Employees do not have to be United States citizens to be employed, but non-citizens must go through proper procedures as stated by the IRCA to have employment status. The I-9 forms must be held for three years after the employee is hired, or a year after the employee leaves the foodservice operation, whichever is later.

Employees Withholding Allowance Certificate

The *W-4*, as it is more commonly known, must be filled out by each employee to inform the employer of his/her marital status and of the number of dependents he/she is claiming. Federal Income Tax withholdings are based on the gross income, marital status, and the number of dependents claimed. Some employees may be "exempt" from Federal Income Tax withholding. Employees who did not have any income tax liability in the preceding year and who do not expect any in the current year may claim an exemption from Federal Income Taxes. Employees who claim an exempt status on their W-4 must file a new W-4 every year of employment by February 15 to claim this exemption. These employees must still contribute to Social Security and Medicare. If an employee has not filed an Employee's Withholding Allowance Certificate with the employer by the end of the first payroll period, the employer may withhold tax as if the employee were claiming a single status with no withholding allowances.

Tip Declaration

All tips received by employees are considered taxable income and are subject to Federal Income Tax, Social Security, and Medicare withholdings. If employees are involved in some kind of tip splitting, the employee need only declare his/her share of the tips earned. There are two types of tipped employees. *Directly tipped* employees are those who receive gratuities directly from the customer. *Indirectly tipped* employees are those who receive gratuities from the directly tipped employee tip pool. It is the responsibility of all employees who receive tips to report 100% of their share of tips earned to their employer. Federal guidelines regarding how and when to report tips are explained below.

U.S. Department of Justice
Immigration and Naturalization Service

OMB No. 1115-0136
Employment Eligibility Verification

Please read instructions carefully before completing this form. The instructions must be available during completion of this form. **ANTI-DISCRIMINATION NOTICE.** It is illegal to discriminate against work eligible individuals. Employers **CANNOT** specify which document(s) they will accept from an employee. The refusal to hire an individual because of a future expiration date may also constitute illegal discrimination.

Section 1. Employee Information and Verification. To be completed and signed by employee at the time employment begins

Print Name: Last	First	Middle Initial	Maiden Name

Address *(Street Name and Number)*	Apt. #	Date of Birth *(month/day/year)*

City	State	Zip Code	Social Security #

I am aware that federal law provides for imprisonment and/or fines for false statements or use of false documents in connection with the completion of this form.

I attest, under penalty of perjury, that I am (check one of the following):
☐ A citizen or national of the United States
☐ A Lawful Permanent Resident (Alien # A_____)
☐ An alien authorized to work until ___/___/___
(Alien # or Admission # _____)

Employee's Signature	Date *(month/day/year)*

Preparer and/or Translator Certification. *(To be completed and signed if Section 1 is prepared by a person other than the employee.) I attest, under penalty of perjury, that I have assisted in the completion of this form and that to the best of my knowledge the information is true and correct.*

Preparer's/Translator's Signature	Print Name

Address (Street Name and Number, City, State, Zip Code)	Date *(month/day/year)*

Section 2. Employer Review and Verification. To be completed and signed by employer. **Examine one document from List A OR examine one document from List B and one from List C** as listed on the reverse of this form and record the title, number and expiration date, if any, of the document(s)

List A	OR	List B	AND	List C
Document title: _____		_____		_____
Issuing authority: _____		_____		_____
Document #: _____		_____		_____
Expiration Date *(if any):* ___/___/___		___/___/___		___/___/___
Document #: _____				
Expiration Date *(if any):* ___/___/___				

CERTIFICATION - I attest, under penalty of perjury, that I have examined the document(s) presented by the above-named employee, that the above-listed document(s) appear to be genuine and to relate to the employee named, that the employee began employment on *(month/day/year)* ___/___/___ **and that to the best of my knowledge the employee is eligible to work in the United States. (State employment agencies may omit the date the employee began employment).**

Signature of Employer or Authorized Representative	Print Name	Title

Business or Organization Name	Address (Street Name and Number, City, State, Zip Code)	Date *(month/day/year)*

Section 3. Updating and Reverification. To be completed and signed by employer

A. New Name *(if applicable)*	B. Date of rehire *(month/day/year) (if applicable)*

C. If employee's previous grant of work authorization has expired, provide the information below for the document that establishes current employment eligibility.

Document Title:_____ Document #:_____ Expiration Date (if any): ___/___/___

I attest, under penalty of perjury, that to the best of my knowledge, this employee is eligible to work in the United States, and if the employee presented document(s), the document(s) I have examined appear to be genuine and to relate to the individual.

Signature of Employer or Authorized Representative	Date *(month/day/year)*

Form I-9 (Rev. 11-21-91) N

FIGURE 13.2 I-9

LISTS OF ACCEPTABLE DOCUMENTS

LIST A		LIST B		LIST C
Documents that Establish Both Identity and Employment Eligibility	**OR**	**Documents that Establish Identity**	**AND**	**Documents that Establish Employment Eligibility**

LIST A

Documents that Establish Both Identity and Employment Eligibility

1. U.S. Passport (unexpired or expired)

2. Certificate of U.S. Citizenship *(INS Form N-560 or N-561)*

3. Certificate of Naturalization *(INS Form N-550 or N-570)*

4. Unexpired foreign passport, with *I-551 stamp or* attached INS Form I-94 indicating unexpired employment authorization

5. Alien Registration Receipt Card with photograph *(INS Form I-151 or I-551)*

6. Unexpired Temporary Resident Card *(INS Form I-688)*

7. Unexpired Employment Authorization Card *(INS Form I-688A)*

8. Unexpired Reentry Permit *(INS Form I-327)*

9. Unexpired Refugee Travel Document *(INS Form I-571)*

10. Unexpired Employment Authorization Document issued by the INS which contains a photograph *(INS Form I-688B)*

OR

LIST B

Documents that Establish Identity

1. Driver's license or ID card issued by a state or outlying possession of the United States provided it contains a photograph or information such as name, date of birth, sex, height, eye color, and address

2. ID card issued by federal, state, or local government agencies or entities provided it contains a photograph or information such as name, date of birth, sex, height, eye color, and address

3. School ID card with a photograph

4. Voter's registration card

5. U.S. Military card or draft record

6. Military dependent's ID card

7. U.S. Coast Guard Merchant Mariner Card

8. Native American tribal document

9. Driver's license issued by a Canadian government authority

For persons under age 18 who are unable to present a document listed above:

10. School record or report card

11. Clinic, doctor, or hospital record

12. Day-care or nursery school record

AND

LIST C

Documents that Establish Employment Eligibility

1. U.S. social security card issued by the Social Security Administration *(other than a card stating it is not valid for employment)*

2. Certification of Birth Abroad issued by the Department of State *(Form FS-545 or Form DS-1350)*

3. Original or certified copy of a birth certificate issued by a state, county, municipal authority or outlying possession of the United States bearing an official seal

4. Native American tribal document

5. U.S. Citizen ID Card *(INS Form I-197)*

6. ID Card for use of Resident Citizen in the United States *(INS Form I-179)*

7. Unexpired employment authorization document issued by the INS *(other than those listed under List A)*

Illustrations of many of these documents appear in Part 8 of the Handbook for Employers (M-274)

Form I-9 (Rev. 11-21-91) N

FIGURE 13.2 I-9 (continued)

Form **W-4**	**Employee's Withholding Allowance Certificate**	OMB No. 1545-0010
Department of the Treasury Internal Revenue Service	▶ **For Privacy Act and Paperwork Reduction Act Notice, see reverse.**	

1 Type or print your first name and middle initial	Last name	**2** Your social security number

Home address (number and street or rural route)

3 ☐ Single ☐ Married ☐ Married, but withhold at higher Single rate.
Note: *If married, but legally separated, or spouse is a nonresident alien, check the Single box.*

City or town, state, and ZIP code

4 If your last name differs from that on your social security card, check here and call 1-800-772-1213 for a new card . . . . . . ▶ ☐

5 Total number of allowances you are claiming (from line G above or from the worksheets on page 2 if they apply) . **5**

6 Additional amount, if any, you want withheld from each paycheck . . . . **6** $

7 I claim exemption from withholding for 1997, and I certify that I meet **BOTH** of the following conditions for exemption:
- Last year I had a right to a refund of **ALL** Federal income tax withheld because I had **NO** tax liability; **AND**
- This year I expect a refund of **ALL** Federal income tax withheld because I expect to have **NO** tax liability.

If you meet both conditions, enter "EXEMPT" here . . . . ▶ **7**

Under penalties of perjury, I certify that I am entitled to the number of withholding allowances claimed on this certificate or entitled to claim exempt status.

Employee's signature ▶   Date ▶   , 19

8 Employer's name and address (Employer: Complete 8 and 10 only if sending to the IRS)	**9** Office code (optional)	**10** Employer identification number

Cat. No. 10220Q

FIGURE 13.3 W-4

Employee Responsibilities to TIP Declaration

If an employee earns less than $20 in TIPS per month while working for an employer, the employee may choose not to report those tips to their employer, but must include the tips earned on his/her federal income tax return. If an employee receives more than $20 in TIPS per month while working for any one employer, the employee must report the tips to the employer so that the appropriate taxes are withheld. It is also the employee's responsibility to keep a daily record of all TIPS earned and to identify tips received as cash or credit card receipts from customers or other employees. An employee must also keep records of all TIPS distributed to other employees through tip sharing; the name of the person to whom the shared tips were distributed and the amount distributed must be recorded daily. The Internal Revenue Service (IRS) Form 4070A, Employee's Daily Record of Tips, is recommended. Employee tip tracking responsibilities must be conveyed to all employees receiving tips. Information concerning federal regulations in declaring tips should also be provided to the employee. Tip declarations to employers ensure that proper withholdings are taken from the employee's pay.

Employer Responsibilities to TIP Declaration

In large foodservice operations (operations that employ 10 employees per day and where tipping is customary), employers must develop a system to insure that at least 8% of the business' food and beverage sales are declared as earned income by tipped employees. At the end of every year, employers at large foodservice operations must file an IRS Form 8027 to report the foodservice operation's food and beverage sales and the total employee tips (cash and charge) declared to the employer. By filing IRS Form 8027, the employer is able to identify whether or not the 8% of food and beverage sales have been met (through the declaration of tips). If the tips reported are greater than the required 8%, the employer

Form **8027**

Department of the Treasury
Internal Revenue Service

**Employer's Annual Information Return of
Tip Income and Allocated Tips**

OMB No. 1545-0714

**Use IRS label.
Make any
necessary
changes.
Otherwise,
please type o
print.**

Name of establishment

Number and street (See instructions.)

City or town, state, and ZIP code

Employer identification number

Type of establishment (check only one box)

☐ **1** Evening meals only

☐ **2** Evening and other meals

☐ **3** Meals other than evening meals

☐ **4** Alcoholic beverages

Employer's name

Establishment number
(See instructions.)

Number and street (P.O. box, if applicable.)

Apt. or suite no.

City, town or post office, state, and ZIP code (If a foreign address, enter city, province or state, postal code, and country.)

Check the box if applicable: Final Return ☐   Amended Return ☐

1	Total charged tips for 1996	**1**
2	Total charged receipts (other than nonallocable receipts) showing charged tips	**2**
3	Total amount of service charges of less than 10% paid as wages to employees	**3**
4a	Total tips reported by indirectly tipped employees	**4a**
b	Total tips reported by directly tipped employees	**4b**
c	Total tips reported (Add lines 4a and 4b.)	**4c**
5	Gross receipts from food or beverage operations (other than nonallocable receipts). . .	**5**

6 Multiply line 5 by 8% (.08) or the lower rate shown here ▶ _____ granted by the
district director. Attach a copy of the district director's determination letter to this return . **6**

Note: *If you have allocated tips using other than the calendar year (semimonthly, biweekly, quarterly, etc.), put an X on line 6 and enter the amount of allocated tips from your records on line 7.*

7 Allocation of tips. If line 6 is more than line 4c, enter the excess here **7**
This amount must be allocated as tips to tipped employees working in this establishment.
Check the box below that shows the method used for the allocation. (Show the portion, if any, attributable to each employee in box 8 of the employee's Form W-2.)
a Allocation based on hours-worked method (See instructions for restriction.) . . . ☐
Note: *If you checked line 7a, enter the average number of employee hours worked per business day during the payroll period. (See instructions.)* _____
b Allocation based on gross receipts method . . . . ☐
c Allocation based on good-faith agreement (Attach copy of agreement.) . . . . . ☐

8 Enter the total number of directly tipped employees at this establishment during 1996 ▶

Under penalties of perjury, I declare that I have examined this return, including accompanying schedules and statements, and to the best of my knowledge and belief, it is true, correct, and complete.

Signature ▶   Title ▶   Date ▶

For Paperwork Reduction Act Notice, see the separate instructions.   Cat. No. 49989U   Form **8027** (1996)

✿ *Printed on recycled paper*   *U.S. Government Printing Office: 1996 — 417-677/40202

FIGURE 13.4 IRS Form 8027

has done his/her job in ensuring that tips have been properly declared. If the tips reported to the employer do not meet the required 8% of food and beverage sales, the employer must then allocate the difference to directly tipped employees. Allocating tips is a process of assigning additional amounts of income as tips to directly tipped employees. Employers may allocate tips based on gross receipts, hours worked, or upon good faith (Figure 13.4).

To alleviate the process of tip allocation at year's end, employers should implement a system throughout the year to monitor tip declaration by employees. A common method used to monitor tip declaration is known as the Gross Sales Method. To use the Gross Sales Method, employers must require that directly tipped employees record their daily gross sales on the same form on which they declare TIPS. The employer can then compare the tips declared by the employee to the 8% of each employee's gross sales. Indirectly tipped employees must be instructed to declare 100% of all tips earned. Although it is not the employer's responsibility to declare tips for employees, monitoring the tips throughout the year will prevent the allocation of tips at the end of the year (a process that employees often consider unfair).

Pre-Payroll Preparation

Most foodservice operations pay their employees on a weekly or biweekly basis. Salaried employees receive a standard weekly compensation, while hourly wage earners are paid based on the number of hours they work. Before payroll preparation can be performed, the chef/manager must devise a schedule to inform the wage earners of their work schedule. Employers must also implement a system to track the number of hours actually worked by each employee.

Schedule Preparation

The schedule preparation discussion that follows will assume that the payroll is prepared on a weekly basis. Schedules for the hourly wage earners are normally prepared by the manager or department head on a weekly basis. It is a commonly known fact that foodservice operations are like no other businesses since foodservice operations are in a constant progression of peak and non-peak work periods. Peak periods can be thought of seasonally, weekly, or even daily. Daily peak periods are normally those times when the foodservice provides customer service. Daily non-peak periods refer to those hours between meals when preparation takes place. It is uncommon that a full staff is needed during the non-peak periods. This is where the chef/manager must use creativity in scheduling employees to control labor costs. Figure 13.5 illustrates the three scheduling methods discussed below.

It is rare that chef/managers need a full staff from 7:00 a.m. to 3:00 p.m. and a full staff from 3:00 p.m. to 11:00 p.m. Chef/managers try to maximize the efficiency of their labor cost dollar and their work force by using an employee scheduling technique that effectively handles non-peak and peak periods. By scheduling different start times and finish times for almost every employee, the maximum number of staff needed during the day is present during the foodservice operation's peak periods. *Irregular scheduling* allows employees to work a scheduled eight hour shift.

Kitchen Schedule   **Meals Served: Lunch and Dinner**   **Week Ending: April 1**

Employee Name	Monday	Tuesday	Wednesday	Thursday	Friday	Saturday	Sunday
Sally Sous Chef	3–11	3–11	3–11	off	off	9–5	9–5
Larry Line Cook	9–5	9–5	3–11	3–11	3–11	off	off
Lucy Line Cook	off	off	9–5	9–5	3–11	3–11	3–11
Luke Line Cook	10–6	10–6	12–8	12–8	off	9–5	off
Laura Line Cook	3–11	3–11	off	off	9–5	10–2/6–10	3–11
Leon Line Cook	12–8	12–8	off	3–11	9–5	off	12–8
Lou Line Cook	off	off	10–6	9–5	10–2/6–10	3–11	9–5
Totals	2-1-2	2-1-2	2-1-2	2-1-2	3-3	3-3	2-1-2

FIGURE 13.5 Weekly Scheduling Strategies

Another scheduling method that is illustrated in Figure 13.5 is the Swing Shift. The *swing shift* is an eight hour shift during which an employee actually works two peak periods rather than one. A third scheduling method that is not always well received by the employee is the Split Shift. When an employee works two peak periods during a given day but has a lengthy break between the two short four-hour shifts rather that one continuous eight hour shift, this is known as a *split shift*. Some employees dread this type of shift because the hours between the two short shifts do not allow enough time for one to actually get home, relax, and get back. Other employees don't mind the split shift at all. For instance, a line cook might work from 10:00 a.m. to 2:00 p.m. and return from 6:00 p.m. to 10:00 p.m. This type of shift allows a parent to meet a child at the school bus, get him/her home, relax until the other parent gets home, and then return to work. The split shift is also often welcomed by front of the house employees. Working the lunch peak period, going home, and then returning to work the dinner peak period is similar to working two days in one and receiving gratuities for both meal periods worked. Be careful not to use the split shift as a regular schedule for an employee unless it is requested by the employee. Once the weekly schedule is prepared informing the employees of days on and off, the work schedule can be used as a guideline for payroll preparation.

Monitoring Wage Earners' Hours

Traditionally, foodservice operations use a time card with either a time clock or a management signing technique to control the hours worked by employees. The employee arrives on schedule and finds his/her time card in the time card rack. He/she punches the time clock that records the time he/she starts work. At the end of the work shift, the employee again pulls the card from the rack and punches out. Some of the more sophisticated time clock systems do not allow an employee to clock in more than five minutes ahead or five minutes after the scheduled time without a management OK. The time clock is easy to use, but unfortunately it does not provide the control many foodservice operations desire.

The use of a time card with a management signing process insures that the manager is aware of the exact arrival and departure time of the employee. But the management signing techniques can become bothersome to a busy manager. Many foodservice operations employ both techniques to guarantee time accuracy and management knowledge and control.

Hours worked by employees are now often tracked through the point of sale computerized cash register system. This computerized system allows the manager to program the weekly schedule into the computer. The employee punches a code or slides an ID card through the register system to "clock in" and "clock out." The code or ID card prevents employees from improperly clocking other employees in and out. The computer cash register system is an investment for foodservice operations that can be used in a number of ways, including the tracking of wage earners' hours.

Payroll Preparation

When the pay period ends, the manager gathers and totals the hours clocked on the time cards or takes a register print out of hourly wage earner activity. It is a good control method to compare the hours worked by each employee to their posted work schedule. If a discrepancy is identified, find out why. Was it caused by an unauthorized schedule change? Did a dedicated employee replace a sick employee? Or was it a scam performed by not so sincere employees who agree to let the last person out punch everyone else out? Chef/managers must develop systems to insure that excessive labor costs do not occur because of employee dishonesty.

In the foodservice industry today, it is rare that foodservice operations prepare their own payroll. Even the foodservice operation that employs a full time bookkeeper rarely prepares payroll as it is such a time consuming procedure. It is imperative that payroll be well prepared to insure that employees are paid properly and on time. If not, poor morale may result and the foodservice operation may lose out in other ways.

The amount of payroll preparation activity that most foodservice operations perform is limited to simply totaling and checking the hours worked by wage earners. The hours are then posted to payroll sheets prepared by the payroll company. Foodservice operators also post the tips declared by each employee so that the employee can be taxed appropriately. Normally when a foodservice operation sets up a payroll account with a payroll preparation company, all the hourly wage and W-4 information is provided to the company so that the payroll can be easily processed. At the end of the year and as part of the payroll company's employment agreement, the payroll company prepares all the payroll tax documents needed (W-2, Wage and Tax Statements, etc.). The cost of the payroll service varies depending upon the number of employees on staff. Be certain to first research the payroll company that you select.

As more foodservice operations become computerized, payroll preparation programs are being implemented into these operations. If a foodservice operation prepares its own payroll, the person preparing the payroll should be well versed in payroll and labor laws. It is usually a good idea to leave payroll preparation to the experts. It will prove to be well worth the cost charged by a payroll preparation company to prevent payment and tax withholding errors.

Calculating Gross Pay and Taxable Income

Whether the foodservice prepares its own payroll or hires a payroll preparation company, it is important that the payroll be calculated correctly and that the difference between the employee's gross pay and net pay be understood. Gross income is the total dollar amount that an employee earns before any payroll taxes and benefits are with-held. Gross income is the amount on which most payroll taxes and benefits are calculated. Net income is the actual dollar amount the employee receives after payroll taxes and benefits have been withheld. Most foodservice operations will have two checking accounts, one for accounts payable and a second for payroll only. When the foodservice operator deposits money into its payroll account, the dollar amount deposited should be equal to gross pay plus any other taxes the employer contributes (such as FICA as previously explained). By depositing this amount of money, the foodservice operator guarantees that all payroll checks will clear and that all payroll taxes will be covered when they come due.

The following payroll sample information is for four employees of the University Inn. We will calculate the weekly net pay for the four employees in Figure 13.6.

Employee	Marital Status	W-4 Allowances	Hourly Wage	Weekly Salary
Mary Manager	S	1	_____	$450.00
Larry Line Cook	M	3	$8.50	_____
William Waiter	M	2	$2.58	_____
Bette Busperson	S	EXEMPT	$5.15	_____

Employee Name	MS	WA	Hours Worked	Hourly Wage	Weekly Salary	Gross Pay	TIPS	Taxable Income	Federal Tax	Social Security	Medi-Care	Total Deduct	Net Pay
Mary Manager	S	1	—	—	$450.00	$450.00	—	$450.00	$ 53.00	$27.90	$6.53	$87.43	$362.57
Larry Line Cook	M	3	44	$8.50	—	$391.00	—	$391.00	$ 18.00	$24.24	$5.67	$47.91	$343.09
William Waiter	M	2	38	$2.58	—	$ 98.04	$375	$473.04	$ 37.00	$29.33	$6.86	$73.19	$ 24.85
Bette Busperson	S	EX	15	$5.15	—	$ 77.25	$ 50	$127.25	-0-	$ 7.89	$1.85	$ 9.74	$ 67.51

FIGURE 13.6 Payroll Ledger

The week ended April 1, and the hours were totaled and checked with the weekly schedule. The totals are as follows:

Employee	Hours Worked	Regular Hours	Overtime Hours	Tips Declared
Mary Manager	Salary			
Larry Line Cook	44	40	4	
William Waiter	38	38	-0-	$375.00
Bette Busperson	15	15	-0-	$ 50.00

To calculate the gross pay for hourly wage earners, multiply regular hours worked by the hourly wage. Then multiply the overtime hours worked by the overtime wage. Add both totals. To calculate the gross pay for salaried personnel, simply transfer the stated weekly salary to the gross pay column.

Taxable Income for non-tipped employees is found in the gross pay column. Taxable income for all tipped employees is a combination of gross pay and tips declared. Remember, Federal Income Tax, Social Security, and Medicare are based on *direct income* (wages, salaries, and tips declared).

Determining Payroll Deductions and Net Pay

To calculate the Federal Income Tax to be withheld for each employee, look to Appendix E, Federal Income Tax Tables. In order to calculate the *Federal Income Tax* to be withheld, the taxable income, marital status and number of withholding allowances claimed must be known. Marital status and number of withholding allowances claimed are taken from the W-4 filed by the employee. To read the Federal Income Tax tables, first identify the filing status of the individual. There are separate charts for single and married employees. Next, look down the left hand column until the taxable income amount determined falls between the range of "at least"– "but less than." The last step in reading the Federal Income Tax Tables is to travel across the top line of the chart that reads "And the number of with-holdings allowances claimed is." Stop at the number claimed. With one hand, travel vertically down the number of withholding allowances claimed, and with the other hand, travel horizontally across the "at least" "but less than" line. Where the line and column intersect the amount of taxes to be withheld is found. Post the Federal Income Tax to the appropriate column on the payroll ledger. Many states will also have a State Income Tax that must be withheld from the employee's gross income. Every state has a different system and the State Income Tax authority should be contacted before preparing payroll.

Social Security taxes are 6.2% of taxable income. Social Security must be taken weekly until employees have earned the taxable wage base. Medicare taxes are 1.45% of taxable income and are taken out throughout the year because there is no taxable wage base for Medicare. Multiply each percentage by the taxable income column and post the tax to the appropriate column. Total the three deductions and post the total to the Total Deductions column. Subtract the Total Deductions from the Gross Pay column and thus determine the Net Pay.

The gross income paid to the four employees in the example illustrates the wages and salaries of these four employees. In addition to the Gross Income that must be deposited into the foodservice operation's payroll account to cover the employees' net pay and the employees' contributions to Federal and FICA taxes, employers must also deposit their 6.2% contribution to Social Security, 1.45% to Medicare, and an additional 6.2% for FUTA so that these taxes might be paid when due.

A knowledge of payroll calculation and labor laws is very important with regards to labor cost control. This chapter concentrates on just a few of the payroll taxes/benefits that must be paid by each employer. Much of the information needed to prepare payroll is published annually by the Internal Revenue Service and is available to all interested. Publication 15 and Circular E (the Employers Tax Guide) keep employers current concerning taxes to be withheld, and the responsibilities of employers.

Review Questions

1.   Explain the federal law regarding:
    Federal Minimum Wage
    Overtime Wage
    TIP Credit
    Meal Credit
    Minimum Wage for under 18 years
    Social Security
    Medicare
    FUTA

2.   Name and explain the purpose of the two documents that must be held in each employee's file.

3.   Explain the difference between the employee's responsibility and the employer's responsibility regarding TIP declaration.

4.   Explain in detail the three scheduling methods discussed within this chapter.

5.   Using the payroll ledger worksheet provided in Appendix F and the following information, calculate the net pay for the following employees. How much money must be deposited in the payroll account to cover all payroll taxes discussed in this chapter?

Employee	Marital Status	W-4 Allowances	Hourly Wage	Weekly Salary
Mike Manager	M	3	_____	$550.00
Lucy Line Cook	S	1	$9.25	_____
Wanda Waiter	S	1	$2.58	_____
Bob Busperson	S	1	$5.15	_____

Employee	Hours Worked	Regular Hours	Overtime Hours	Tips Declared
Mike Manager	Salary	_____	_____	_____
Lucy Line Cook	40	40	-0-	_____
Wanda Waiter	45	40	5	$ 450.00
Bob Busperson	35	35	-0-	$ 75.00

6.   Using the spreadsheet program of your professor's choice, set up a payroll ledger to calculate the payroll illustrated above.

Bibliography

Department of the Treasury. Internal Revenue Service. *Publication 15, Circular E, Employer's Tax Guide, Cat. No. 10000W*. Philadelphia: January 1997.

Johnson, Richard C. and Diane L. Bridge. *The Legal Problem Solver for Foodservice Operators*, 6th. ed., Washington D.C.: National Restaurant Association, 1993.

Miller, Jack E., Mary Porter and Karen Eich Drummond. *Supervision in the Hospitality Industry*, 2d. ed. New York: John Wiley & Sons, Inc.

Menu Equipment Analysis

objectives

Upon completion of this chapter, the student should be able to:

1. purchase foodservice equipment without over purchasing.
2. complete a menu equipment analysis and establish a listing of foodservice equipment that indicates the capacity of the equipment.
3. list six guidelines to procuring equipment.

key terms

Forecasting
Guarantee
Leasing

Renting
Warranty

Introduction

This chapter should help to guide the reader in the selection of cooking equipment. The process of selecting equipment for the foodservice operation, especially the major pieces of cooking equipment, can be complicated. The amount of money spent on equipment represents the second highest expense category in a budget. The lease/mortgage expense category is first. Procuring the correct type of equipment is essential in producing a smooth transition of menu dishes from the kitchen to the customer. With a properly equipped kitchen, the chef, cooks, and service staff can keep a low food cost and sell more dinners, thus increasing sales and profit.

Guidelines to Procuring Equipment

It is always important to justify the purchase of each piece of equipment. Know why you are purchasing an item. Analyze which cooking techniques will be used to cook the dishes on the menu. Match the cooking techniques with the equipment needed to produce that technique. If a particular piece of equipment is not needed to produce the items on your menu, do not purchase that piece of equipment.

Seek professional assistance after the menu equipment analysis has been completed. Consult a professional foodservice equipment dealer to help you purchase the correct equipment. The foodservice equipment dealer is there to help you succeed. Although it is the job of the foodservice operator to know what to purchase, it is the job of the professional foodservice equipment dealers to know the facts about the equipment they are selling. "Professional" foodservice equipment dealers do not oversell equipment.

Purchase new equipment if the aesthetic appearance of the equipment is essential to establishing an ambiance for customers to enjoy themselves. If the foodservice operator has a sufficient budget and is willing to spend it, purchase new equipment. The advantages of new equipment include: a full warranty and guarantee, a better energy efficiency rate, a greater aesthetic value in the kitchen, and easy to clean and sanitize equipment. New equipment can also be depreciated. Chefs and cooks usually have more respect for their jobs, the equipment, and the foodservice owner, when provided with new equipment.

Research the equipment's warranty and guarantee. A *warranty* is issued by the manufacturer and covers the major components (such as a motor), and typically for a five year life time period. A *guarantee* is issued by the dealership that sells the equipment, and covers small parts of a piece of equipment and maintenance for a time period ranging from 30 days to two years, depending on the type of equipment. Guarantees and warranties vary so read them carefully. Always make a copy of these documents and file them separately from the originals. Do not throw them away with the boxes.

Select equipment that can be sanitized, especially smallware. Equipment that has been tested to withstand washing in abrasive chemicals will be stamped by the National Sanitation Foundation (NSF). The NSF certifies that the finishing material on the equipment will withstand the reaction of the abrasive chemicals during the cleaning process. The Board of Health also examines equipment to see that it can be disassembled for cleaning and sanitizing. It is a good idea to purchase equipment with the NSF label.

Determine if leasing or renting equipment is best for you. The term *leasing* means renting with the option to purchase the equipment. The title of ownership will transfer to the foodservice operator once the terms of the lease have been met. When *renting* equipment there is no option to purchase the equipment; the title of ownership will always remain with the renting company. The main advantages of renting and/or leasing equipment are numerous. Here are some reasons to rent and/or lease equipment:

1.   When something goes wrong with the equipment the foodservice operator does not have to pay for the service charge.

2.   If the equipment breaks while in operation, the foodservice operator does not have to pay for the spare parts or repairs.

3.   When a foodservice operator leases equipment, the operating capital that is needed to open the foodservice operation is less. More money is needed to purchase the equipment than to rent or lease equipment.

Menu Equipment Analysis

The purpose of the menu equipment analysis chart (Figure 14.1) is to establish the type of equipment needed to produce a menu and to determine the volume of the equipment necessary. There are three factors to consider when evaluating the results of the analysis. An important element that influences the end result of the analysis is how the food is purchased. Food is purchased in a frozen, fresh, or convenience form. Each form requires that the chef does a different amount of work to prepare, cook, and serve that particular menu item or ingredient. The decision of how to purchase the food is based on how the foodservice operator and the chef want the menu items to be cooked. A food product that comes in a

Menu Equipment Analysis

Menu Item	Portions To Prepare Per Hour	Weight or Volume Per Portion	Total Amount Produced	Cooking Technique	Equipment			Cooking Equipment Needs
					Preparation	Production	Holding For Service	
Broiled N.Y. Sirloin Strip	20	6 oz.	120 oz. 20 Steaks	Broiling	Reach-in Table Sheet Pan	Broiler	None	Broiler 21 + 15 + 20 = 56 items*
Prime Rib	27	11 slices to the rib	33 slices 3–10 lb. ribs	Roasting	Walk-in Table Roasting Pan	Oven	Oven	Oven 2 racks
Sautéed Tenderloin Tips	10	6 oz.	60 oz. 3.75 lb.	Sauté	Walk-in Table Sauté Pan	Range Top Burner	Steamtable	Range Top Burners** 10 + 3 + 8 + 16 + 21 + 12 + 27 = 97 Items 8 Burners
Broiled Salisbury Steak	15	8 oz.	120 oz. 7.5 lb. 15 steaks	Broiling	Walk-in Table Mixing Bowl	Broiler	None	
Beef Stew	3	6 oz.	18 oz.	Sauté Simmer	Walk-in Sink Table Stock Pot	Range Top Burner	Steamtable	

* The total menu items are derived from both beef and pasta forecasted menus.

** To establish the number of range top burners, first determine the average sauté time for menu items. Next divide the average sauté time into one hour. This equals the number of menu items one burner will produce in an hour. For example, if the average sauté time for one menu item is 5 minutes, divide 60 minutes by 5 minutes to get 12 sautéed items per hour per burner. The total number of sautéed items is 97. Lastly, divide the 97 items by the 12 items to arrive at 8 burners.

FIGURE 14.1 Menu Equipment Analysis Chart

ready to cook form usually requires less equipment. Broiled sirloin strip steaks that are prefabricated and received fresh need only to be taken out of the reach-in box and cooked on the broiler. A fresh, whole tenderloin strip must be weighed and cut into strips and then cooked on the broiler. When the sirloin strips are purchased as a whole tenderloin, there are two extra steps: weighing and cutting. These two steps require additional pieces of equipment: a scale, and a cutting board and knife.

A second element to consider is whether the chef cooks to order or batch cooks to produce the items on the menu. Both methods require different types and different volumes of equipment. The point to remember in completing the menu equipment analysis chart is that no two chefs purchase, prepare, cook, and serve the items on a menu in the same way.

The third factor of the menu equipment analysis to be examined is the per hour production rate of equipment. During the busiest hour in the kitchen, equipment output of food is evaluated. The major pieces of heavy duty production equipment are rated based on the amount of food a piece of equipment will produce. Foodservice equipment specifications usually indicate the capacity of each piece of equipment. The capacity is expressed in food produced per load/per hour. For example, a broiler grid, model ABC, will physically hold 20 sirloin strip steaks that are 3 inches wide, 6 inches long, and 1.5 inches thick. It takes 10 minutes to cook the steaks. Model ABC will produce a total of 120 steaks in one hour. Divide 10 minutes into 60 minutes to arrive at 6 (loads per hour). six loads per hour × 20 steaks = 120 steaks per hour.

When evaluating the equipment needed, the first step is to establish the menu and list the menu items. The second step is to identify the busiest meal period during the week (usually Friday or Saturday dinner). Next establish the total number of customers to be served during the busiest hour. To find this number multiply the dining room seating capacity by the hourly turnover rate. For example, a property with a capacity of 180, which has an hourly turnover rate of 1.5, would accommodate 270 customers. Assuming that 270 customers order an entrée, we then forecast (*forecasting* means to predict) which entrées the customers will select. As a starting point only, we can distribute equally the 270 orders amongst all entrée categories. If a menu contains five entrée categories: beef, pasta, seafood, poultry and fish, each category is allotted 54 orders. 270 orders ÷ 5 categories = 54 orders per category.

The forecast would be presented in this way:

Forecasted Portions to Prepare: 270

Beef	54 orders
Pasta	54 orders
Seafood	54 orders
Poultry	54 orders
Fish	54 orders

Obviously this forecast is unrealistic as it does not take into account a number of factors.

Factors to be Considered Include:

A. the amount of time it takes to cook the entrée.

B. the price of the entrée. (Is the price in the highest, lowest, or middle category listing?)

C. the popularity of an item.

D. the amount of advertising or marketing done to promote the entrée.

E.   the quality of flavor (taste) of the offering.

F.   the attractiveness of the presentation.

G.   the product promotion by the service staff.

H.   the placement of the item on the menu.

I.   the seasonal appeal of the dish.

J.   the total number of entrées listed on the menu.

All these factors will influence the sale of each entrée. If an Italian family style restaurant is featuring beef dishes and pasta dishes as their signature items, the forecast would reflect these promotions. The forecast would be presented in this way:

Forecasted Portions to Prepare: 270

Beef	75 orders
Pasta	84 orders
Seafood	26 orders
Poultry	64 orders
Fish	21 orders

The next step is to forecast the number of entrées the customers will order within each entrée category. On this menu, the chef has selected the following entrées: five beef, seven pasta, five seafood, five poultry, and five fish. Once again, as a starting point, evenly distribute the Forecasted number of entrées in each category. The beef and pasta categories might look like this:

Forecasted Portions to Prepare in the Beef Entrée Category:

Beef—75 portions

Broiled N.Y. Sirloin Strip Steak	$11.95	15 orders
Prime Rib	$10.95	15 orders
Sautéed Tenderloin Tips	$ 9.95	15 orders
Broiled Salisbury Steak	$ 7.95	15 orders
Beef Stew	$ 6.95	15 orders

Forecasted Portions to Prepare in the Pasta Entrée Category:

Pasta—84 portions

Spaghetti with Meatballs	$ 5.95	12 orders
Pasta Marinara	$ 6.95	12 orders
Broiled Chicken with Penne Pasta	$ 8.95	12 orders
Linguine and Shrimp	$10.95	12 orders
Fettuccine Alfredo	$11.95	12 orders
Shrimp Scampi with Angel Hair Pasta	$12.95	12 orders
Ravioli with Scallops	$13.95	12 orders

Now adjust the forecasting factors in the beef and pasta categories to fit your sales goals. Possibly . . .

Beef—75 portions

Broiled N.Y. Sirloin Strip Steak	$11.95	20 orders
Prime Rib	$10.95	27 orders
Sautéed Tenderloin Tips	$ 9.95	10 orders
Broiled Salisbury Steak	$ 7.95	15 orders
Beef Stew	$ 6.95	3 orders

Pasta—84 portions

Spaghetti with Meatballs	$ 5.95	8 orders
Pasta Marinara	$ 6.50	16 orders
Broiled Boneless Chicken Breast and Pasta Penne	$ 8.95	21 orders
Linguine and Shrimp	$10.95	12 orders
Fettuccine Alfredo	$11.95	10 orders
Shrimp Scampi with Angel Hair Pasta	$12.95	11 orders
Ravioli with Scallops	$13.95	6 orders

The same Forecasted process would be applied to each entrée category and the dishes within that category.

The third step is to assign a portion size, expressed in weight or volume. For example, the broiled N.Y. sirloin strip steak weighs six ounces. The fourth step is to calculate the total amount of food to be produced during the busiest hour. Multiply the portions to prepare column by the weight or volume per portion column to equal the total amount of food to be produced (Figure 14.1). The number of strip steak portions to prepare is 20, and each steak is 6 ounces, equaling 80 ounces (5 lb.), or 20 steaks per hour. Knowing the total quantity of sirloin to be produced for that hour, in addition to knowing the remaining quantity of sirloin needed throughout the meal period, help to forecast purchasing needs.

The fifth step is to identify the cooking techniques used in the menu and the remaining equipment needed to prepare, produce (production), and serve the menu item. The above menu includes broiling, roasting (Prime Rib), sautéing and simmering (beef stew and cooking the pasta). As you can see, the cooking techniques are determined by how the chef wants to cook the various menu items. Once the cooking techniques have been identified, determine the total quantity of food that needs to be prepared with each cooking technique. If there are 20 N.Y. Sirloin Strip Steaks, 15 Salisbury Steaks, and 21 Chicken Breasts, a total of 56 broiled portions must be prepared during the hour.

The sixth step is to determine what size broiler is needed. Once the chef knows that he/she needs to produce 56 broiled items per hour, he/she needs to research foodservice equipment catalogs or to talk to a salesperson to find out which broiler model will match or come as close to accommodating these needs. By carefully studying the menu and the methods of preparation used to prepare the offerings, you can intelligently estimate equipment needs.

Here are some helpful hints to remember when completing a menu equipment analysis chart:

- Needs vary greatly, depending on how the chef decides to purchase, prepare, produce, and serve the menu items.

- Soups, sauces, gravies, and other products with volume are usually made prior to the busiest production hour and will not be listed in the production column.

- Some menu items will list two or three pieces of equipment (in the product column), while others may not use any.

- The menu equipment analysis establishes a shopping list for the major heavy duty cooking equipment. Smallware such as plates, knives, and cutting boards should be placed on an independent list.

Review Questions

1. What are the advantages and disadvantages of renting and leasing equipment?

2. Define and explain a production load.

3. Why is accurate forecasting difficult?

4. List and explain five forecasting factors a chef must take into consideration when forecasting portions to prepare.

5. What is the purpose of a menu equipment analysis?

National Restaurant Association's Accuracy in Menus*

Accuracy in Menus offers foodservice operators specific guidelines for the proper representation of products served. Truthful representation involves more than just item description. Photographs, graphic illustrations, printed advertisements, and verbal depiction by employees must also be accurately presented. This guide outlines some common misrepresentations which can be easily avoided by clarification of terms.

Customer satisfaction and prevention of government intervention depends on accuracy in menu offerings. Care should be taken that all written or spoken words are substantiated with product, invoice, or label.

Representation of Quantity

Proper operational procedures should preclude any misinterpretations regarding size or quantity.

Steaks are often merchandised by weight. It is generally assumed that declared weight is that prior to cooking and can be safely listed as such. "Jumbo" eggs should mean exactly that, since Jumbo is a recognized egg standard (30 ounces). Similarly, "Petite" and "Super Colossal" are official size descriptions for olives. Check with your suppliers for official standards or purchase a copy of *Specs, The Comprehensive Foodservice Purchasing and Specification Manual*, published by CBI Publishing Company, Inc., Boston, MA.

Although double martinis are obviously twice the size of the normal drink, the use of terms such as "extra large drink" should be verified. Also, remember the implied meaning of words: a bowl of soup contains more than a cup of soup.

Representation of Quality

Federal and state standards of quality grades exist for many restaurant products, including meat, poultry, eggs, dairy products, fruits, and vegetables. Terminology used to describe grades include Prime, Grade A, Good, No. 1, Choice, Fancy, Grade AA, and Extra Standard.

Menu descriptions which use these words may imply certain quality and must be accurate. An item appearing as "Choice sirloin of beef" connotes the use of USDA

Choice Grade sirloin of beef. The term "prime rib" is an exception to this rule; prime rib is a long established, accepted description for a cut of beef (the "prime" ribs, the sixth to twelfth ribs) and does not represent the grade quality unless USDA is used in conjunction.

The USDA definition of ground beef is just what the name implies. No extra fat, water, extenders, or binders are permitted. The fat limit is 30 percent. Seasonings may be added as long as they are identified. These requirements identify only product ground and packaged in federal or state-inspected plants.

Representation of Price

If your pricing structure includes a cover charge, service charge, or gratuity, these must be appropriately brought to your customers' attention. If extra charges are made for requests, such as "all white meat" or "no ice drinks," these should also be stated at the time of ordering.

Any coupon or premium promotion restrictions must be clearly defined.

If a price promotion involves a multi-unit company, clearly indicate which units are participating.

Representation of Brand Names

Any brand name product that is advertised must be the one served. A registered or copywritten trademark or brand name must not be used generically to refer to a product. Several examples of brand name restaurant products are:

Armour Bacon, Sanka, Log Cabin Syrup, Coca-Cola, Seven-Up, Swift Premium Ham, Pepsi-Cola, Starkist Tuna, Ry-Krisp, Jello, Heinz Catsup, Maxwell House Coffee, Folgers Coffee, Kraft Cheese, Tabasco Sauce, Ritz Crackers, Seven and Seven, and Miracle Whip.

Your own house brand of a product may be so labeled, even when prepared by an outside source if its manufacturing was to your specifications.

Representation of Product Identification

Substituting one food item for another is common. These substitutions may be due to nondelivery, availability, merchandising considerations, or price. Menus must accurately specify all substitutions that are made. Common examples are:

Maple syrup and maple-flavored syrup

Boiled ham and baked ham

Chopped and shaped veal pattie and veal cutlet

Ice Milk and ice cream

Powered eggs and fresh eggs

Picnic-style pork shoulder and ham

Ground beef and ground sirloin of beef

Capon and chicken

Standard ice cream and French-style ice cream

Cod and haddock

Noodles and egg noodles

Light meat tuna and white meat tuna

Milk and skim milk

Pure jams and pectin jams

Whipped topping and whipped cream

Turkey and chicken

Hereford beef and Black Angus beef

Peanut oil and corn oil

Beef liver and calves' liver

Cream and half & half

Margarine and butter

Nondairy creamers or whiteners and cream

Pollack and haddock

Flounder and sole

Cheese food and processed cheese

Cream sauce and nondairy cream sauce

Bonito and tuna fish

Roquefort cheese and blue cheese

Tenderloin tips and diced beef

Mayonnaise and salad dressing

Representation of Points of Origin

Products identified by their points of origin must be authentic. Claims may be substantiated by packaging labels, invoices, or other documentation provided by the product's supplier. Mistakes are possible as sources of supply change and availability of product shifts. The following are common assertions of points of origin:

Lake Superior whitefish

Idaho potatoes

Maine lobster

Imported Swiss cheese

Puget Sound sockeye salmon

Bay scallops

Gulf shrimp

Florida orange juice

Smithfield ham

Wisconsin cheese

Danish blue cheese

Louisiana frog legs

Florida stone crabs

Chesapeake Bay oysters

Colorado brook trout

Alaskan king crab

Imported ham

Long Island duckling

Colorado beef

There is widespread use of geographic names used in a generic sense to describe methods of preparation or service. Such terminology is commonly understood and accepted by the customer and need not be restricted. Examples are:

Russian dressing

French toast

New England clam chowder

Country fried steak

Irish stew

Denver sandwich

Country ham

French dip

French fries

Swiss steak

Danish pastries

German potato salad

Russian service

French service

English muffins

Manhattan clam chowder

Swiss cheese

Representation of Merchandising Terms

Exaggerations in advertising are acceptable if they do not mislead. "We serve the best gumbo in town" is understood by consumers for what it is—boasting for advertising's sake. However, "We use only the finest beef" implies that USDA Prime beef is used since a standard exists for this product. Similarly, a customer who orders a "mile-high pie" would expect it to be heaped with a fluffy topping. However, to advertise a "foot-long hotdog" and then serve something less would be in error.

Mistakes are possible in properly identifying steak cuts. The National Association of Meat Purveyors' *Meat Buyer's Guide* lists industry standards which should be used.

Since most foodservice sanitation ordinances prohibit the preparation of foods in home facilities, the term "homemade" should not be used when describing menu offerings. "Homestyle," "homemade style," or "our own" are suggested alternatives.

Use of the following terms should be verifiable:

Fresh daily

Fresh roasted

Flown in daily

Kosher meat

Black Angus beef

Aged steaks

Milk-fed chicken

Corn-fed porkers

Slept in Chesapeake Bay

Finest quality

Center-cut ham

Own special sauce

Low calorie

Representation of Means of Preservation

Menus often list foods which have been canned, chilled, bottled, frozen, or dehydrated. If these terms are used to describe menu selections, they must be accurate. Frozen orange juice is not fresh, canned peas are not frozen, and bottled applesauce is not canned.

Representation of Food Preparation

The means of food preparation is often the determining factor in the customer's selection of a menu entree. Absolute accuracy is a must. Readily understood terms include:

Charcoal-broiled	Roasted
Stir-fried	Poached
Sauteed	Fried in butter
Deep-fried	Mesquite-grilled
Baked	Grilled
Smoked	Steamed
Broiled	Rotisseried
Prepared from scratch	Barbecued

Representation of Verbal and Visual Presentation

Menus, wall placards, or other advertising which contain a pictorial representation of a meal or platter must not be misleading. Examples of visual misrepresentation include:

- mushroom caps pictured in a sauce when mushroom pieces are actually used
- whole strawberries pictured on a shortcake when sliced strawberries are actually used
- single thick slice of meat pictured when numerous thin slices are actually used
- six shrimp pictured when five shrimp are actually used
- vegetables or other extras pictured with a meal when they are not actually included
- a sesame seed-topped bun pictured when a plain bun is actually used

Servers must also provide accurate descriptions of products. Examples of verbal misrepresentations include:

- the question "Would you like sour cream or butter with your potatoes?" when in fact an imitation sour cream or margarine is served
- the statement "The pies are baked in our kitchen" when in fact the pies were baked elsewhere

Success in Business Mathematics

The following is a tool to help even the "non-math lover" to succeed in solving business math problems.

The Percentage Formula

When working with percentages it is important that before you try so solve the equation, you first understand the parts of the equation. If you understand how to identify each part and what each part represents, you will be able to solve any kind of problem that involves percentages.

There are three parts to every equation involving percentages: the Base, the Portion, and the Rate. Within each equation to be solved, two parts are given, and the third is unknown. Before the problem solver actually sets up the equation to solve the unknown, he/she must first identify the two given numbers. The first step in solving a percentage equation is to identify the Base, the Portion, and the Rate. The following definitions will help.

The Base is identified as the whole, or total available. If there are 38 students in a classroom, the 38 students are the whole (or the total). If a guest check totals $120, the total of the guest check is the whole or the Base. If a business brings in $4,500 in sales, the $4,500 is the whole. Unless you are analyzing different types of sales dollars (food sales, beverage sales, room sales), sales will always be identified as the base. When looking at an equation or a word problem and having difficulty in determining which number is the base, look for the word "of." The word "of" always introduces the base to the problem solver.

The Portion is identified as part of the whole. Of the 38 students in the classroom mentioned above, there are 20 women. The 20 women are the Portion or part of the whole. If a guest check totals $120, and the guest wants to leave an $18 tip, the amount of the tip is part of the whole. If a business spends $1,350 in labor cost to produce $4,500 in sales, the $1,350 in labor cost is the Portion or part of the whole. Unless the problem solver is analyzing different categories of the same type of costs (labor cost: line cooks, prep cooks, dishwashers), costs will always be identified as a portion. When looking at an equation or a word problem and having a difficulty in determining which is the portion, look for the word "is" or the "="sign. "Is" or "equal to" will either introduce the portion or immediately follow the numeral that represents the Portion.

The Rate is identified as the percentage that corresponds to the part of the whole. It is always a percent. But remember, a percent may also be represented in decimal form. For example, 35% has the decimal equivalent of .35.

To change a decimal to a percent, the decimal is multiplied by 100. .35 × 100 = 35%, the equivalent of moving the decimal point two places to the right. Decimal to Percent: move two places to the right (D to P: P is to the right of D in the alphabet therefore move the decimal point to the right two decimal places).

To change a percent to a decimal, the percent is divided by 100. 35% ÷ 100 = .35, the equivalent of moving the decimal point two places to the left. Percent to Decimal: Move two places to the left (P to D: D is to the left of P in the alphabet therefore move the decimal point to the left two decimal places).

In a classroom of 38 students, 20 are women; what percent are women? (52.6%). Leaving a gratuity of $18 of a $120 guest check would yield a 15% rate. When spending $1,350 in labor cost of the $4,500 in sales, the rate would be 30%. At this point do not be concerned about how these answers are derived. Instead, concentrate on how to identify the Base, the Portion, and the Rate.

In the following problems, identify the Base, the Portion, and the Rate. Again, at this time, do not try to solve these problems. Try to identify only the parts of the equation. This process is the foundation to all business analysis.

Example 1: A recipe costs a foodservice operation $3.50 to prepare, and the business wants to maintain a 28% food cost. What is the minimum sales price that must be charged to maintain the desired food cost %? Identify   the Base.

the Portion.

the Rate.

Example 2: 8% of $132 is? Identify   the Base.

the Portion.

the Rate.

Example 3: A guest check total is $125.00, and the guest leaves a $30.00 gratuity. What percent gratuity did the customer leave? Identify   the Base.

the Portion.

the Rate.

The base, rate, and portion of the preceding problems are listed below.

	Base:	**Portion:**	**Rate:**
Example 1:	(?)	$ 3.50	28%
Example 2:	$132.00	(?)	8%
Example 3:	$125.00	$30.00	(?)

Now that the Base, Portion, and Rate have been identified, set up the equation solving for the unknown.

When solving for Base:	Base	=	Portion	÷	Rate
When solving for Portion:	Portion	=	Base	×	Rate
When solving for Rate:	Rate	=	Portion	÷	Base

All three of these equations can be housed within a tool called the Percentage Formula Triangle.

Example 1—Solving for Base. Cover the letter B as the Base is the unknown. Covering the B will leave P ÷ R. Now insert the identified numbers and solve.

B = P ÷ R

B = $3.50 ÷ 28%

B = $3.50 ÷ .28 (28% ÷ 100)

B = $12.50

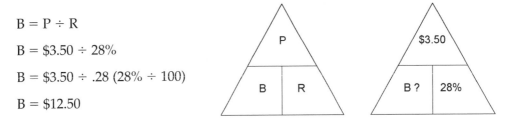

Example 2—Solving for Portion. If you cover the letter P on the triangle, the formula to solve for Portion is identified as B × R. Post the appropriate numbers and solve.

B × R

P = B × R

P = $132.00 × 8%

P = $132.00 × .08 (8% ÷ 100)

P = $10.56

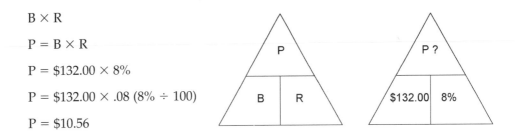

Example 3—Solving for Rate. Cover the letter R on the triangle, the formula to solve for Rate is identified as P ÷ B.

R = P ÷ B

R = $30.00 ÷ $125.00

R = .24 × 100

R = 24%

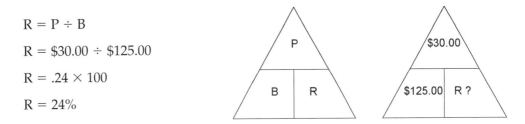

Other variations of this percentage formula triangle can be just as helpful.

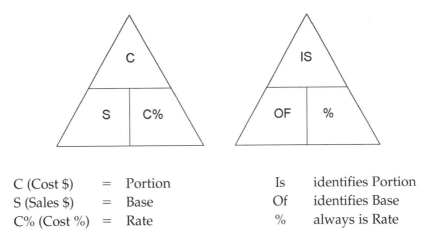

C (Cost $)	=	Portion		Is	identifies Portion
S (Sales $)	=	Base		Of	identifies Base
C% (Cost %)	=	Rate		%	always is Rate

Practice identifying the Base, Rate, and Portion. The Percentage Formula is a tool that can be applied to almost every cost control formula used in industry. The better the Base, Rate, and Portion concept is understood, the easier the math formulas will be to calculate.

Problems

Please round off your answers to the nearest cent and nearest .1%

1. 16 is what percent of 48?

2. 125 is what percent of 50?

3. Four college friends go out and spend $60 on lunch. They all pitch in and leave a $10 gratuity. What percent gratuity do they leave?

4. 40% of 300 is?

5. 150% of 20 is?

6. A guest check totals $152.50. The foodserver adds a 6% Sales Tax. How much is the Sales Tax?

7. 50 is 10% of?

8. $3.25 is 28% of?

9. Labor cost normally represents 35% of the sales dollar. If a restaurant expects to pay $4,200 in Labor Cost this week, what is the amount of sales needed to maintain a 35% labor cost?

10. A foodservice operation brings in $75,000 in food sales in January and wants to increase its food sales by 8% next month. What is the dollar amount of food sales needed in February?

A p p e n d i x   C

Measurement Equivalents and Edible Yield %

The following information is taken from the *Food Buying Guide for Child Nutrition Programs*. It is prepared by the Nutritional and Technical Services Division and the Human Nutrition Information Service of the United States Department of Agriculture and the National Marine Fisheries Service of the United States Department of Commerce. It was originally presented in January 1984, and revised in May 1990. The purpose of the information provided here is to help the student determine measurement equivalents. Edible yields are included so that the student can use this information in costing and purchasing procedures in foodservice operations.

I. Measurement Equivalents

Metric Equivalents

US Weight	=	Metric	Metric	=	US Fluid Ounces
1 ounce	=	28 grams	1.75 liters	=	59.2 ounces
1 lb.	=	454 grams	1.5 liters	=	50.7 ounces
2.2 lbs.	=	1 kg	1.0 liters	=	33.8 ounces
1.05 quarts	=	1 liter	750 milliliters	=	25.4 ounces

Volume Equivalents

3 tsps.	=	1 Tbsp.	1 peck	=	8 quarts
2 Tbsps	=	1 fl. oz.	1 bushel	=	4 pecks
8 fl. oz.	=	1 c.	2 pts.	=	1qt.
2 c.	=	1 pt.	4 qts.	=	1 gal.

Appendix C: Measurement Equivalents and Edible Yield %

Scoops: The number of the scoop shows the number of scoops needed to equal 1 quart

#6	2/3 cup
#8	1/2 cup
#10	3/8 cup
#12	1/3 cup
#16	1/4 cup
#20	3 1/3 tablespoons
#24	2 tablespoons

Ladles: The number on the ladle refers to the number of fl. ounces it holds.

1 ounce	=	1/8 cup
2 ounce	=	1/4 cup
4 ounce	=	1/2 cup
6 ounce	=	3/4 cup
8 ounce	=	1 cup
12 ounce	=	1.5 cups

Can Sizes:	*Approximate Weight or Volume*		
No. 10	96 oz.	to	117 oz.
No. 3 Cyl.	51 oz.	or	46 fl. oz.
No. 2 1/2	26 oz.	to	30 oz.
No. 2 Cyl.	24 fl. oz.		
No. 2	20 oz.	or	18 fl. oz.
No. 303	16 oz.	to	17 oz.
No. 300	14 oz.	to	16 oz.
No. 2 (vac)	12 oz.		
No. 1 (pinic)	10.5 oz.	to	12 oz.
8 oz.	8 oz.		

Appendix C: Edible Yields % after Cooking

Beef	One Pound As Purchased	=	Edible (Cooked) Yield %
Brisket, Corned (boned)		=	70%
Brisket, Fresh (boned)		=	69%
Ground Meats (26% fat)		=	72%
Ground Meats (20% fat)		=	74%
Ground Meats (15% fat)		=	75%
Ground Meats (10% fat)		=	76%
Heart (trimmed)		=	57%
Roast, Chuck (without bone)		=	63%
Roast, Chuck (with bone)		=	54%
Rump (without bone)		=	68%
Rump (with bone)		=	62%
Steak, flank		=	73%
Steak, round (without bone)		=	63%
Stew meat		=	61%
Tongue		=	58%

Poultry			
Chicken Breast Halves		=	66% w/skin
(approx. 6.1 oz. with ribs)		=	56% w/o skin
Chicken Breast Halves		=	55% w/skin
(approx. 7.5 oz. with backs)		=	47% w/o skin
Turkey		=	53% w/skin
		=	47% w/o skin

Other Meats			
Lamb Chops, Shoulder with bone		=	46%
Lamb Roast (Leg) without bone		=	61%
Lamb Roast (Shoulder) without bone		=	54%
Lamb Stew Meat		=	65%
Veal cutlets		=	54%
Pork Chops Loin		=	54%
Pork Roasts (leg) without bone		=	57%
Pork Roasts (leg) with bone		=	46%
Pork Loin without bone		=	58%
Pork Loin with bone		=	45%

Shoulder/Boston Butt without bone	=	60%
Shoulder/Boston Butt with bone	=	52%
Shoulder/picnic without bone	=	57%
Shoulder/picnic with bone	=	42%
Canadian Bacon	=	69%
Ham without bone	=	63%
Ham with bone	=	53%

Appendix C: Edible Yield % of Fresh Vegetables and Fruits

One Pound Purchased	=	Edible Yield %
Apples	=	91%
Apricots	=	93%
Asparagus	=	53%
Avocados	=	67%
Bananas	=	65%
Beans, Green	=	88%
Beans, Lima	=	44%
Beans, Wax (Yellow)	=	88%
Beet Greens	=	48%
Beets	=	77%
Broccoli	=	81%
Brussels Sprouts	=	76%
Cabbage	=	87%
Cabbage, Red	=	64%
Cantaloupe	=	52%
Carrots	=	70%
Cauliflower	=	62%
Celery	=	83%
Chard, Swiss	=	92%
Cherries	=	98%
Chicory	=	89%
Collards	=	57%
Corn, cob	=	33%

One Pound Purchased	=	Edible Yield %
Cranberries	=	95%
Cucumbers	=	84%
Eggplant	=	81%
Endive, Escarole	=	78%
Grapefruit	=	52%
Grapes	=	97%
Honeydew Melon	=	46%
kale	=	67%
kohlrabi	=	45%
Lemons	=	43% (3/4 cup juice)
Lettuce, head	=	76%
Lettuce, leaf	=	66%
Lettuce, Romaine	=	64%
Limes	=	47% (7/8 cup juice)
Mangoes	=	69%
Mushrooms	=	98%
Mustard Greens	=	93%
Nectarines	=	91%
Okra	=	87%
Onions, Green	=	83%
Onions	=	88%
Oranges	=	71%
Papaya	=	67%
Parsley	=	92%
Parsnips	=	83%
Peaches	=	76%
Pears	=	92%
Peas, Green	=	38%
Peppers, Green	=	80%
Pineapple	=	54%
Plantains, Green	=	62%
Plantains, Ripe	=	65%
Plums	=	94%
Potatoes, White	=	81%
Pumpkin	=	70%
Radishes	=	94%
Raspberries	=	96%

One Pound Purchased	=	Edible Yield %
Rhubarb	=	86%
Rutabagas	=	85%
Spinach	=	88%
Squash, Summer	=	95%
Squash, Zucchini	=	94%
Squash, Acorn	=	70%
Squash, Butternut	=	84%
Squash, Hubbard	=	64%
Strawberries	=	88%
Sweet Potatoes	=	80%
Tangerines	=	74%
Tomatoes	=	99%
Tomatoes, Cherry	=	97%
Turnips, Greens	=	70%
Turnips	=	79%
Watercress	=	92%
Watermelon	=	57%

Sample Chart of Accounts Based on Uniform System of Accounts for Restaurants

Below is a partial listing of accounts from the sample Chart of Accounts numbering system for the income and expense classifications as seen in the Appendix of the seventh edition of the *Uniform System of Accounts for Restaurants* (National Restaurant Association, 1986). The purpose of the Chart of Accounts system is to guide foodservice operations in organizing income and expense data using a consistent format, so that foodservice operations may compare their results to those of other foodservice establishments. The purpose of this numbering system is to provide you with a solid foundation concerning expenses incurred by foodservice operations. It is strongly recommended that as you climb up the chain of command, you become very familiar with this Chart of Accounts numbering system. You should also purchase the *Uniform System of Accounts for Restaurants* from the National Restaurant Association.

Chart of Accounts

(4000)	Sales
4100	**Food Sales**
4200	**Beverage Sales**
(5000)	Cost of Sales (Detailed sub-accounts, if desired, will vary by type of restaurant)
5100	**Cost of Sales: Food**
5200	**Cost of Sales: Beverage**
(6000)	Other Income
(7000)	Operating Expenses
7100	**Salaries and Wages**
7105	Service
7110	Preparation
7115	Sanitation
7120	Beverages
7125	Administrative
7130	Purchasing and Storing
7135	Other
7200	**Employee Benefits**
7205	FICA
7205	Federal Unemployment Tax

7210	State Unemployment Tax
7215	Workmen's Compensation
7225	Group Insurance
7230	State Health Insurance
7245	Accident and Health Insurance
7250	Hospitalization, Blue Cross, Blue Shield
7255	Employee Meals
7260	Employee Instruction and Education
7265	Employee Parties
7270	Employee Sports Activities
7285	Awards and Prizes
7290	Transportation and Housing
7300	**Occupancy Cost**
7305	Rent, minimum or fixed
7310	Percentage rent
7315	Ground rental
7320	Equipment rental
7325	Real Estate Taxes
7330	Personal Property Taxes
7335	Other Municipal Taxes
7340	Franchise tax
7345	Capital stock tax
7350	Partnership or corporation license fees
7355	Insurance on building and contents
7370	Depreciation
7371	Buildings
7372	Amortization of leasehold
7373	Amortization of leasehold improvements
7374	Furniture, fixtures and equipment
7400	**Direct Operating Expenses**
7402	Uniforms
7404	Laundry and Dry Cleaning
7406	Linen Rental
7408	Linen
7410	China and Glassware
7412	Silverware
7414	Kitchen Utensils
7416	Auto and truck expense

7418	Cleaning Supplies
7420	Paper Supplies
7422	Guest Supplies
7424	Bar Supplies
7426	Menus and Wine Lists
7428	Contract Cleaning
7430	Exterminating
7432	Flowers and Decorations
7436	Parking Lot Expense
7438	Licenses and Permits
7440	Banquet Expenses
7498	Other Operating Expenses
7500	**Music and Entertainment**
7505	Musicians
7510	Professional entertainers
7520	Mechanical music
7525	Contracted wire service
7530	Piano rental and tuning
7535	Films, records, tapes, and sheet music
7540	Programs
7550	Royalties to ASCAP, BMI
7560	Meals to Musicians
7600	**Marketing**
7601	Selling and Promotion
7604	Direct Mail
7605	Telephone
7606	Complimentary Food and Beverage
7607	Postage
7610	Advertising
7611	Newspaper
7612	Magazines and Trade Journals
7613	Circulars, brochures, post cards, other mailing
7614	Outdoor Signs
7615	Radio and Television
7616	Programs, directories, and guides
7620	Public Relations and Publicity
7621	Civic and Community Projects
7622	Donations

7623	Souvenirs, favors, treasure chest
7630	Fees and Commissions
7640	Research
7641	Travel in connection with research
7642	Outside Research agency
7643	Product testing
7700	**Utilities**
7705	Electric
7710	Electric Bulbs
7715	Water
7720	Waste Removal
7725	Other Fuel
7800	**Administrative and General Expenses**
7805	Office Stationary
7810	Data Processing
7815	Postage
7820	Telegrams and Telephones
7825	Dues and Subscriptions
7830	Traveling Expenses
7835	Insurance—general
7840	Credit card commissions
7845	Provisions for Doubtful Accounts
7850	Cash over or <short>
7855	Professional Fees
7860	Protective and Bank Pick Up Service
7865	Bank Charges
7870	Miscellaneous
7900	**Repairs and Maintenance**
7902	Furniture and Fixtures
7904	Kitchen Equipment
7906	Office Equipment
7908	Refrigeration
7910	Air Conditioning
7912	Plumbing and Heating
7914	Electrical and Mechanical
7916	Floors and Carpets
7918	Buildings
7920	Parking Lot

7922	Gardening and Grounds Maintenance
7924	Building Alterations
7928	Painting, Plastering, and Decorating
7990	Maintenance Contracts
7996	Autos and Trucks
7998	Other
(8000)	Interest and Corporate Overhead
8100	**Interest**
8105	Notes Payable
8110	Long-term debt
8115	Other
8200	**Corporate or Executive Office Overhead**
9000	**Income Taxes**
9010	Federal
9020	State

Sample Federal Income Tax Tables

SINGLE Persons—WEEKLY Payroll Period

If the wages are-		And the number of withholding allowances claimed is—										
At least	But less than	0	1	2	3	4	5	6	7	8	9	10
		The amount of income tax to be withheld is—										
$0	$55	0	0	0	0	0	0	0	0	0	0	0
55	60	1	0	0	0	0	0	0	0	0	0	0
60	65	2	0	0	0	0	0	0	0	0	0	0
65	70	2	0	0	0	0	0	0	0	0	0	0
70	75	3	0	0	0	0	0	0	0	0	0	0
75	80	4	0	0	0	0	0	0	0	0	0	0
80	85	5	0	0	0	0	0	0	0	0	0	0
85	90	5	0	0	0	0	0	0	0	0	0	0
90	95	6	0	0	0	0	0	0	0	0	0	0
95	100	7	0	0	0	0	0	0	0	0	0	0
100	105	8	0	0	0	0	0	0	0	0	0	0
105	110	8	1	0	0	0	0	0	0	0	0	0
110	115	9	2	0	0	0	0	0	0	0	0	0
115	120	10	2	0	0	0	0	0	0	0	0	0
120	125	11	3	0	0	0	0	0	0	0	0	0
125	130	11	4	0	0	0	0	0	0	0	0	0
130	135	12	5	0	0	0	0	0	0	0	0	0
135	140	13	5	0	0	0	0	0	0	0	0	0
140	145	14	6	0	0	0	0	0	0	0	0	0
145	150	14	7	0	0	0	0	0	0	0	0	0
150	155	15	8	0	0	0	0	0	0	0	0	0
155	160	16	8	1	0	0	0	0	0	0	0	0
160	165	17	9	1	0	0	0	0	0	0	0	0
165	170	17	10	2	0	0	0	0	0	0	0	0
170	175	18	11	3	0	0	0	0	0	0	0	0
175	180	19	11	4	0	0	0	0	0	0	0	0
180	185	20	12	4	0	0	0	0	0	0	0	0
185	190	20	13	5	0	0	0	0	0	0	0	0
190	195	21	14	6	0	0	0	0	0	0	0	0
195	200	22	14	7	0	0	0	0	0	0	0	0
200	210	23	15	8	0	0	0	0	0	0	0	0
210	220	25	17	9	2	0	0	0	0	0	0	0
220	230	26	18	11	3	0	0	0	0	0	0	0
230	240	28	20	12	5	0	0	0	0	0	0	0
240	250	29	21	14	6	0	0	0	0	0	0	0
250	260	31	23	15	8	0	0	0	0	0	0	0
260	270	32	24	17	9	2	0	0	0	0	0	0
270	280	34	26	18	11	3	0	0	0	0	0	0
280	290	35	27	20	12	5	0	0	0	0	0	0
290	300	37	29	21	14	6	0	0	0	0	0	0
300	310	38	30	23	15	8	0	0	0	0	0	0
310	320	40	32	24	17	9	1	0	0	0	0	0
320	330	41	33	26	18	11	3	0	0	0	0	0
330	340	43	35	27	20	12	4	0	0	0	0	0
340	350	44	36	29	21	14	6	0	0	0	0	0
350	360	46	38	30	23	15	7	0	0	0	0	0
360	370	47	39	32	24	17	9	1	0	0	0	0
370	380	49	41	33	26	18	10	3	0	0	0	0
380	390	50	42	35	27	20	12	4	0	0	0	0
390	400	52	44	36	29	21	13	6	0	0	0	0
400	410	53	45	38	30	23	15	7	0	0	0	0
410	420	55	47	39	32	24	16	9	1	0	0	0
420	430	56	48	41	33	26	18	10	3	0	0	0
430	440	58	50	42	35	27	19	12	4	0	0	0
440	450	59	51	44	36	29	21	13	6	0	0	0
450	460	61	53	45	38	30	22	15	7	0	0	0
460	470	62	54	47	39	32	24	16	9	1	0	0
470	480	64	56	48	41	33	25	18	10	2	0	0
480	490	65	57	50	42	35	27	19	12	4	0	0
490	500	67	59	51	44	36	28	21	13	5	0	0
500	510	68	60	53	45	38	30	22	15	7	0	0
510	520	71	62	54	47	39	31	24	16	8	1	0
520	530	74	63	56	48	41	33	25	18	10	2	0
530	540	77	65	57	50	42	34	27	19	11	4	0
540	550	80	66	59	51	44	36	28	21	13	5	0
550	560	82	68	60	53	45	37	30	22	14	7	0
560	570	85	71	62	54	47	39	31	24	16	8	1
570	580	88	74	63	56	48	40	33	25	17	10	2
580	590	91	77	65	57	50	42	34	27	19	11	4
590	600	94	79	66	59	51	43	36	28	20	13	5

SINGLE Persons—WEEKLY Payroll Period

If the wages are-		And the number of withholding allowances claimed is—										
At least	But less than	0	1	2	3	4	5	6	7	8	9	10
		The amount of income tax to be withheld is—										
$600	$610	96	82	68	60	53	45	37	30	22	14	7
610	620	99	85	71	62	54	46	39	31	23	16	8
620	630	102	88	73	63	56	48	40	33	25	17	10
630	640	105	91	76	65	57	49	42	34	26	19	11
640	650	108	93	79	66	59	51	43	36	28	20	13
650	660	110	96	82	68	60	52	45	37	29	22	14
660	670	113	99	85	70	62	54	46	39	31	23	16
670	680	116	102	87	73	63	55	48	40	32	25	17
680	690	119	105	90	76	65	57	49	42	34	26	19
690	700	122	107	93	79	66	58	51	43	35	28	20
700	710	124	110	96	82	68	60	52	45	37	29	22
710	720	127	113	99	84	70	61	54	46	38	31	23
720	730	130	116	101	87	73	63	55	48	40	32	25
730	740	133	119	104	90	76	64	57	49	41	34	26
740	750	136	121	107	93	79	66	58	51	43	35	28
750	760	138	124	110	96	81	67	60	52	44	37	29
760	770	141	127	113	98	84	70	61	54	46	38	31
770	780	144	130	115	101	87	73	63	55	47	40	32
780	790	147	133	118	104	90	75	64	57	49	41	34
790	800	150	135	121	107	93	78	66	58	50	43	35
800	810	152	138	124	110	95	81	67	60	52	44	37
810	820	155	141	127	112	98	84	70	61	53	46	38
820	830	158	144	129	115	101	87	72	63	55	47	40
830	840	161	147	132	118	104	89	75	64	56	49	41
840	850	164	149	135	121	107	92	78	66	58	50	43
850	860	166	152	138	124	109	95	81	67	59	52	44
860	870	169	155	141	126	112	98	84	69	61	53	46
870	880	172	158	143	129	115	101	86	72	62	55	47
880	890	175	161	146	132	118	103	89	75	64	56	49
890	900	178	163	149	135	121	106	92	78	65	58	50
900	910	180	166	152	138	123	109	95	80	67	59	52
910	920	183	169	155	140	126	112	98	83	69	61	53
920	930	186	172	157	143	129	115	100	86	72	62	55
930	940	189	175	160	146	132	117	103	89	75	64	56
940	950	192	177	163	149	135	120	106	92	77	65	58
950	960	194	180	166	152	137	123	109	94	80	67	59
960	970	197	183	169	154	140	126	112	97	83	69	61
970	980	200	186	171	157	143	129	114	100	86	72	62
980	990	203	189	174	160	146	131	117	103	89	74	64
990	1,000	206	191	177	163	149	134	120	106	91	77	65
1,000	1,010	208	194	180	166	151	137	123	108	94	80	67
1,010	1,020	211	197	183	168	154	140	126	111	97	83	68
1,020	1,030	214	200	185	171	157	143	128	114	100	86	71
1,030	1,040	217	203	188	174	160	145	131	117	103	88	74
1,040	1,050	220	205	191	177	163	148	134	120	105	91	77
1,050	1,060	222	208	194	180	165	151	137	122	108	94	80
1,060	1,070	225	211	197	182	168	154	140	125	111	97	82
1,070	1,080	228	214	199	185	171	157	142	128	114	100	85
1,080	1,090	231	217	202	188	174	159	145	131	117	102	88
1,090	1,100	235	219	205	191	177	162	148	134	119	105	91
1,100	1,110	238	222	208	194	179	165	151	136	122	108	94
1,110	1,120	241	225	211	196	182	168	154	139	125	111	96
1,120	1,130	244	228	213	199	185	171	156	142	128	114	99
1,130	1,140	247	231	216	202	188	173	159	145	131	116	102
1,140	1,150	250	234	219	205	191	176	162	148	133	119	105
1,150	1,160	253	237	222	208	193	179	165	150	136	122	108
1,160	1,170	256	240	225	210	196	182	168	153	139	125	110
1,170	1,180	259	244	228	213	199	185	170	156	142	128	113
1,180	1,190	262	247	231	216	202	187	173	159	145	130	116
1,190	1,200	266	250	234	219	205	190	176	162	147	133	119
1,200	1,210	269	253	237	222	207	193	179	164	150	136	122
1,210	1,220	272	256	240	224	210	196	182	167	153	139	124
1,220	1,230	275	259	243	227	213	199	184	170	156	142	127
1,230	1,240	278	262	246	231	216	201	187	173	159	144	130
1,240	1,250	281	265	249	234	219	204	190	176	161	147	133

| $1,250 and over | Use Table 1(a) for **a SINGLE person** on page 34. Also see the instructions on page 32. |

MARRIED Persons—WEEKLY Payroll Period

If the wages are-		And the number of withholding allowances claimed is—										
At least	But less than	0	1	2	3	4	5	6	7	8	9	10
		The amount of income tax to be withheld is—										
$0	$125	0	0	0	0	0	0	0	0	0	0	0
125	130	1	0	0	0	0	0	0	0	0	0	0
130	135	1	0	0	0	0	0	0	0	0	0	0
135	140	2	0	0	0	0	0	0	0	0	0	0
140	145	3	0	0	0	0	0	0	0	0	0	0
145	150	4	0	0	0	0	0	0	0	0	0	0
150	155	4	0	0	0	0	0	0	0	0	0	0
155	160	5	0	0	0	0	0	0	0	0	0	0
160	165	6	0	0	0	0	0	0	0	0	0	0
165	170	7	0	0	0	0	0	0	0	0	0	0
170	175	7	0	0	0	0	0	0	0	0	0	0
175	180	8	0	0	0	0	0	0	0	0	0	0
180	185	9	1	0	0	0	0	0	0	0	0	0
185	190	10	2	0	0	0	0	0	0	0	0	0
190	195	10	3	0	0	0	0	0	0	0	0	0
195	200	11	3	0	0	0	0	0	0	0	0	0
200	210	12	5	0	0	0	0	0	0	0	0	0
210	220	14	6	0	0	0	0	0	0	0	0	0
220	230	15	8	0	0	0	0	0	0	0	0	0
230	240	17	9	1	0	0	0	0	0	0	0	0
240	250	18	11	3	0	0	0	0	0	0	0	0
250	260	20	12	4	0	0	0	0	0	0	0	0
260	270	21	14	6	0	0	0	0	0	0	0	0
270	280	23	15	7	0	0	0	0	0	0	0	0
280	290	24	17	9	1	0	0	0	0	0	0	0
290	300	26	18	10	3	0	0	0	0	0	0	0
300	310	27	20	12	4	0	0	0	0	0	0	0
310	320	29	21	13	6	0	0	0	0	0	0	0
320	330	30	23	15	7	0	0	0	0	0	0	0
330	340	32	24	16	9	1	0	0	0	0	0	0
340	350	33	26	18	10	3	0	0	0	0	0	0
350	360	35	27	19	12	4	0	0	0	0	0	0
360	370	36	29	21	13	6	0	0	0	0	0	0
370	380	38	30	22	15	7	0	0	0	0	0	0
380	390	39	32	24	16	9	1	0	0	0	0	0
390	400	41	33	25	18	10	2	0	0	0	0	0
400	410	42	35	27	19	12	4	0	0	0	0	0
410	420	44	36	28	21	13	5	0	0	0	0	0
420	430	45	38	30	22	15	7	0	0	0	0	0
430	440	47	39	31	24	16	8	1	0	0	0	0
440	450	48	41	33	25	18	10	2	0	0	0	0
450	460	50	42	34	27	19	11	4	0	0	0	0
460	470	51	44	36	28	21	13	5	0	0	0	0
470	480	53	45	37	30	22	14	7	0	0	0	0
480	490	54	47	39	31	24	16	8	1	0	0	0
490	500	56	48	40	33	25	17	10	2	0	0	0
500	510	57	50	42	34	27	19	11	4	0	0	0
510	520	59	51	43	36	28	20	13	5	0	0	0
520	530	60	53	45	37	30	22	14	7	0	0	0
530	540	62	54	46	39	31	23	16	8	0	0	0
540	550	63	56	48	40	33	25	17	10	2	0	0
550	560	65	57	49	42	34	26	19	11	3	0	0
560	570	66	59	51	43	36	28	20	13	5	0	0
570	580	68	60	52	45	37	29	22	14	6	0	0
580	590	69	62	54	46	39	31	23	16	8	0	0
590	600	71	63	55	48	40	32	25	17	9	2	0
600	610	72	65	57	49	42	34	26	19	11	3	0
610	620	74	66	58	51	43	35	28	20	12	5	0
620	630	75	68	60	52	45	37	29	22	14	6	0
630	640	77	69	61	54	46	38	31	23	15	8	0
640	650	78	71	63	55	48	40	32	25	17	9	2
650	660	80	72	64	57	49	41	34	26	18	11	3
660	670	81	74	66	58	51	43	35	28	20	12	5
670	680	83	75	67	60	52	44	37	29	21	14	6
680	690	84	77	69	61	54	46	38	31	23	15	8
690	700	86	78	70	63	55	47	40	32	24	17	9
700	710	87	80	72	64	57	49	41	34	26	18	11
710	720	89	81	73	66	58	50	43	35	27	20	12
720	730	90	83	75	67	60	52	44	37	29	21	14
730	740	92	84	76	69	61	53	46	38	30	23	15

MARRIED Persons—WEEKLY Payroll Period

If the wages are-		And the number of withholding allowances claimed is—										
At least	But less than	0	1	2	3	4	5	6	7	8	9	10
		The amount of income tax to be withheld is—										
$740	$750	93	86	78	70	63	55	47	40	32	24	17
750	760	95	87	79	72	64	56	49	41	33	26	18
760	770	96	86	81	73	66	58	50	43	35	27	20
770	780	98	90	82	75	67	59	52	44	36	29	21
780	790	99	92	84	76	69	61	53	46	38	30	23
790	800	101	93	85	78	70	62	55	47	39	32	24
800	810	102	95	87	79	72	64	56	49	41	33	26
810	820	104	96	88	81	73	65	58	50	42	35	27
820	830	105	98	90	82	75	67	59	52	44	36	29
830	840	107	99	91	84	76	68	61	53	45	38	30
840	850	108	101	93	85	78	70	62	55	47	39	32
850	860	110	102	94	87	79	71	64	56	48	41	33
860	870	111	104	96	88	81	73	65	58	50	42	35
870	880	113	105	97	90	82	74	67	59	51	44	36
880	890	116	107	99	91	84	76	68	61	53	45	38
890	900	118	108	100	93	85	77	70	62	54	47	39
900	910	121	110	102	94	87	79	71	64	56	48	41
910	920	124	111	103	96	88	80	73	65	57	50	42
920	930	127	113	105	97	90	82	74	67	59	51	44
930	940	130	115	106	99	91	83	76	68	60	53	45
940	950	132	118	108	100	93	85	77	70	62	54	47
950	960	135	121	109	102	94	86	79	71	63	56	48
960	970	138	124	111	103	96	88	80	73	65	57	50
970	980	141	127	112	105	97	89	82	74	66	59	51
980	990	144	129	115	106	99	91	83	76	68	60	53
990	1,000	146	132	118	108	100	92	85	77	69	62	54
1,000	1,010	149	135	121	109	102	94	86	79	71	63	56
1,010	1,020	152	138	123	111	103	95	88	80	72	65	57
1,020	1,030	155	141	126	112	105	97	89	82	74	66	59
1,030	1,040	158	143	129	115	106	98	91	83	75	68	60
1,040	1,050	160	146	132	118	108	100	92	85	77	69	62
1,050	1,060	163	149	135	120	109	101	94	86	78	71	63
1,060	1,070	166	152	137	123	111	103	95	88	80	72	65
1,070	1,080	169	155	140	126	112	104	97	89	81	74	66
1,080	1,090	172	157	143	129	114	106	98	91	83	75	68
1,090	1,100	174	160	146	132	117	107	100	92	84	77	69
1,100	1,110	177	163	149	134	120	109	101	94	86	78	71
1,110	1,120	180	166	151	137	123	110	103	95	87	80	72
1,120	1,130	183	169	154	140	126	112	104	97	89	81	74
1,130	1,140	186	171	157	143	128	114	106	98	90	83	75
1,140	1,150	188	174	160	146	131	117	107	100	92	84	77
1,150	1,160	191	177	163	148	134	120	109	101	93	86	78
1,160	1,170	194	180	165	151	137	123	110	103	95	87	80
1,170	1,180	197	183	168	154	140	125	112	104	96	89	81
1,180	1,190	200	185	171	157	142	128	114	106	98	90	83
1,190	1,200	202	188	174	160	145	131	117	107	99	92	84
1,200	1,210	205	191	177	162	148	134	120	109	101	93	86
1,210	1,220	208	194	179	165	151	137	122	110	102	95	87
1,220	1,230	211	197	182	168	154	139	125	112	104	96	89
1,230	1,240	214	199	185	171	156	142	128	114	105	98	90
1,240	1,250	216	202	188	174	159	145	131	116	107	99	92
1,250	1,260	219	205	191	176	162	148	134	119	108	101	93
1,260	1,270	222	208	193	179	165	151	136	122	110	102	95
1,270	1,280	225	211	196	182	168	153	139	125	111	104	96
1,280	1,290	228	213	199	185	170	156	142	128	113	105	98
1,290	1,300	230	216	202	188	173	159	145	130	116	107	99
1,300	1,310	233	219	205	190	176	162	148	133	119	108	101
1,310	1,320	236	222	207	193	179	165	150	136	122	110	102
1,320	1,330	239	225	210	196	182	167	153	139	125	111	104
1,330	1,340	242	227	213	199	184	170	156	142	127	113	105
1,340	1,350	244	230	216	202	187	173	159	144	130	116	107
1,350	1,360	247	233	219	204	190	176	162	147	133	119	108
1,360	1,370	250	236	221	207	193	179	164	150	136	122	110
1,370	1,380	253	239	224	210	196	181	167	153	139	124	111
1,380	1,390	256	241	227	213	198	184	170	156	141	127	113

$1,390 and over	Use Table 1(b) for a **MARRIED person** on page 34. Also see the instructions on page 32.

Worksheets and Project Forms

Corresponding Chapter	Form Name
Chapter 2	Developing a Concept
Chapter 6	Profit and Loss Statement
Chapter 7	Yield Test Cost Form
	Cooking Loss Cost Form
	Standard Recipe Cost Form
Chapter 8	Product Specification
	Order Sheet
	Purveyor Bid Sheet
	Purchase Order
Chapter 9	Purchase Distribution Journal
	Receiving Report Form
Chapter 10	Inventory Sheet
	Bin Card
	Transfer Memo
Chapter 11	Daily Cost %: Simple Approach
	Daily Food Cost %—Accurate Approach
	Daily Beverage Cost %—Accurate Approach

Chapter 12   Sales Journal

                              Menu Engineering Worksheet

Chapter 13   Weekly Schedule

                              Payroll Ledger

The Concept

Foodservice Category: Check The Appropriate Answer

    Quick Serve   _____

    Family   _____

    Dinner House   _____

    Fine Dining   _____

Style Of Menu: A La Carte____, Semi A La Carte ____, Table d Hote____, Prix Fixe____

Cuisine:

    American Regional   _____ Region_____

    French   _____

    Mexican   _____

    Italian   _____

    Cajun   _____

    German   _____

    Kosher   _____

    Other   _____

Days Open: Monday_____, Tuesday_____, Wednesday_____,

                    Thursday_____, Friday_____, Saturday_____, Sunday_____.

Total Days Open Per Year: _____

Capacity:

    Dining Room(s)   seats_____

    Lounge   seats_____

    Bar   seats_____

    Banquet Facilities   seats_____

    Other_____   seats_____

    Total Capacity   _____

Turnover Rate Per Hour:

    Dining Room(s)   _____

Check Average Per Person:

    Breakfast $_____

    Lunch $_____

    Dinner $_____

    Afternoon Tea $_____

    Brunch $_____

    Other $_____

Meal Period(s) Opened: Serving Time:

    Breakfast   _____   _____am to_____am/pm

    Lunch   _____   _____am to_____pm

    Dinner   _____   _____pm to_____pm

    Afternoon Tea _____   _____pm to_____pm

    Brunch   _____   _____pm to_____pm

    Other_____   _____pm to_____pm

The Concept
Page Two

Type Of Service	self	counter	table
Breakfast			
Lunch			
Dinner			
Afternoon Tea			
Brunch			
Banquet			
Other			

Type Of Service	American	French	Family	Buffet	Banquet	Other
Breakfast						
Lunch						
Dinner						
Afternoon Tea						
Brunch						
Banquet						
Other						

Atmosphere:

Describe the exterior and interior design of the foodservice operation. Describe the image the operation is trying to project. Include items such as type of landscaping, exterior colors, interior color scheme, type of floors, color of carpet or tile, type of wallpaper, style of table setting, tablecloth, china pattern, type of lighting, style of music and the style of uniform.

Give the bank manager a clear and complete image of the ambiance or atmosphere of the foodservice operation. Include a description of the decor including pictures, etc.

The Concept
Page Three

Type Of Customer:

    Family   _____

    Professional / Businnes Person   _____

    Blue Collar Employee   _____

    White Collar Employee   _____

    Single   _____

    Married   _____

Students:

    Graduate   _____

    Undergraduate   _____

    High School   _____

Age Group: Must Equal 100%

    Children   1 – 5 _____

                         6 – 10 _____

                        11 – 13 _____

                        14 – 17 _____

    Adults   18 – 22 _____   46 – 50 _____

                        23 – 29 _____   51 – 55 _____

                        30 – 35 _____   56 – 60 _____

                        36 – 40 _____   61 – 65 _____

                        41 – 45 _____   66 – 45+ _____

Occupation:

Office Clerk	_____	Lawyer	_____
Electrician	_____	Salesperson	_____
Plumber	_____	Doctor	_____
Painter	_____	Business Executive	_____
Factory Worker	_____	Teacher	_____
Police Officer	_____	Politician	_____
Other	_____	Other	_____

Income Bracket: Must Equal 100%

    Under $16,000   _____

    $16,000 – $25,000   _____

    $26,000 – $35,000   _____

    $36,000 – $45,000   _____

    $46,000 – $55,000   _____

    $56,000 – $65,000   _____

    $66,000 – $75,000   _____

    $76,000 – $100,000   _____

    Above $100,000   _____

Ethnic Origin:

    Hispanic   (Spanish Origin)   _____

    Oriental   (Asian Origin)   _____

    Black   (African Origin)   _____

    White   (Caucasian)   _____

    Other   _____

Gender Ratio: Must Equal 100%

    Male _____   Female _____

The Concept
Page Four

Education:

Less Than 9th Grade	_____
9th to 12th Grade, No Diploma	_____
High School Graduate	_____
Associate Degree	_____
Bachelor's Degree	_____
Graduate or Professional Degree	_____

Community Geographics

Select a specific location and review the geographies of that community. Using this data (include actual data) as well as other information, draw conclusions on your targeted customers' preferences: dining times, preferred dining out day, and examine foodservice needs. Identify a minimum of five direct and indirect competitors and discuss the characteristics of each.

Location:

Address: Street _____

City _____, State _____

Zip Code _____, Area Code _____

Community Name _____

Urban _____ or Surburban _____

Population: _____, Increase _____

Population Growth # _____   _____%

Population Decrease #_____   _____%

School Enrollment:

Preprimary School(s)	_____	# of Students	_____
Elementary School(s)	_____	# of Students	_____
Middle School(s)	_____	# of Students	_____
High School(s)	_____	# of Students	_____
College(s)	_____	# of Students	_____

Number of Households _____

Number of People in Business, Commercial, Mall(s) _____

Average Income Per Household _____

Climate: Summer   Median Temp. _____ Average Rainfall _____

Fall   Median Temp. _____

Winter   Median Temp. _____ Average Snowfall _____

Spring   Median Temp. _____

How many months does each season last? Summer _____, Fall _____,
Winter _____, Spring _____.

Sales Generators:

Type Of Business   1. _____ # of Employees _____

2. _____ # of Employees _____

3. _____ # of Employees _____

Parking: Not Available _____, Limited _____, Ample Space _____

STATEMENT OF INCOME
THE NAME OF THE RESTAURANT
Month / Year Ending _____ 31, 20 ____

SALES

Food $_____   _____%

Beverages $_____   _____%

Total Sales   **$_____**   **100%**

COST OF SALES

Food $_____   _____%

Beverages $_____   _____%

Total Cost of Sales   **$_____**   **_____%**

GROSS PROFIT $_____   _____%

OPERATING EXPENSES

Salaries and wages $_____   _____%

Employee Benefits $_____   _____%

Direct Operating Expenses $_____   _____%

Music and Entertainment $_____   _____%

Marketing $_____   _____%

Utilities Services $_____   _____%

Repairs and Maintenance $_____   _____%

Occupancy Costs $_____   _____%

Depreciation $_____   _____%

General and Administrative Fees $_____   _____%

Total Operating Expenses   **$_____**   **_____%**

Operating Income   **$_____**   **_____%**

Interest $_____   _____%

Income Before Taxes   **$_____**   **_____%**

Yield Test Standard Portion Cost Form:

YIELD TEST STANDARD PORTION COST FORM			MENU LISTING:		
PRODUCT:				STANDARD PORTION SIZE IN OZ.:	
AS PURCHASED COST:		AS PURCHASED WEIGHT:		AS PURCHASED COST/LB.:	
PRODUCT USE	WEIGHT	YIELD %	NUMBER OF PORTIONS	EDIBLE COST/LB.	EDIBLE COST/ PORTION	COST FACTOR PER LB.	COST FACTOR PER PORTION.
	LBs.						
TOTAL WEIGHT:		100%					
TRIM LOSS:							
EDIBLE PRODUCT:							

Cooking Loss Standard Portion Cost Form

COOKING LOSS STANDARD PORTION COST FORM

MENU ITEM:

PRODUCT:

STANDARD PORTION SIZE IN OZs.::

AS PURCHASED COST:

AS PURCHASED WEIGHT IN LBs.::

AS PURCHASED COST/LB.::

PRODUCT USE	WEIGHT IN LBs.	YIELD %	NUMBER OF PORTIONS	EDIBLE COST/LB.	EDIBLE COST/PORTION	COST FACTOR PER LB.	COST FACTOR PER PORTION
TOTAL WEIGHT		100.00%					
TRIM LOSS							
PRE-COOKED WEIGHT							
LOSS IN COOKING							
TRIM AFTER COOKING							
EDIBLE PRODUCT							

Standard Recipe Cost Card

RECIPE NAME:						STANDARD PORTION:				
STANDARD YIELD:						PORTION CONTROL TOOL:				
RECIPE		EY%	AS PURCHASED			INVOICE		RECIPE		INDIVIDUAL INGREDIENT COST
QTY	UNIT		QTY	UNIT	INGREDIENT	COST	UNIT	COST	UNIT	

Garnish:

Method of Preparation:

TOTAL INGREDIENT COST:	$
Q FACTOR %:	
RECIPE COST:	
PORTION COST:	
ADDITIONAL COST:	
ADDITIONAL COST:	
ADDITIONAL COST:	
TOTAL PLATE COST:	
DESIRED COST %:	
PRELIMINARY SELLING PRICE:	
ACTUAL SELLING PRICE:	
ACTUAL COST %:	

Equipment Required:

Product Specification

Product Name:
Intended Use:
Purchase Unit:
Quantity/Packaging Standards:
Quality Standards:
Special Requirements:

Product Name:
Intended Use:
Purchase Unit:
Quantity/Packaging Standards:
Quality Standards:
Special Requirements:

Product Name:
Intended Use:
Purchase Unit:
Quantity/Packaging Standards:
Quality Standards:
Special Requirements:

Product Name:
Intended Use:
Purchase Unit:
Quantity/Packaging Standards:
Quality Standards:
Special Requirements:

Order Sheet

Food Category: _____   **Day/Date:** _____

On Hand	PAR	Order	Ingredient (Special Order)

Prepared by: _____

Purveyor Bid Sheet

Food Category: **Day/Date:**

Ingredient	Purchase Unit	Purveyor 1	Purveyor 2	Purveyor 3

Purveyor 1:

Purveyor 2:

Purveyor 3:

ORIGINAL PURCHASE ORDER   NO.

_____
_____
_____
( )
_____

To: _____   Ship To   _____

       _____   _____

       _____   _____

ship to above unless otherwise noted here

Date	Date Required	Terms	Ship Via	F.O.B.	Requisition #

| Quantity | | ITEM | Unit Price | Amount |
Ordered	Received			
			TOTAL	$

Prepared by _____

Purchase Distribution Journal

Date	Invoice #	Meats	Seafood	Poultry	Produce	Grocery	Dairy	Bakery	Other	Total Invoice

Purchase Distribution Journal   Category: Month/Year:

Receiving Report Form

| Receiving Report Form | | Month: | | | | | | | Page: | |
Date	Invoice #	Purveyor	Description	Food	Beverage	Other	$ Directs	$ Stores	General Info

INVENTORY SHEET

Category:

Page:

Location:

Qty	Unit	Item	Cost	Unit	Extension

Prepared by: _____

_____

Page Total

Total

Bin Card

Stock #: _____

Product Name: _____   Unit Size: _____

Date		Storage In		Storage Out		Balance on Hand	
Month	**Day**	**Units**	**Costs**	**Units**	**Costs**	**Units**	**Costs**

Food and Beverage Transfer

<table>
<tr><td colspan="6" align="center">**Food and Beverage Transfer**</td></tr>
<tr><td colspan="6">**Day/Date:** _____</td></tr>
<tr><td colspan="3">**From Department:** _____</td><td colspan="3">**To Department:** _____</td></tr>
<tr><td>**Quantity**</td><td>**Unit**</td><td>**Item**</td><td colspan="2">**Unit Cost**</td><td>**Total**</td></tr>
<tr><td></td><td></td><td></td><td></td><td></td><td></td></tr>
<tr><td></td><td></td><td></td><td></td><td></td><td></td></tr>
<tr><td></td><td></td><td></td><td></td><td></td><td></td></tr>
<tr><td></td><td></td><td></td><td></td><td></td><td></td></tr>
<tr><td></td><td></td><td></td><td></td><td></td><td></td></tr>
<tr><td></td><td></td><td></td><td></td><td></td><td></td></tr>
<tr><td></td><td></td><td></td><td></td><td></td><td></td></tr>
<tr><td></td><td></td><td></td><td></td><td></td><td></td></tr>
<tr><td></td><td></td><td></td><td></td><td></td><td></td></tr>
<tr><td></td><td></td><td></td><td></td><td></td><td></td></tr>
</table>

Authorized by: _____

Daily Cost %: Simple Approach

Month/Year: _____

Day	Date	Daily Purchases	Daily Sales	Daily Cost %	To-Date Purchases	To-Date Sales	To-Date Cost %

Daily Food Cost %: An Accurate Approach

Month/Year:

Day	Date	Reqs	Direct Purch	Trans To Kitchen	Cost Food Used	Trans from Kitchen	Emp Meals	IHP	Daily Cost of Food Sold	Daily Sales	Daily Food Cost %	To-Date Cost of Food Sold	To-Date Food Sales	To-Date Food Cost %

Daily Beverage Cost %: An Accurate Approach

Month/Year:

Day	Date	Issues	Trans To Bar	Additions	Cost of Bev. Used	Trans From Bar	IHP	Sign Priv	Subtrac- tions	Daily Cost of Bev. Sold	Daily Bev. Sales	Daily Bev. Cost %	To-Date Cost of Bev. Sold	To-Date Bev. Sales	To-Date Bev. Cost %

Sales Journal

Sales Journal Month: _____

	Type of Sale								Method of Payment					
Day	Food Sales	Beverage Sales	Other Sales	Total Sales	Sales Tax	Charge Tips	Total Collected	Cash	Checks	MC/V	AMX	O-CC	Other	Total Payments

Menu Engineering Worksheet

Food Category: _____   **Time Period:** _____

	A	B	C	D	E	F	G	H	I	J	K	L	M
	Menu Items	No. Sold	Sales Mix %	Selling Price	Food Cost	Cont. Margin	Total Sales	Total Food Cost	Total CM	CM %	Sales Mix Category	Cont. Margin Category	Menu Classification
Totals													

Desired Sales Mix %: _____   Average Contribution Margin: _____   Potential Food Cost %: _____

Weekly Schedule

Department: _____   **Meals Served:** _____   **Week Ending:** _____

Employee Name	Monday	Tuesday	Wednesday	Thursday	Friday	Saturday	Sunday
Totals Employees Scheduled							

Payroll Ledger

Week Ending:

Employee Name	MS	WA	Hours Worked	Hourly Wage	Weekly Salary	Gross Pay	TIPS	Taxable Income	Federal Tax	Social Security	Medi-Care	Total Deduct	Net Pay

Index